a bit HAYWIRE

created & illustrated by courtney huddleston

written by scott zirkel

inked by jeff dabu and courtney huddleston

colored by mike garcia

lettered by greg gatlin

Published by Viper Comics
9400 N. MacArthur Blvd., Suite 124-215
Irving, TX 75063
First edition: November 2006
ISBN: 0-9777883-5-0

Jessie Garza president & publisher
Jim Resnowski editor-in-chief & creative director
P.J. Kryfko assistant editor
Jason M. Burns assistant publisher

VIPER COMICS | WWW.VIPERCOMICS.COM | EST. 2001

chapter 1
ONE OF THOSE DAYS

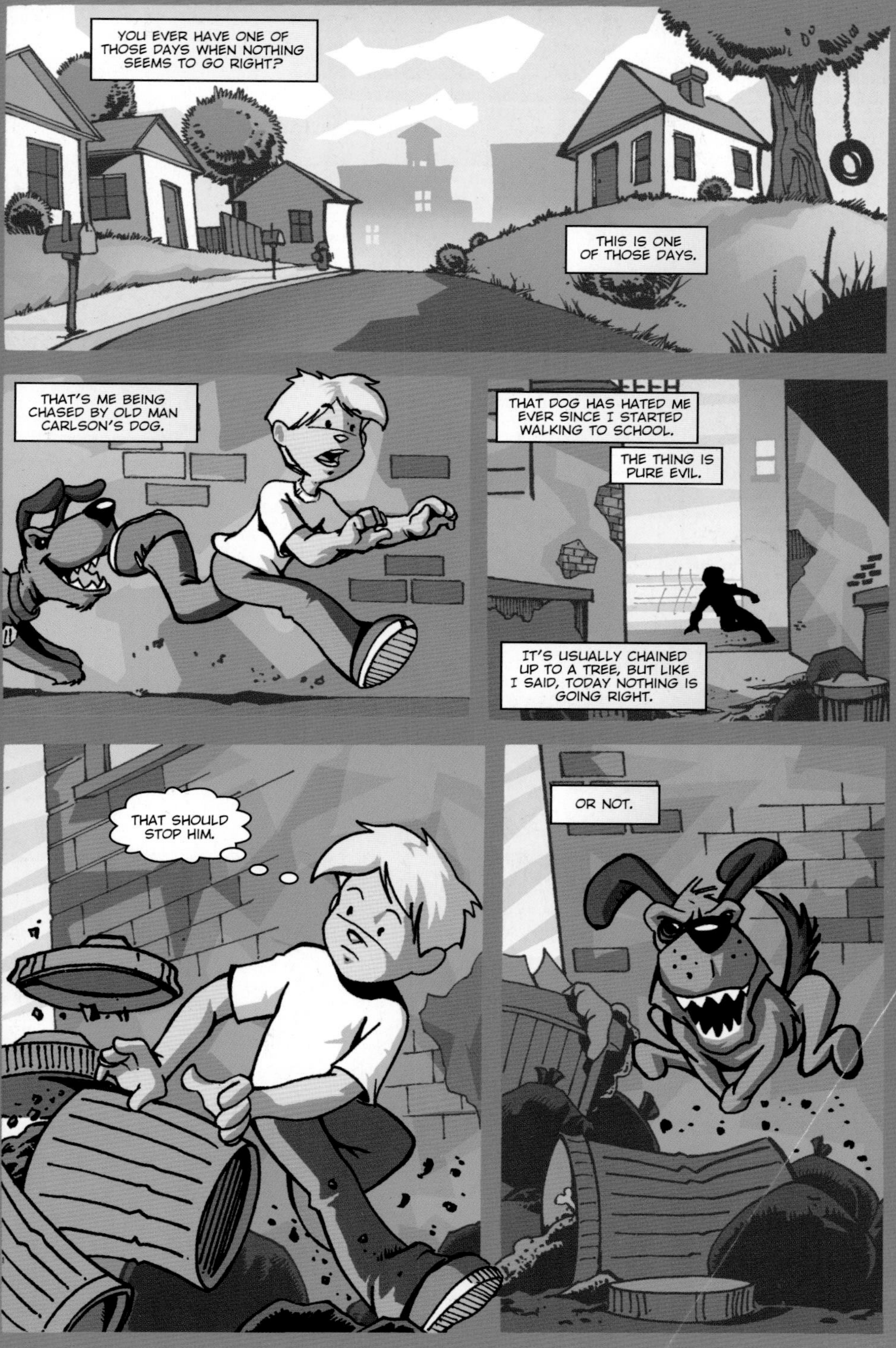
YOU EVER HAVE ONE OF THOSE DAYS WHEN NOTHING SEEMS TO GO RIGHT?
THIS IS ONE OF THOSE DAYS.
THAT'S ME BEING CHASED BY OLD MAN CARLSON'S DOG.
THAT DOG HAS HATED ME EVER SINCE I STARTED WALKING TO SCHOOL.
THE THING IS PURE EVIL.
IT'S USUALLY CHAINED UP TO A TREE, BUT LIKE I SAID, TODAY NOTHING IS GOING RIGHT.
THAT SHOULD STOP HIM.
OR NOT.

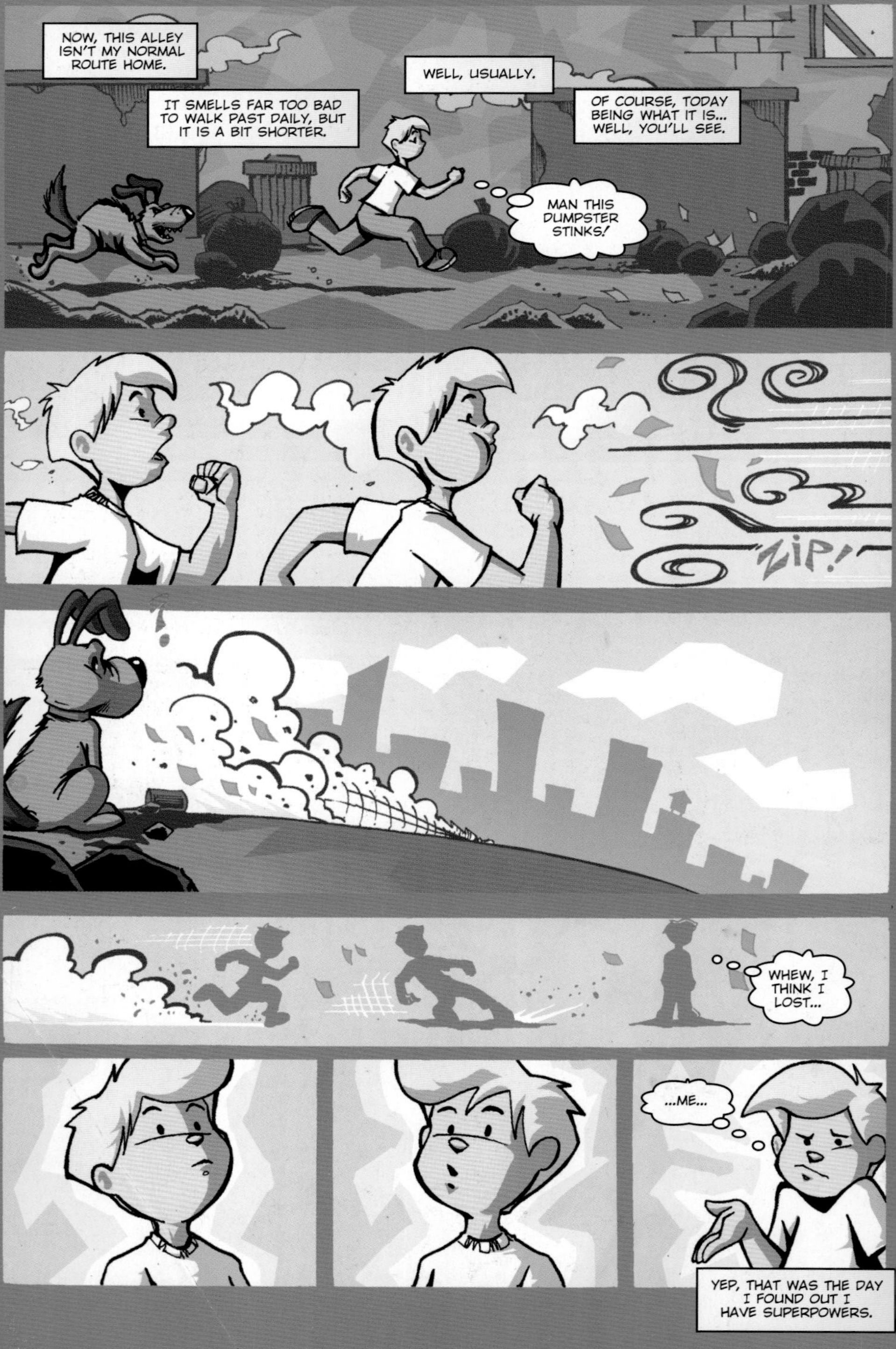
NOW, THIS ALLEY ISN'T MY NORMAL ROUTE HOME.
IT SMELLS FAR TOO BAD TO WALK PAST DAILY, BUT IT IS A BIT SHORTER.
WELL, USUALLY.
OF COURSE, TODAY BEING WHAT IT IS... WELL, YOU'LL SEE.
MAN THIS DUMPSTER STINKS!
ZIP!
WHEW, I THINK I LOST...
...ME...
YEP, THAT WAS THE DAY I FOUND OUT I HAVE SUPERPOWERS.

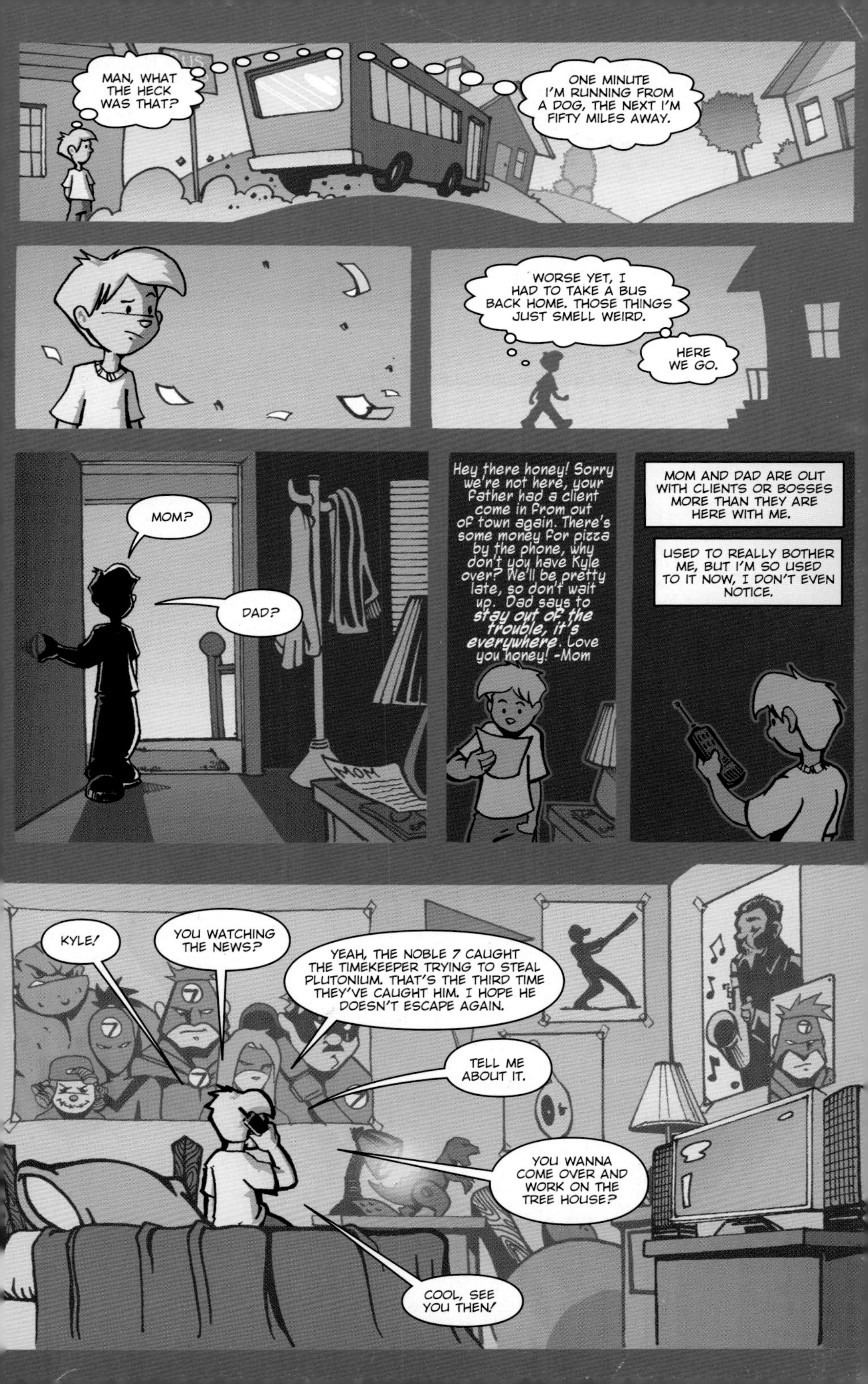
MAN, WHAT THE HECK WAS THAT?
ONE MINUTE I'M RUNNING FROM A DOG, THE NEXT I'M FIFTY MILES AWAY.
WORSE YET, I HAD TO TAKE A BUS BACK HOME. THOSE THINGS JUST SMELL WEIRD.
HERE WE GO.
MOM?
DAD?
MOM
Hey there honey! Sorry we're not here, your father had a client come in from out of town again. There's some money for pizza by the phone, why don't you have Kyle over? We'll be pretty late, so don't wait up. Dad says to stay out of the trouble, it's everywhere. Love you honey! -Mom
MOM AND DAD ARE OUT WITH CLIENTS OR BOSSES MORE THAN THEY ARE HERE WITH ME.
USED TO REALLY BOTHER ME, BUT I'M SO USED TO IT NOW, I DON'T EVEN NOTICE.
KYLE!
YOU WATCHING THE NEWS?
YEAH, THE NOBLE 7 CAUGHT THE TIMEKEEPER TRYING TO STEAL PLUTONIUM. THAT'S THE THIRD TIME THEY'VE CAUGHT HIM. I HOPE HE DOESN'T ESCAPE AGAIN.
TELL ME ABOUT IT.
YOU WANNA COME OVER AND WORK ON THE TREE HOUSE?
COOL, SEE YOU THEN!

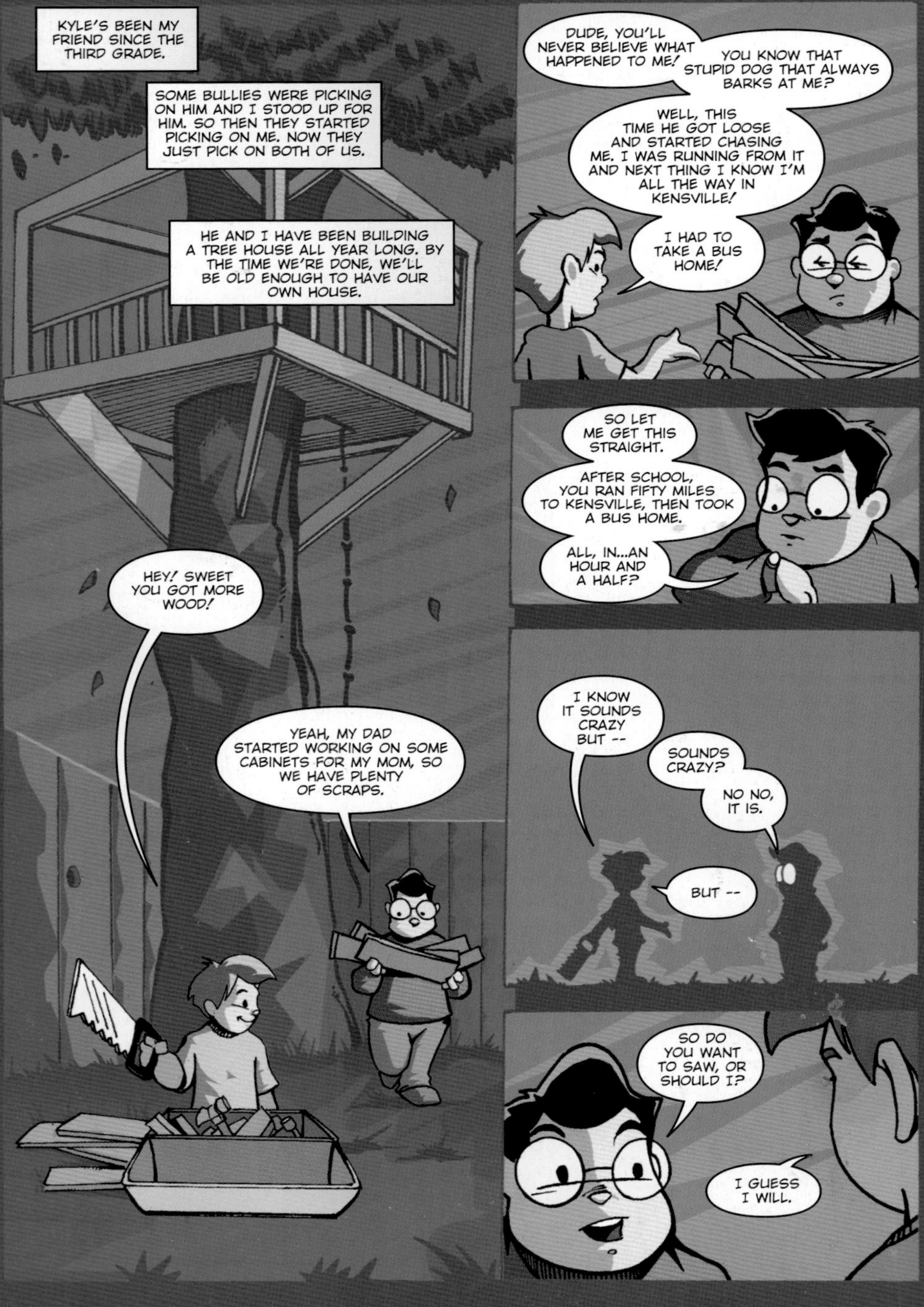
KYLE'S BEEN MY FRIEND SINCE THE THIRD GRADE.
SOME BULLIES WERE PICKING ON HIM AND I STOOD UP FOR HIM. SO THEN THEY STARTED PICKING ON ME. NOW THEY JUST PICK ON BOTH OF US.
HE AND I HAVE BEEN BUILDING A TREE HOUSE ALL YEAR LONG. BY THE TIME WE'RE DONE, WE'LL BE OLD ENOUGH TO HAVE OUR OWN HOUSE.
HEY! SWEET YOU GOT MORE WOOD!
YEAH, MY DAD STARTED WORKING ON SOME CABINETS FOR MY MOM, SO WE HAVE PLENTY OF SCRAPS.
DUDE, YOU'LL NEVER BELIEVE WHAT HAPPENED TO ME!
YOU KNOW THAT STUPID DOG THAT ALWAYS BARKS AT ME?
WELL, THIS TIME HE GOT LOOSE AND STARTED CHASING ME. I WAS RUNNING FROM IT AND NEXT THING I KNOW I'M ALL THE WAY IN KENSVILLE!
I HAD TO TAKE A BUS HOME!
SO LET ME GET THIS STRAIGHT.
AFTER SCHOOL, YOU RAN FIFTY MILES TO KENSVILLE, THEN TOOK A BUS HOME.
ALL, IN...AN HOUR AND A HALF?
I KNOW IT SOUNDS CRAZY BUT --
SOUNDS CRAZY?
NO NO, IT IS.
BUT --
SO DO YOU WANT TO SAW, OR SHOULD I?
I GUESS I WILL.

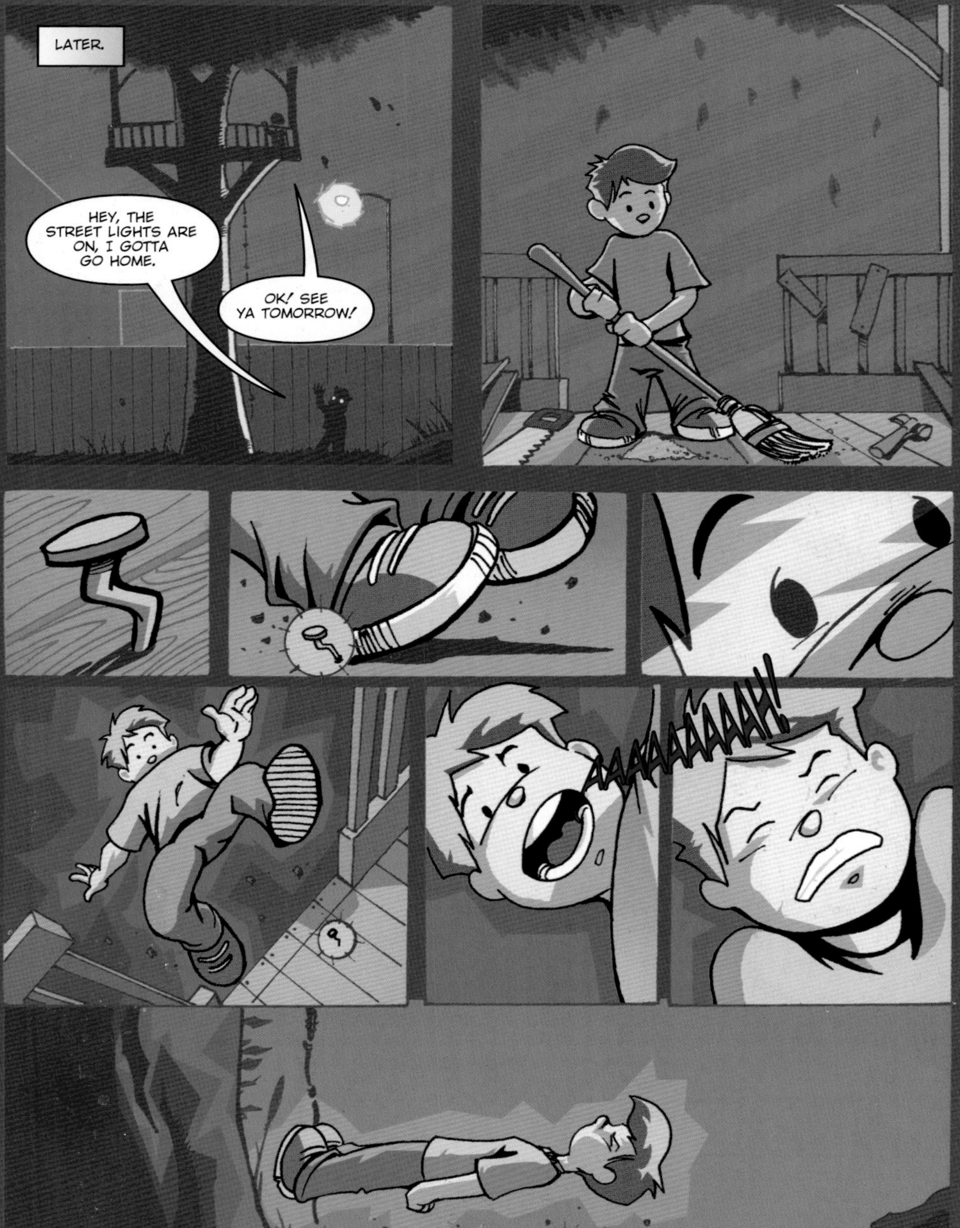
LATER.
HEY, THE STREET LIGHTS ARE ON, I GOTTA GO HOME.
OK! SEE YA TOMORROW!
AAAAAAAAAAH!

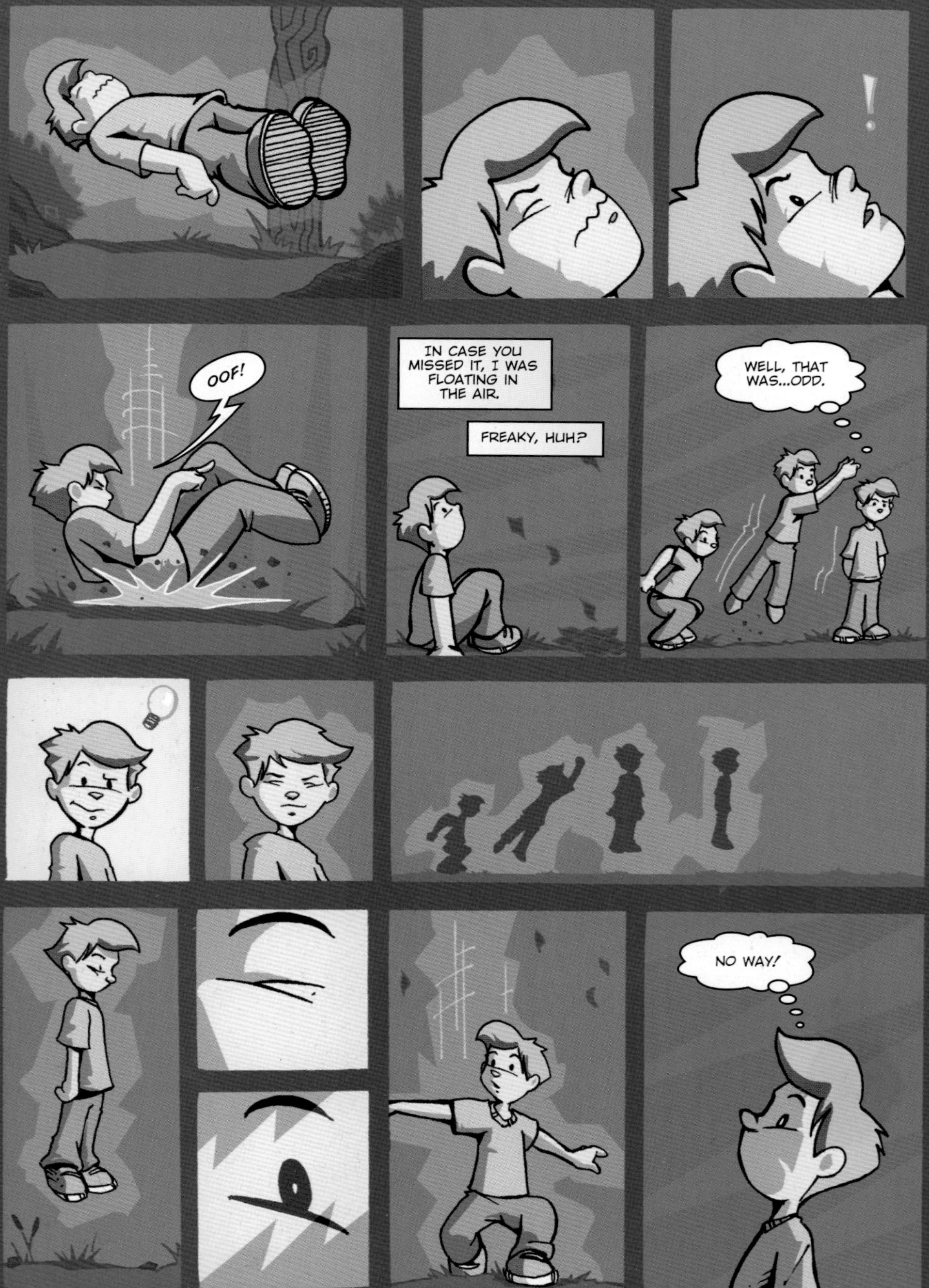
!
OOF!
IN CASE YOU MISSED IT, I WAS FLOATING IN THE AIR.
FREAKY, HUH?
WELL, THAT WAS...ODD.
NO WAY!

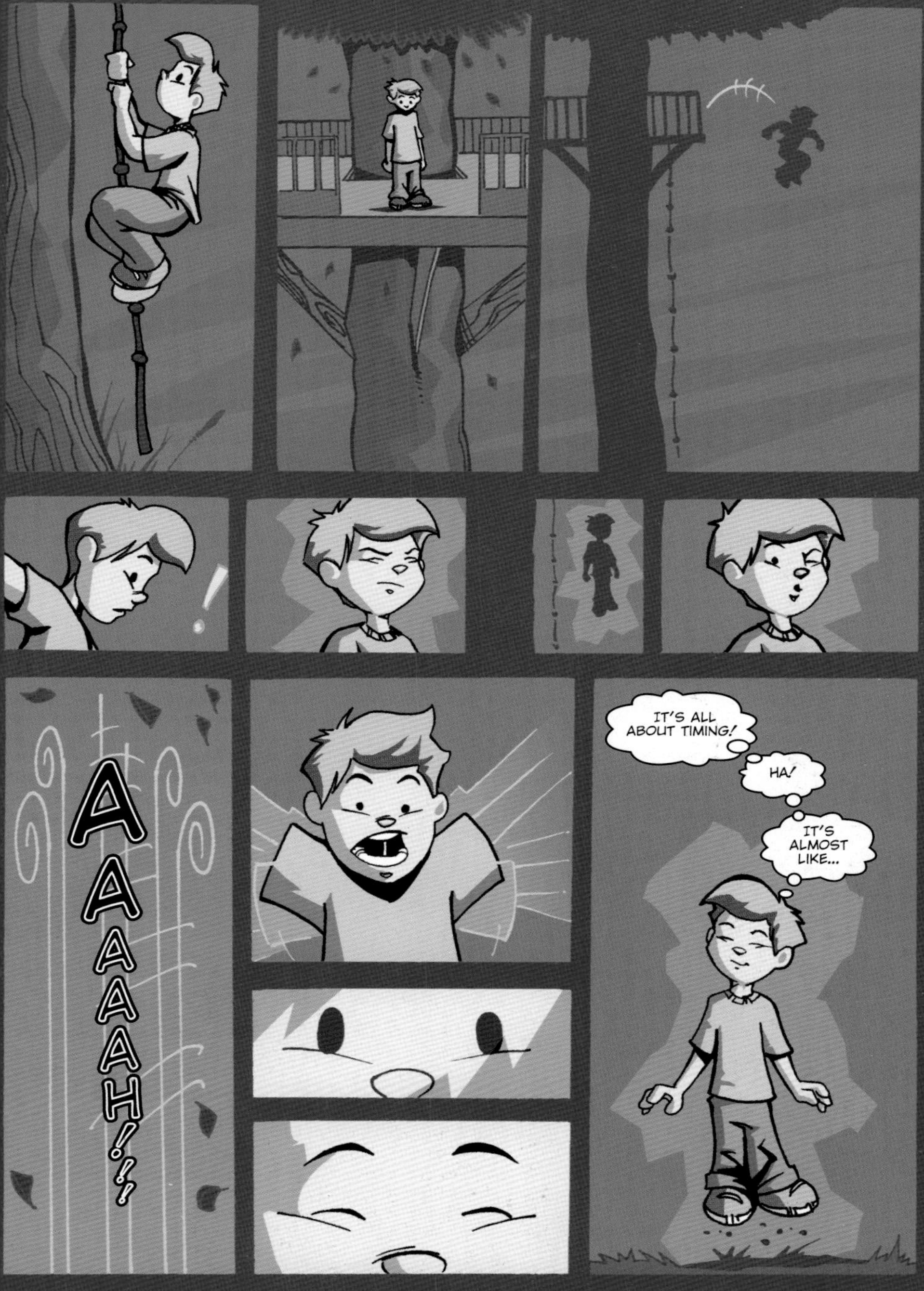
!
AAAAAAH!!!
IT'S ALL ABOUT TIMING!
HA!
IT'S ALMOST LIKE...

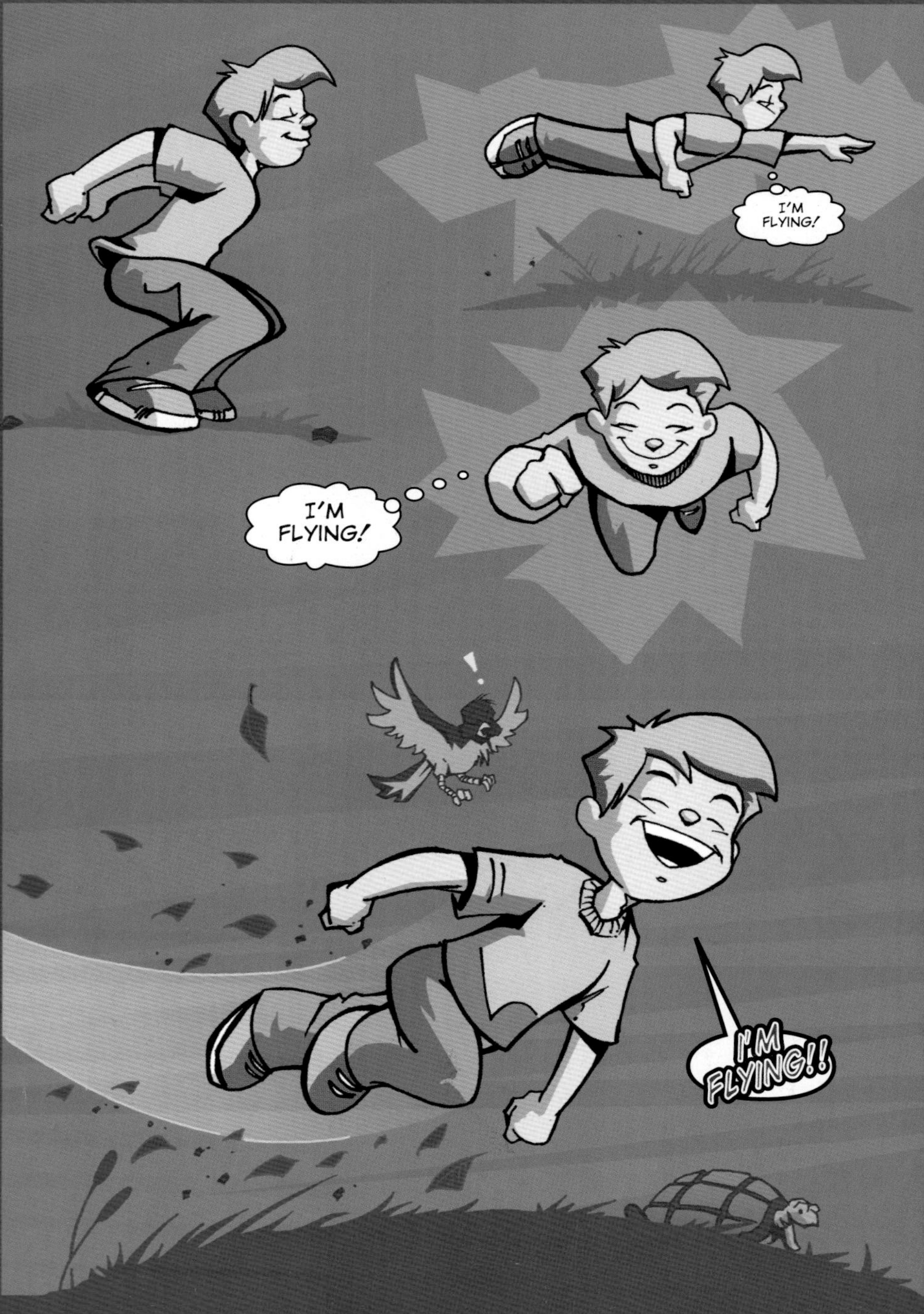
I'M FLYING!
I'M FLYING!
!
I'M FLYING!!

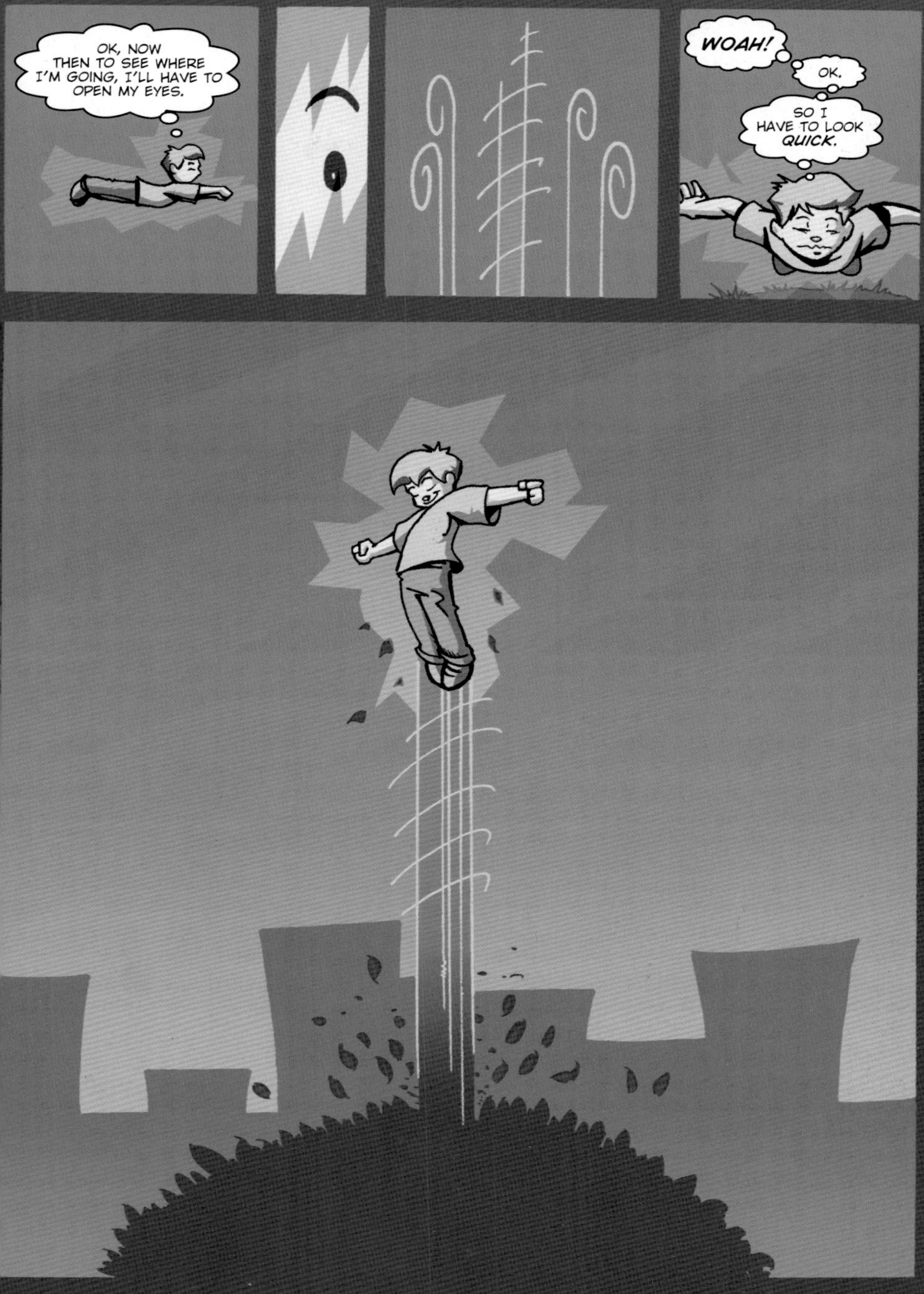
OK, NOW THEN TO SEE WHERE I'M GOING, I'LL HAVE TO OPEN MY EYES.
WOAH!
OK.
SO I HAVE TO LOOK QUICK.

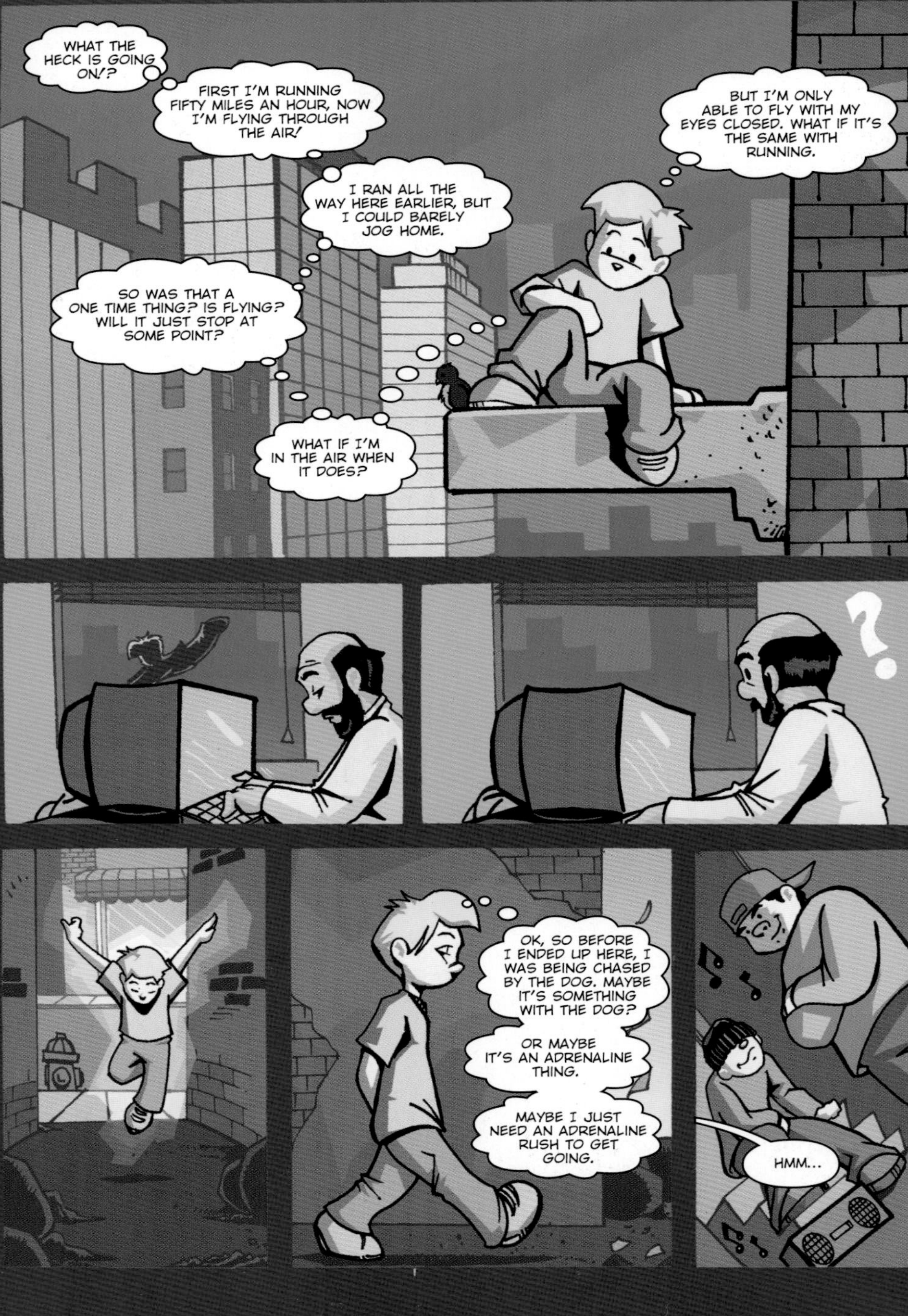
WHAT THE HECK IS GOING ON!?
FIRST I'M RUNNING FIFTY MILES AN HOUR, NOW I'M FLYING THROUGH THE AIR!
I RAN ALL THE WAY HERE EARLIER, BUT I COULD BARELY JOG HOME.
SO WAS THAT A ONE TIME THING? IS FLYING? WILL IT JUST STOP AT SOME POINT?
WHAT IF I'M IN THE AIR WHEN IT DOES?
BUT I'M ONLY ABLE TO FLY WITH MY EYES CLOSED. WHAT IF IT'S THE SAME WITH RUNNING.
?
OK, SO BEFORE I ENDED UP HERE, I WAS BEING CHASED BY THE DOG. MAYBE IT'S SOMETHING WITH THE DOG?
OR MAYBE IT'S AN ADRENALINE THING.
MAYBE I JUST NEED AN ADRENALINE RUSH TO GET GOING.
HMM...

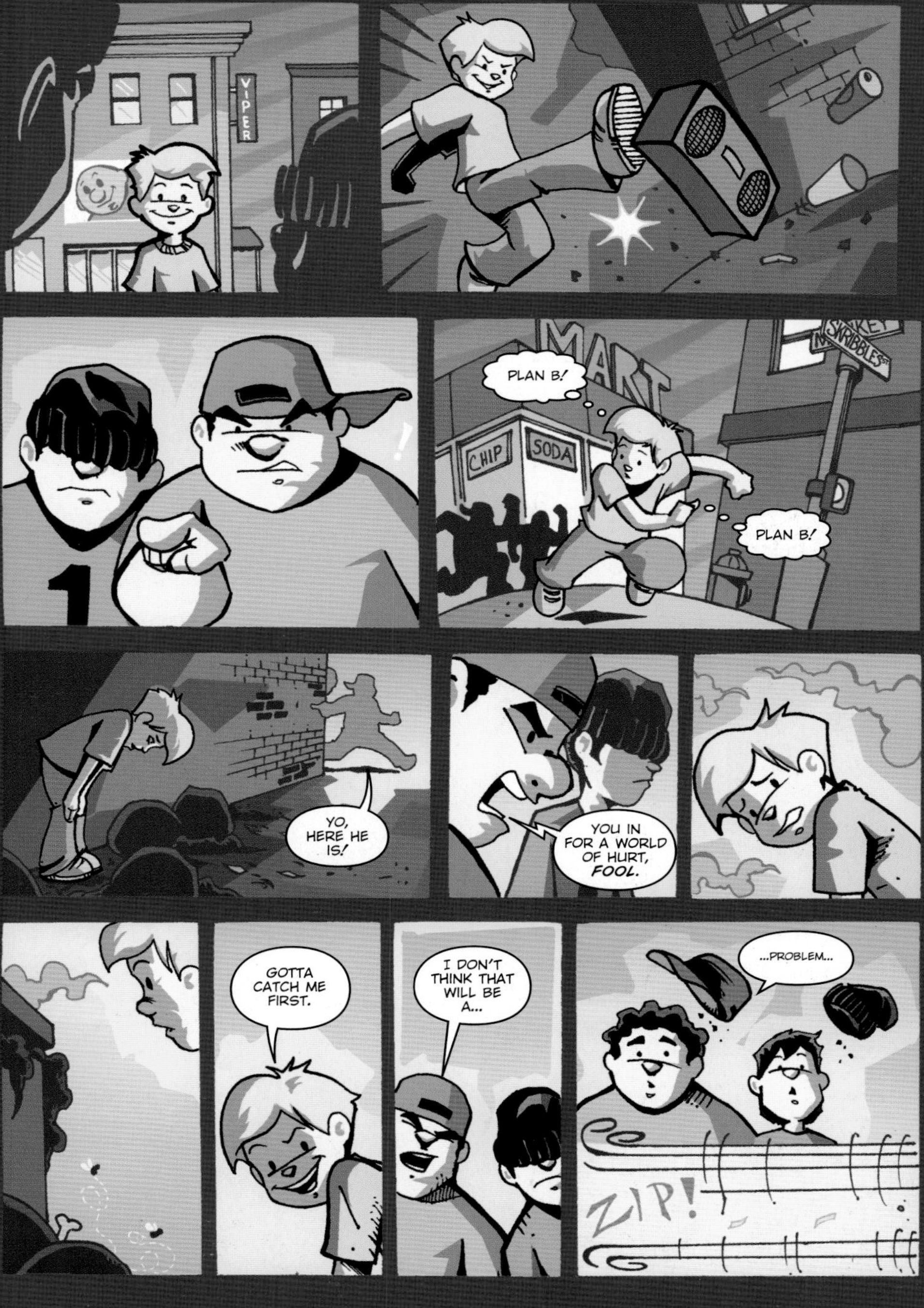
VIPER
MART
SKRIBBLES ST
PLAN B!
CHIP
SODA
PLAN B!
YO, HERE HE IS!
YOU IN FOR A WORLD OF HURT, *FOOL*.
GOTTA CATCH ME FIRST.
I DON'T THINK THAT WILL BE A...
...PROBLEM...
ZIP!

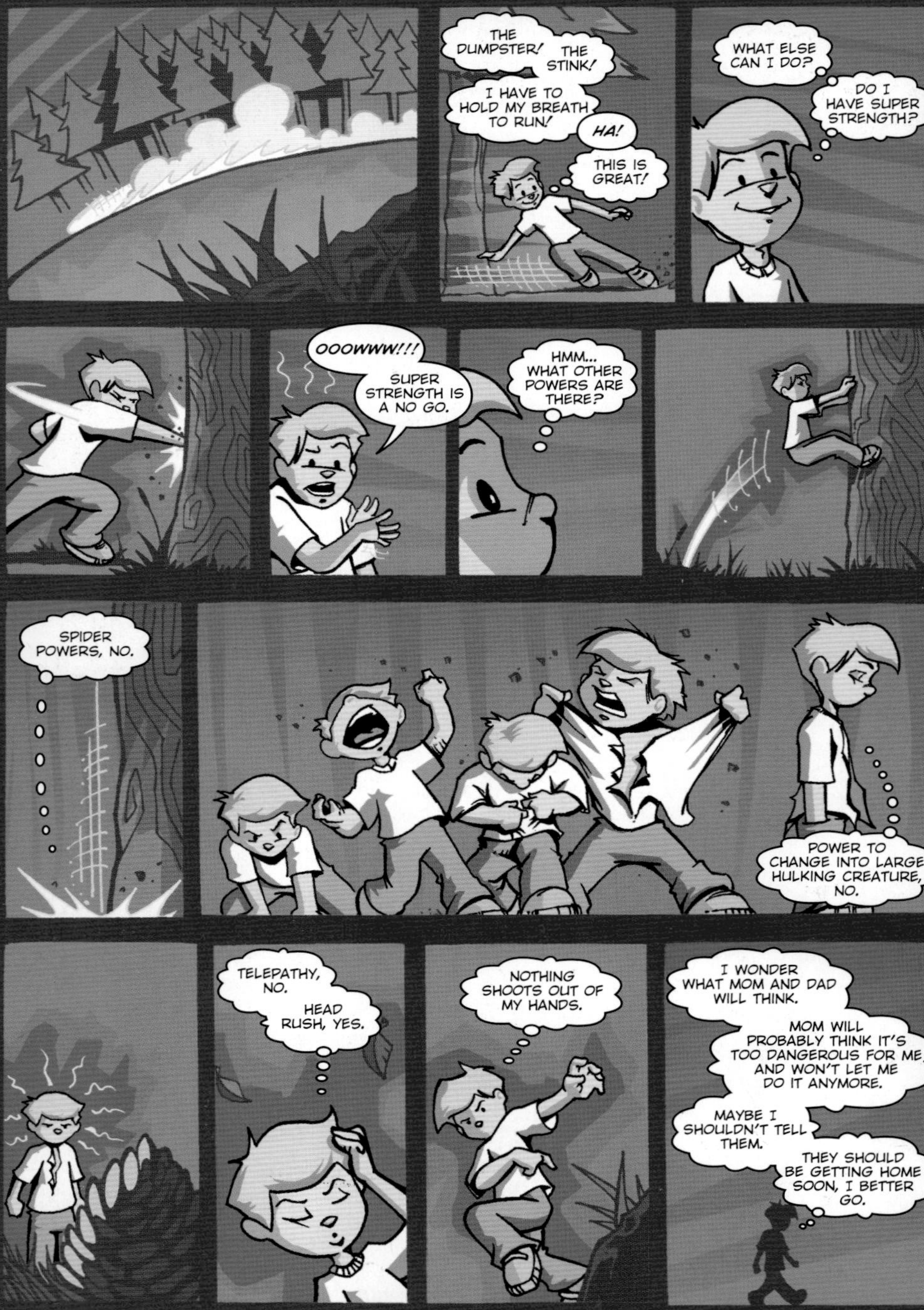
THE DUMPSTER!
THE STINK!
I HAVE TO HOLD MY BREATH TO RUN!
HA!
THIS IS GREAT!
WHAT ELSE CAN I DO?
DO I HAVE SUPER STRENGTH?
OOOWWW!!!
SUPER STRENGTH IS A NO GO.
HMM... WHAT OTHER POWERS ARE THERE?
SPIDER POWERS, NO.
POWER TO CHANGE INTO LARGE HULKING CREATURE, NO.
TELEPATHY, NO.
HEAD RUSH, YES.
NOTHING SHOOTS OUT OF MY HANDS.
I WONDER WHAT MOM AND DAD WILL THINK.
MOM WILL PROBABLY THINK IT'S TOO DANGEROUS FOR ME AND WON'T LET ME DO IT ANYMORE.
MAYBE I SHOULDN'T TELL THEM.
THEY SHOULD BE GETTING HOME SOON, I BETTER GO.

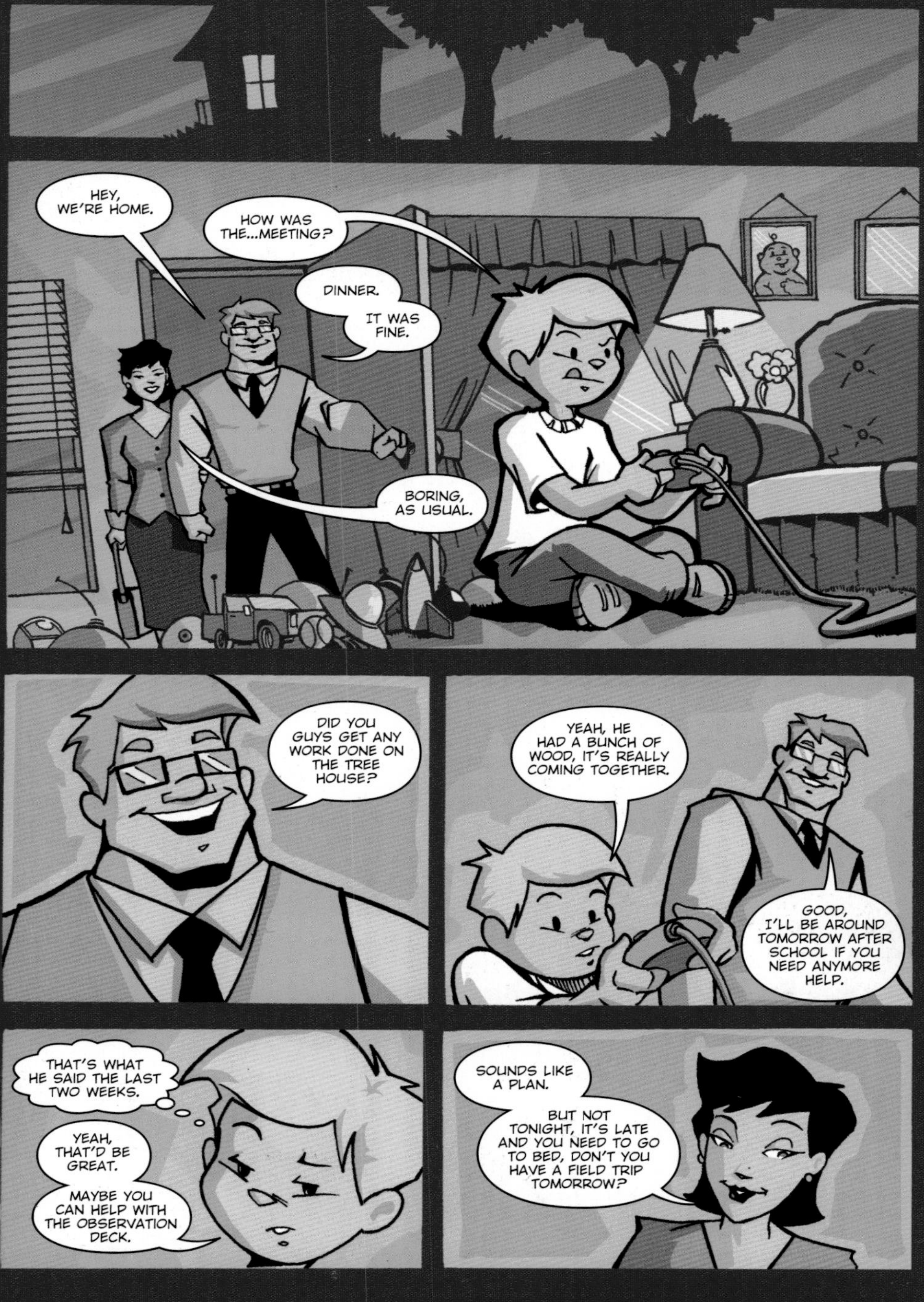
HEY, WE'RE HOME.
HOW WAS THE...MEETING?
DINNER.
IT WAS FINE.
BORING, AS USUAL.
DID YOU GUYS GET ANY WORK DONE ON THE TREE HOUSE?
YEAH, HE HAD A BUNCH OF WOOD, IT'S REALLY COMING TOGETHER.
GOOD, I'LL BE AROUND TOMORROW AFTER SCHOOL IF YOU NEED ANYMORE HELP.
THAT'S WHAT HE SAID THE LAST TWO WEEKS.
YEAH, THAT'D BE GREAT.
MAYBE YOU CAN HELP WITH THE OBSERVATION DECK.
SOUNDS LIKE A PLAN.
BUT NOT TONIGHT, IT'S LATE AND YOU NEED TO GO TO BED, DON'T YOU HAVE A FIELD TRIP TOMORROW?

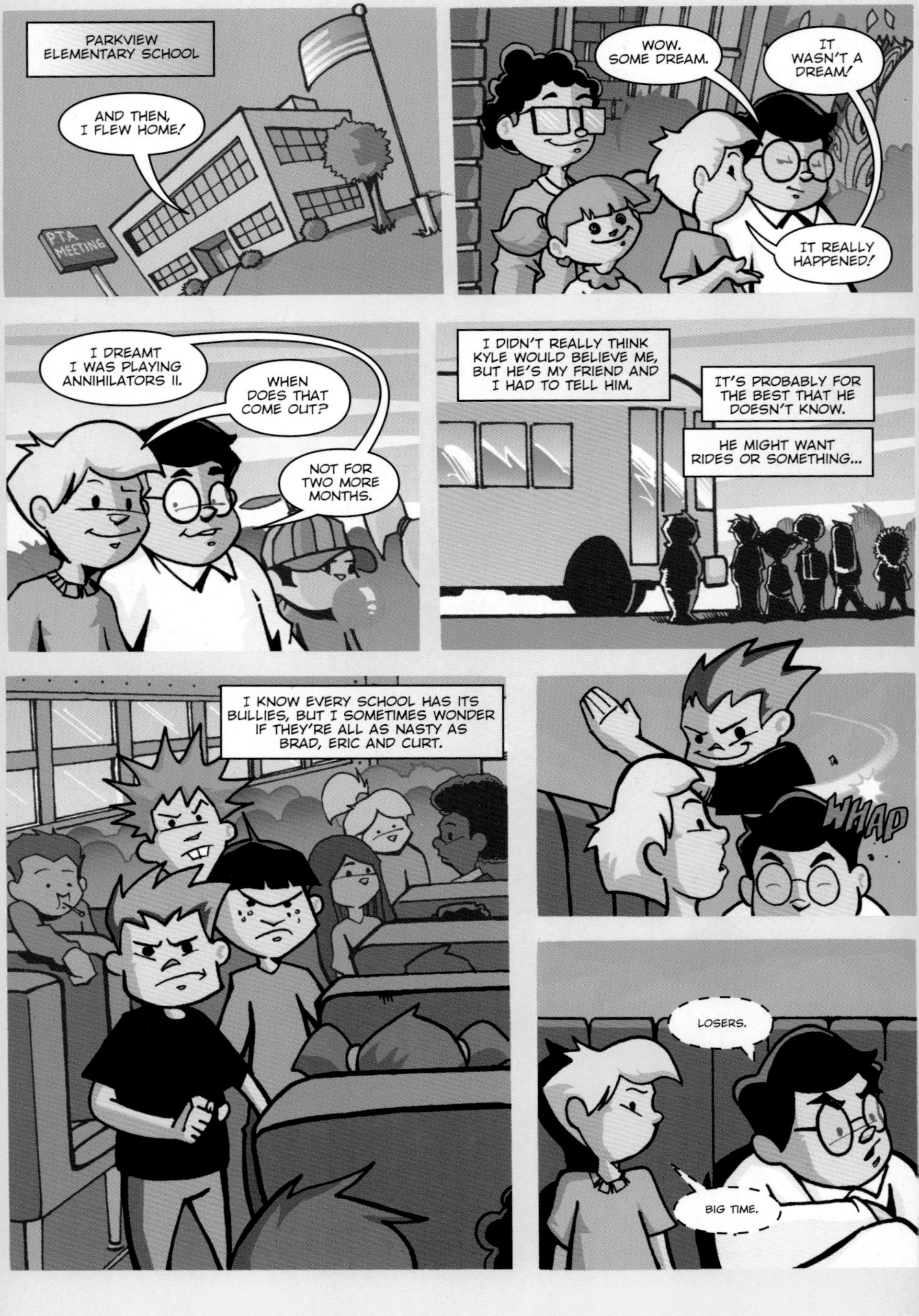

PARKVIEW ELEMENTARY SCHOOL
AND THEN, I FLEW HOME!
PTA MEETING
WOW. SOME DREAM.
IT WASN'T A DREAM!
IT REALLY HAPPENED!
I DREAMT I WAS PLAYING ANNIHILATORS II.
WHEN DOES THAT COME OUT?
NOT FOR TWO MORE MONTHS.
I DIDN'T REALLY THINK KYLE WOULD BELIEVE ME, BUT HE'S MY FRIEND AND I HAD TO TELL HIM.
IT'S PROBABLY FOR THE BEST THAT HE DOESN'T KNOW.
HE MIGHT WANT RIDES OR SOMETHING...
I KNOW EVERY SCHOOL HAS ITS BULLIES, BUT I SOMETIMES WONDER IF THEY'RE ALL AS NASTY AS BRAD, ERIC AND CURT.
WHAP
LOSERS.
BIG TIME.

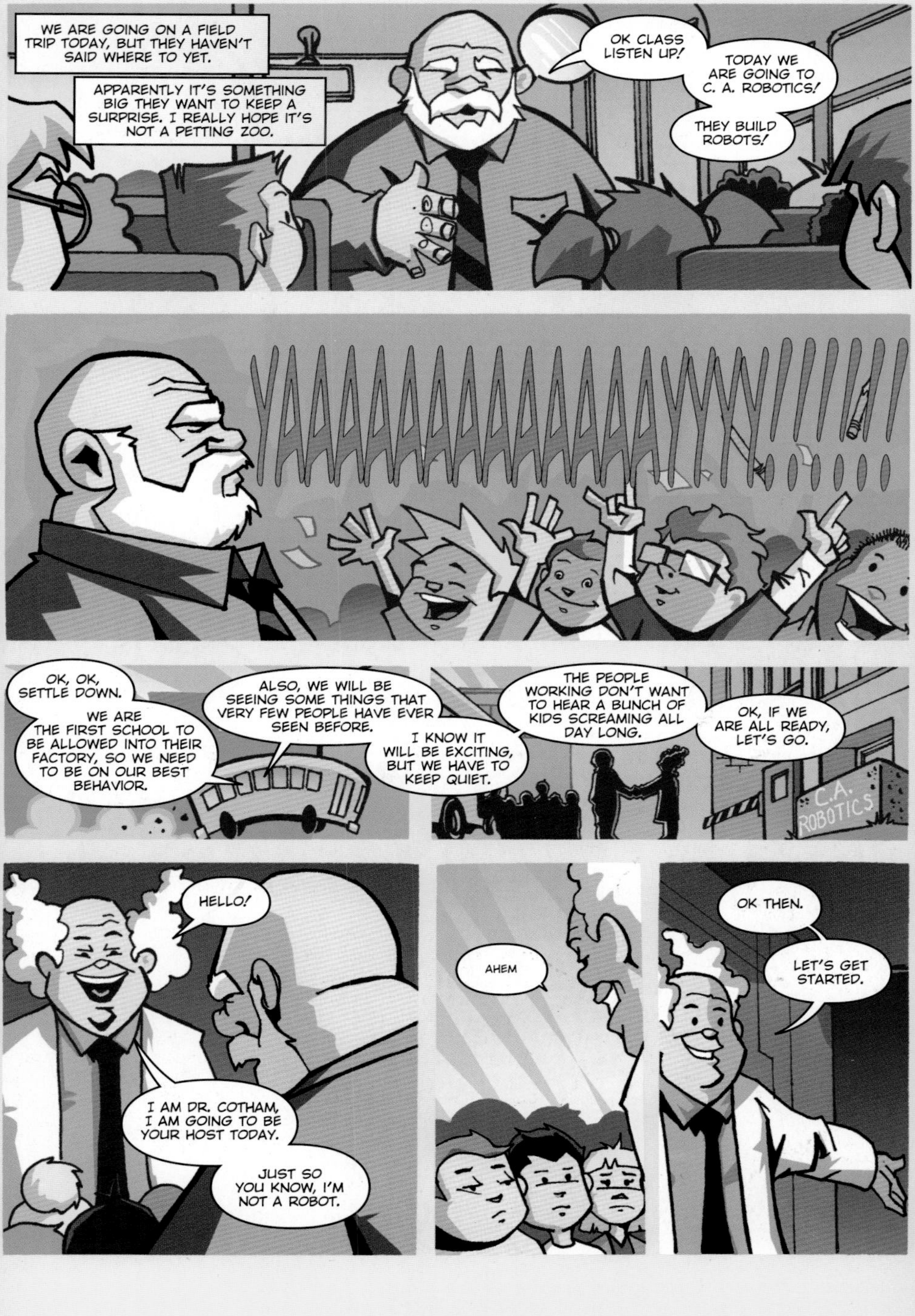
WE ARE GOING ON A FIELD TRIP TODAY, BUT THEY HAVEN'T SAID WHERE TO YET.
APPARENTLY IT'S SOMETHING BIG THEY WANT TO KEEP A SURPRISE. I REALLY HOPE IT'S NOT A PETTING ZOO.
OK CLASS LISTEN UP!
TODAY WE ARE GOING TO C. A. ROBOTICS!
THEY BUILD ROBOTS!
YAAAAAAAAAAAAAAYYYY!!!!!!!
OK, OK, SETTLE DOWN.
WE ARE THE FIRST SCHOOL TO BE ALLOWED INTO THEIR FACTORY, SO WE NEED TO BE ON OUR BEST BEHAVIOR.
ALSO, WE WILL BE SEEING SOME THINGS THAT VERY FEW PEOPLE HAVE EVER SEEN BEFORE.
I KNOW IT WILL BE EXCITING, BUT WE HAVE TO KEEP QUIET.
THE PEOPLE WORKING DON'T WANT TO HEAR A BUNCH OF KIDS SCREAMING ALL DAY LONG.
OK, IF WE ARE ALL READY, LET'S GO.
C.A. ROBOTICS
HELLO!
I AM DR. COTHAM, I AM GOING TO BE YOUR HOST TODAY.
JUST SO YOU KNOW, I'M NOT A ROBOT.
AHEM
OK THEN.
LET'S GET STARTED.

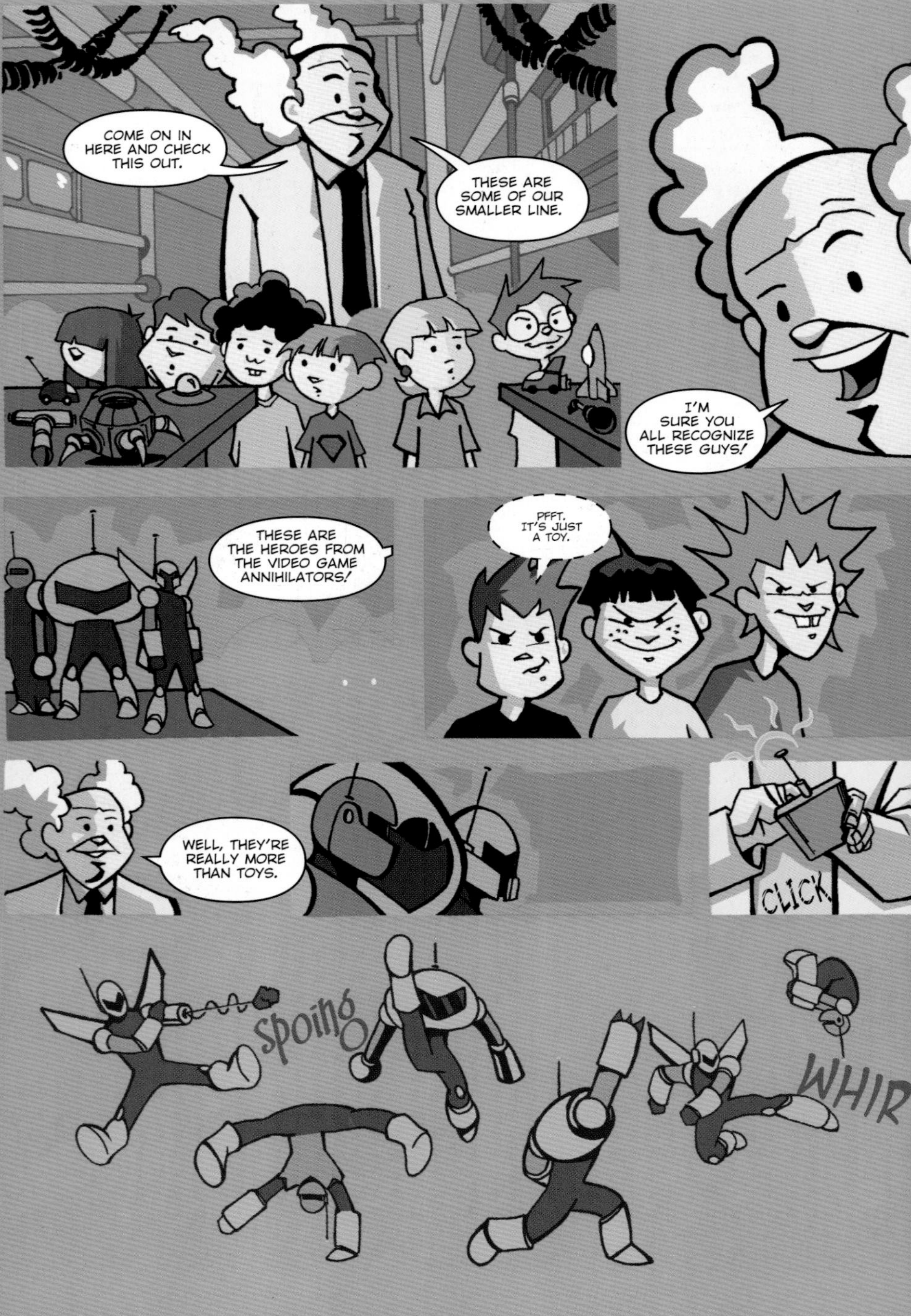

COME ON IN HERE AND CHECK THIS OUT.
THESE ARE SOME OF OUR SMALLER LINE.
I'M SURE YOU ALL RECOGNIZE THESE GUYS!
THESE ARE THE HEROES FROM THE VIDEO GAME ANNIHILATORS!
PFFT. IT'S JUST A TOY.
WELL, THEY'RE REALLY MORE THAN TOYS.
CLICK
SPOING
WHIR

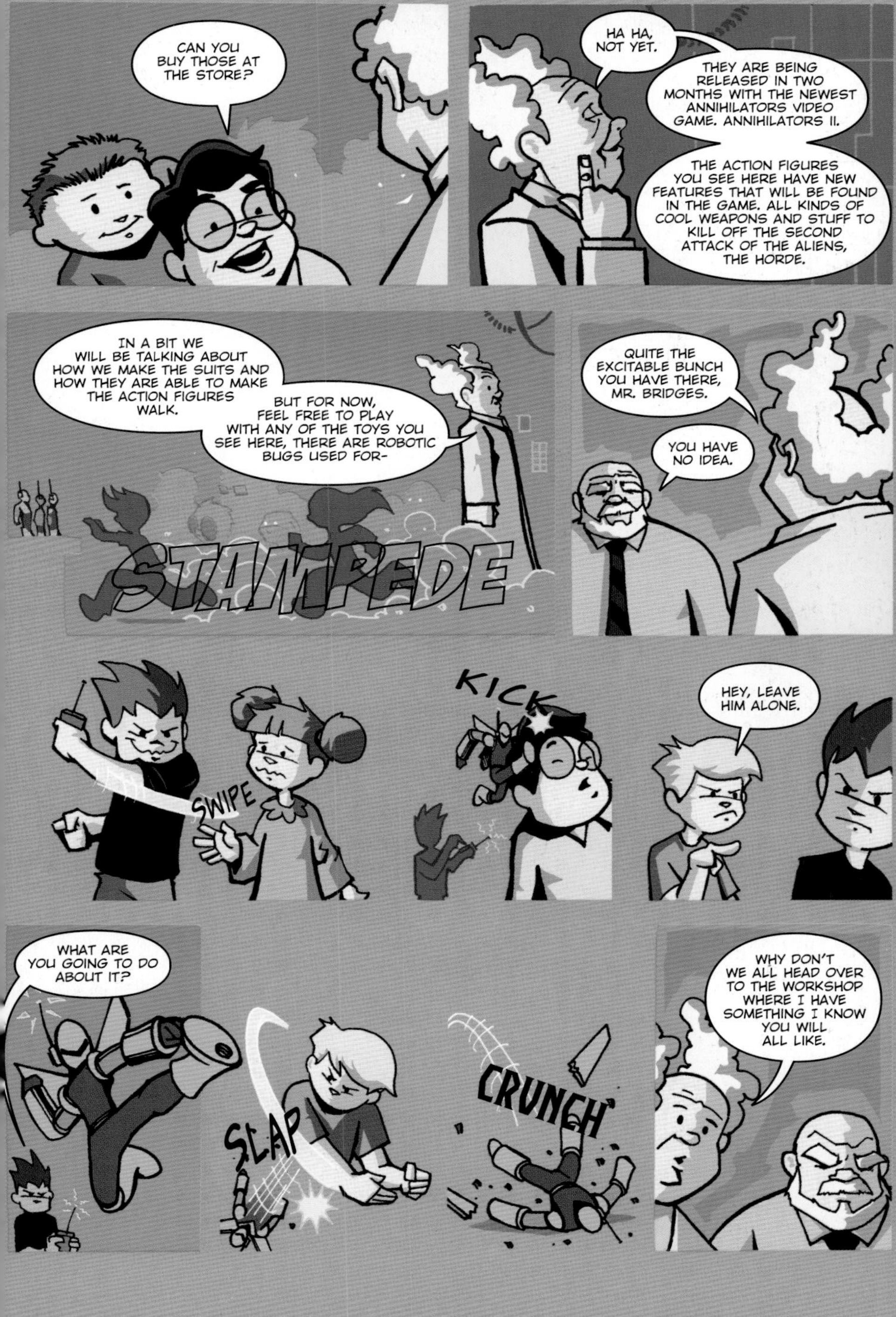
CAN YOU BUY THOSE AT THE STORE?
HA HA, NOT YET.
THEY ARE BEING RELEASED IN TWO MONTHS WITH THE NEWEST ANNIHILATORS VIDEO GAME. ANNIHILATORS II.
THE ACTION FIGURES YOU SEE HERE HAVE NEW FEATURES THAT WILL BE FOUND IN THE GAME. ALL KINDS OF COOL WEAPONS AND STUFF TO KILL OFF THE SECOND ATTACK OF THE ALIENS, THE HORDE.
IN A BIT WE WILL BE TALKING ABOUT HOW WE MAKE THE SUITS AND HOW THEY ARE ABLE TO MAKE THE ACTION FIGURES WALK.
BUT FOR NOW, FEEL FREE TO PLAY WITH ANY OF THE TOYS YOU SEE HERE, THERE ARE ROBOTIC BUGS USED FOR-
STAMPEDE
QUITE THE EXCITABLE BUNCH YOU HAVE THERE, MR. BRIDGES.
YOU HAVE NO IDEA.
SWIPE
KICK
HEY, LEAVE HIM ALONE.
WHAT ARE YOU GOING TO DO ABOUT IT?
SLAP
CRUNCH
WHY DON'T WE ALL HEAD OVER TO THE WORKSHOP WHERE I HAVE SOMETHING I KNOW YOU WILL ALL LIKE.

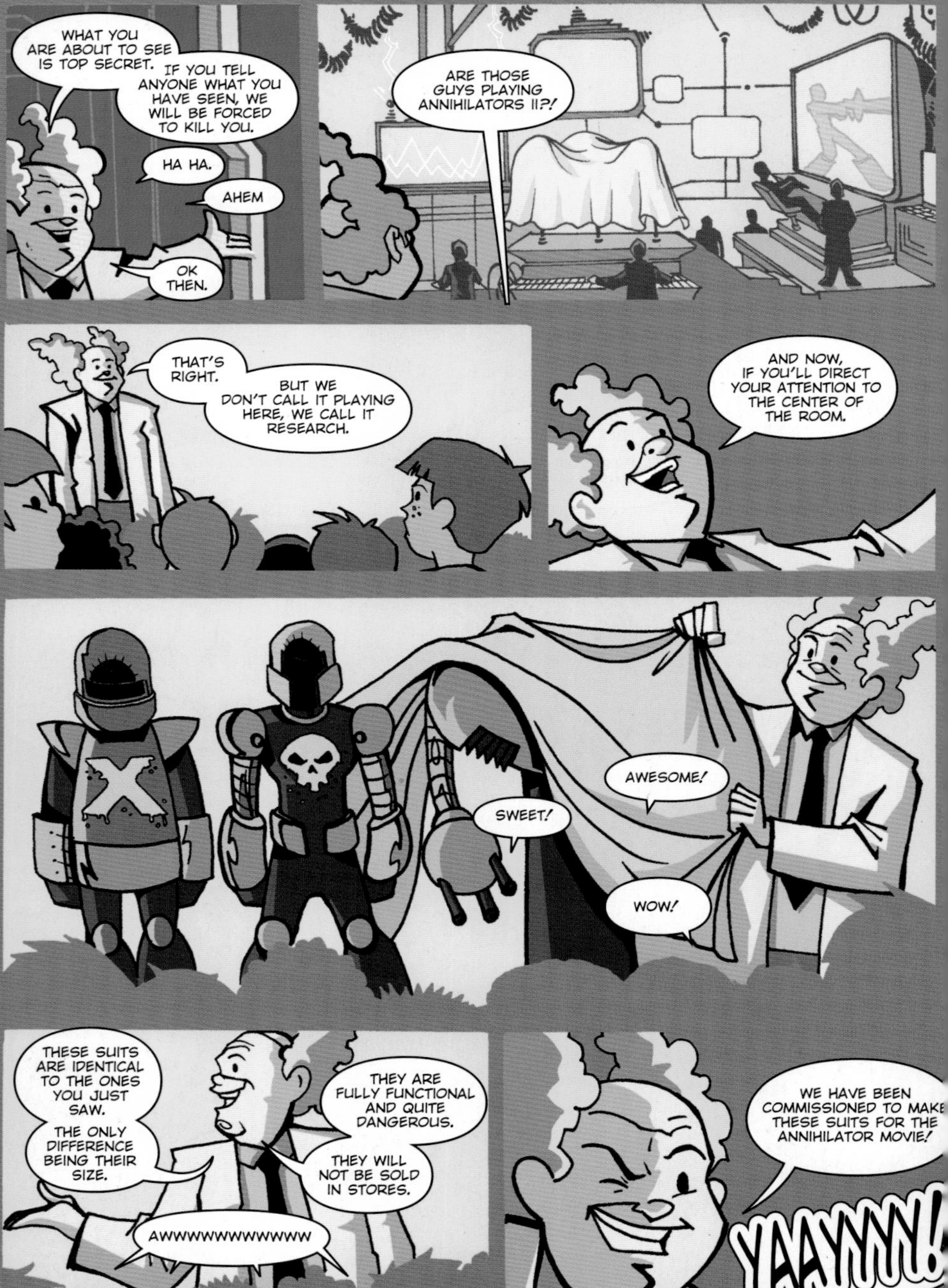
WHAT YOU ARE ABOUT TO SEE IS TOP SECRET.
IF YOU TELL ANYONE WHAT YOU HAVE SEEN, WE WILL BE FORCED TO KILL YOU.
HA HA.
AHEM
OK THEN.
ARE THOSE GUYS PLAYING ANNIHILATORS II?!
THAT'S RIGHT.
BUT WE DON'T CALL IT PLAYING HERE, WE CALL IT RESEARCH.
AND NOW, IF YOU'LL DIRECT YOUR ATTENTION TO THE CENTER OF THE ROOM.
AWESOME!
SWEET!
WOW!
THESE SUITS ARE IDENTICAL TO THE ONES YOU JUST SAW.
THE ONLY DIFFERENCE BEING THEIR SIZE.
THEY ARE FULLY FUNCTIONAL AND QUITE DANGEROUS.
THEY WILL NOT BE SOLD IN STORES.
AWWWWWWWWWWW
WE HAVE BEEN COMMISSIONED TO MAKE THESE SUITS FOR THE ANNIHILATOR MOVIE!
YAAYYY!

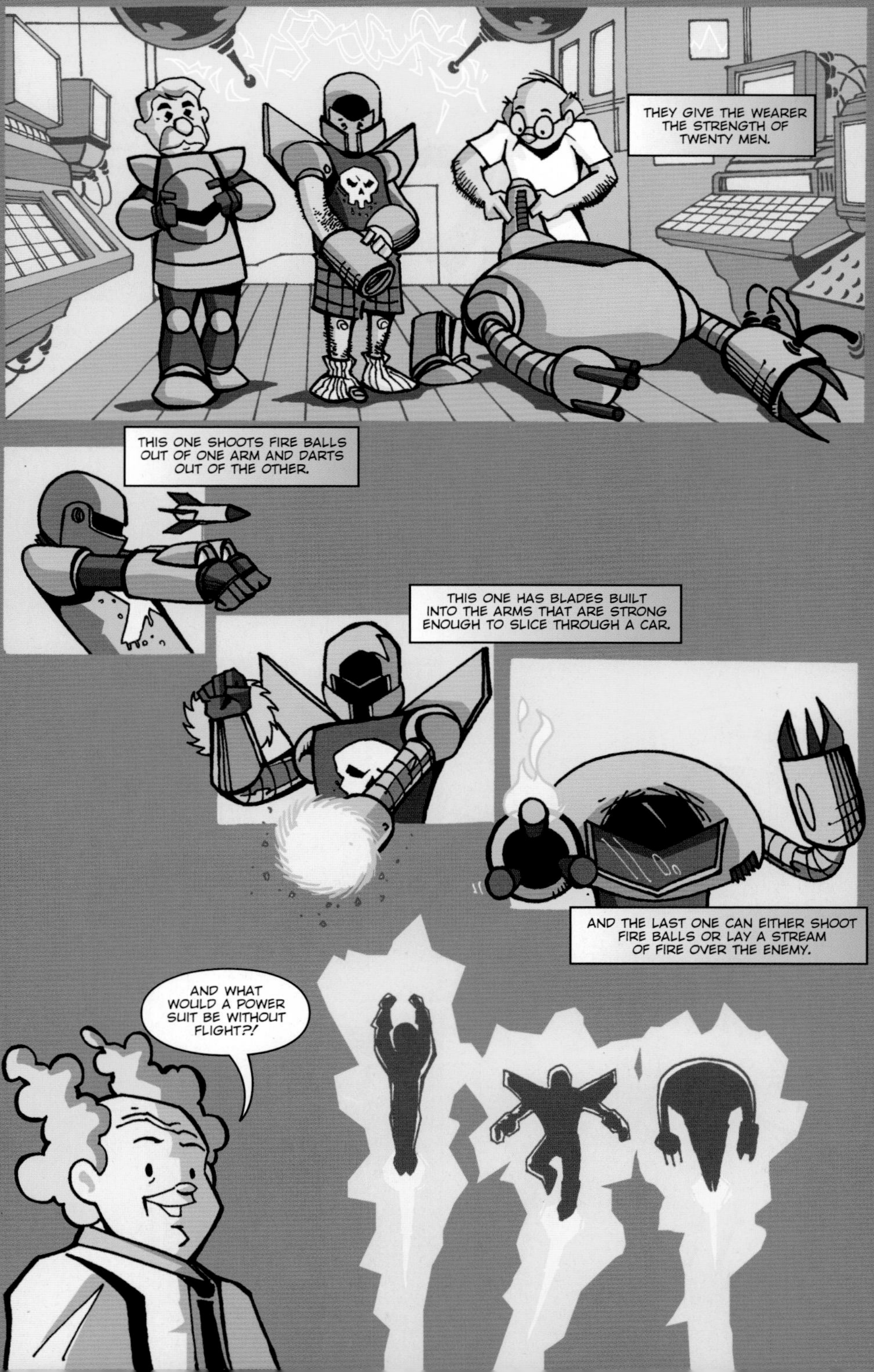
THEY GIVE THE WEARER THE STRENGTH OF TWENTY MEN.
THIS ONE SHOOTS FIRE BALLS OUT OF ONE ARM AND DARTS OUT OF THE OTHER.
THIS ONE HAS BLADES BUILT INTO THE ARMS THAT ARE STRONG ENOUGH TO SLICE THROUGH A CAR.
AND THE LAST ONE CAN EITHER SHOOT FIRE BALLS OR LAY A STREAM OF FIRE OVER THE ENEMY.
AND WHAT WOULD A POWER SUIT BE WITHOUT FLIGHT?!

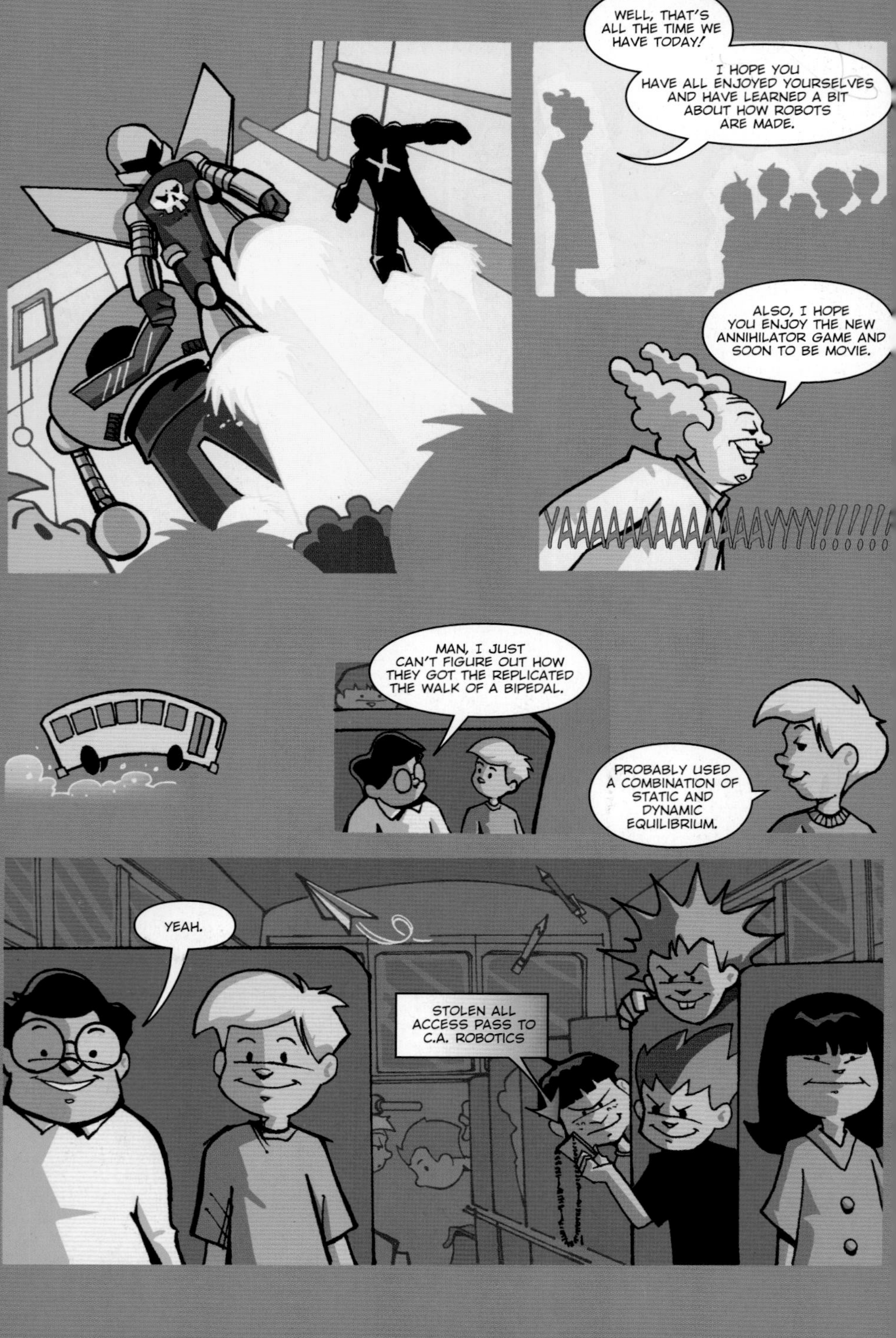
WELL, THAT'S ALL THE TIME WE HAVE TODAY!
I HOPE YOU HAVE ALL ENJOYED YOURSELVES AND HAVE LEARNED A BIT ABOUT HOW ROBOTS ARE MADE.
ALSO, I HOPE YOU ENJOY THE NEW ANNIHILATOR GAME AND SOON TO BE MOVIE.
YAAAAAAAAAAAAAYYYY!!!!!!
MAN, I JUST CAN'T FIGURE OUT HOW THEY GOT THE REPLICATED THE WALK OF A BIPEDAL.
PROBABLY USED A COMBINATION OF STATIC AND DYNAMIC EQUILIBRIUM.
YEAH.
STOLEN ALL ACCESS PASS TO C.A. ROBOTICS

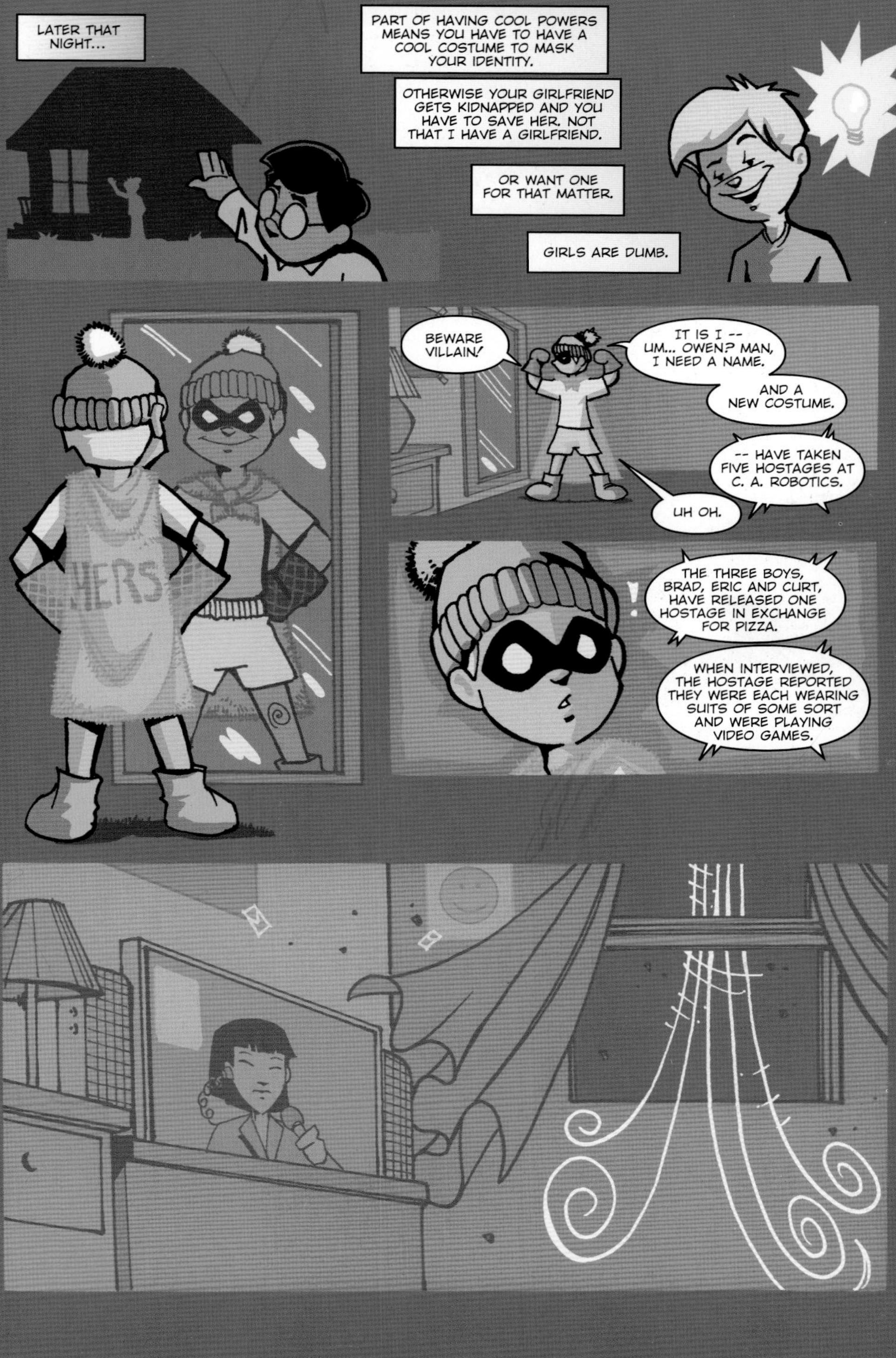
LATER THAT NIGHT...
PART OF HAVING COOL POWERS MEANS YOU HAVE TO HAVE A COOL COSTUME TO MASK YOUR IDENTITY.
OTHERWISE YOUR GIRLFRIEND GETS KIDNAPPED AND YOU HAVE TO SAVE HER. NOT THAT I HAVE A GIRLFRIEND.
OR WANT ONE FOR THAT MATTER.
GIRLS ARE DUMB.
BEWARE VILLAIN!
IT IS I -- UM... OWEN? MAN, I NEED A NAME.
AND A NEW COSTUME.
-- HAVE TAKEN FIVE HOSTAGES AT C. A. ROBOTICS.
UH OH.
THE THREE BOYS, BRAD, ERIC AND CURT, HAVE RELEASED ONE HOSTAGE IN EXCHANGE FOR PIZZA.
WHEN INTERVIEWED, THE HOSTAGE REPORTED THEY WERE EACH WEARING SUITS OF SOME SORT AND WERE PLAYING VIDEO GAMES.

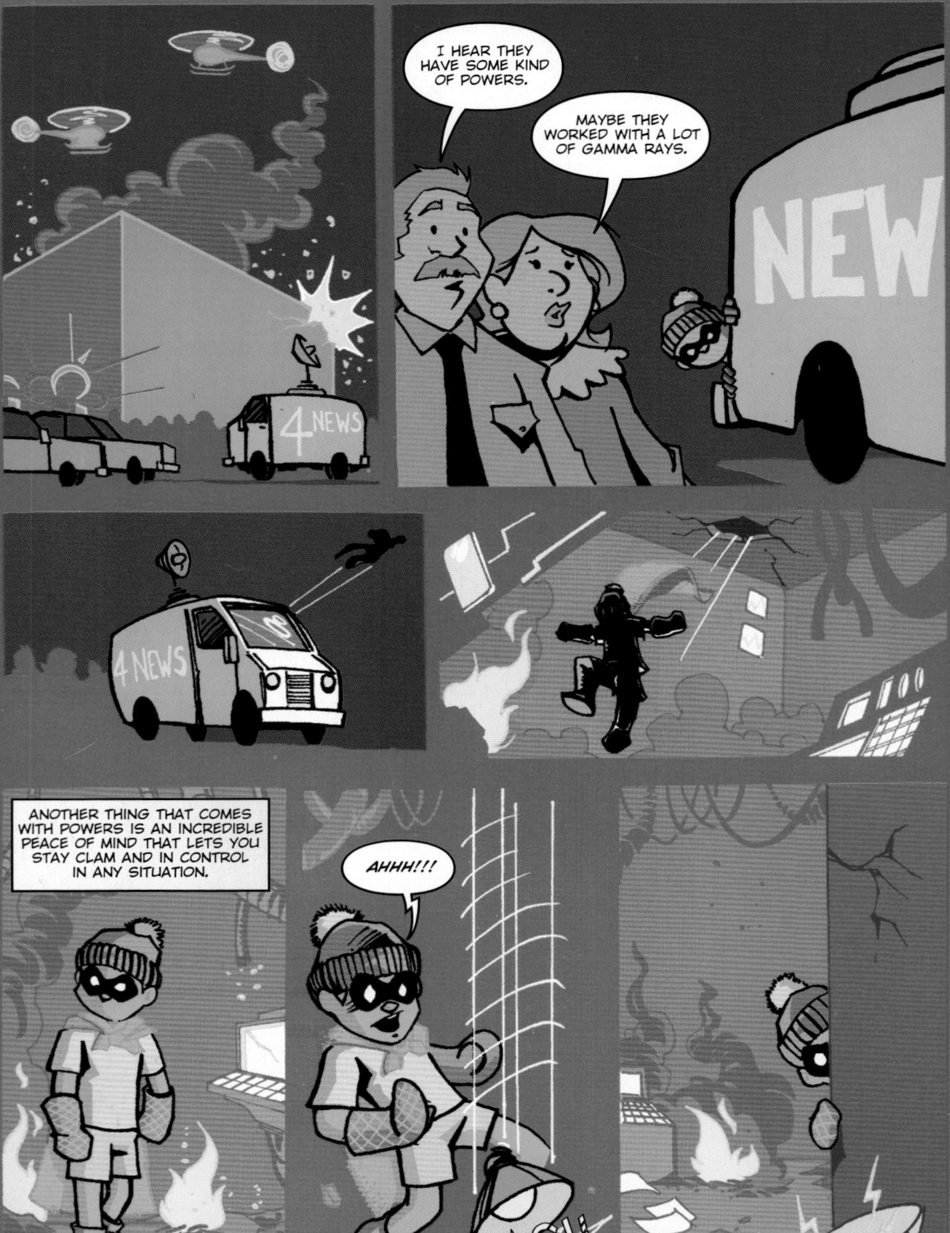
4 NEWS
I HEAR THEY HAVE SOME KIND OF POWERS.
MAYBE THEY WORKED WITH A LOT OF GAMMA RAYS.
NEW
4 NEWS
ANOTHER THING THAT COMES WITH POWERS IS AN INCREDIBLE PEACE OF MIND THAT LETS YOU STAY CLAM AND IN CONTROL IN ANY SITUATION.
AHHH!!!
CRASH

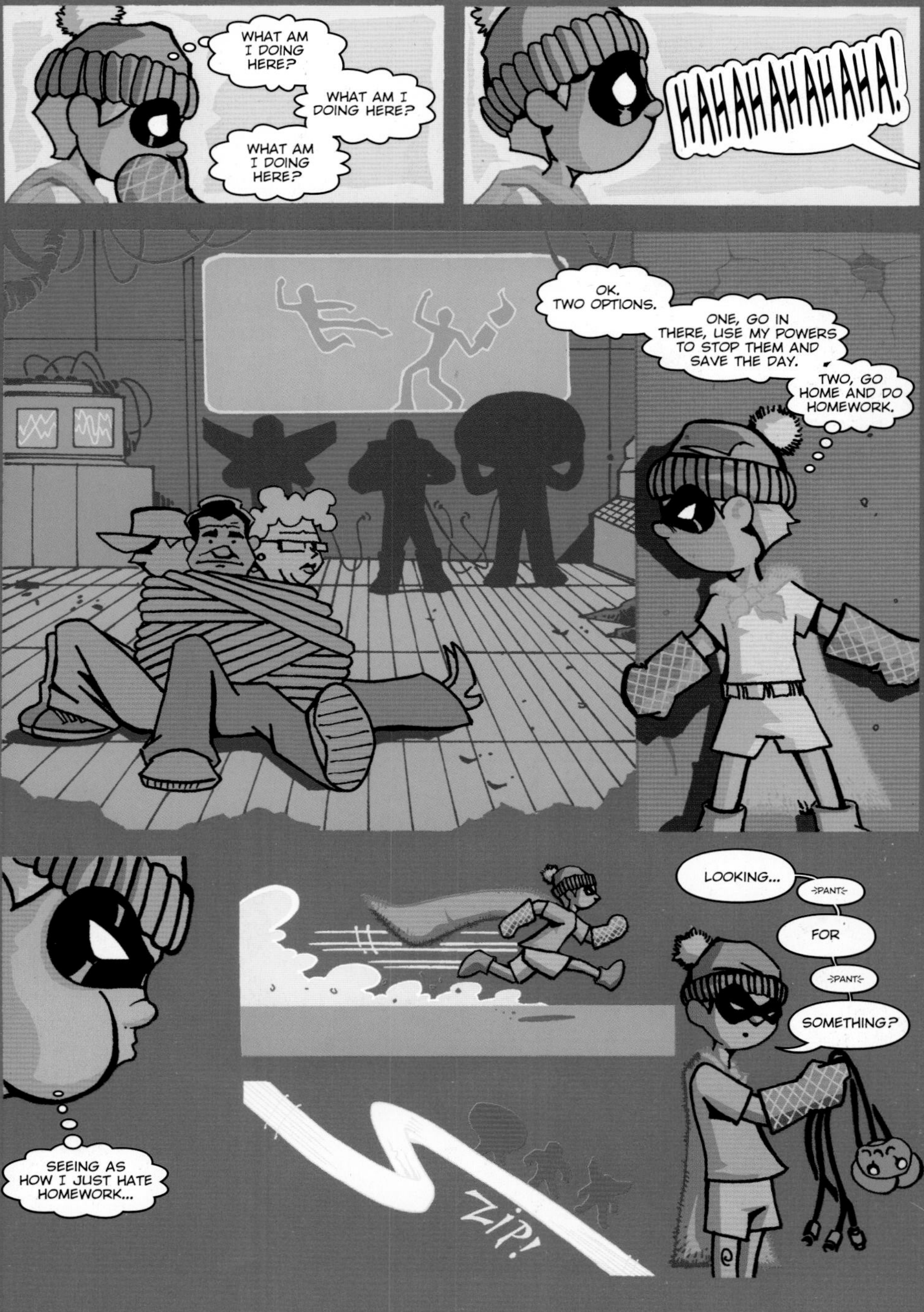
WHAT AM I DOING HERE?
WHAT AM I DOING HERE?
WHAT AM I DOING HERE?
HAHAHAHAHAHA!
OK. TWO OPTIONS.
ONE, GO IN THERE, USE MY POWERS TO STOP THEM AND SAVE THE DAY.
TWO, GO HOME AND DO HOMEWORK.
SEEING AS HOW I JUST HATE HOMEWORK...
ZIP!
LOOKING...
PANT
FOR
PANT
SOMETHING?

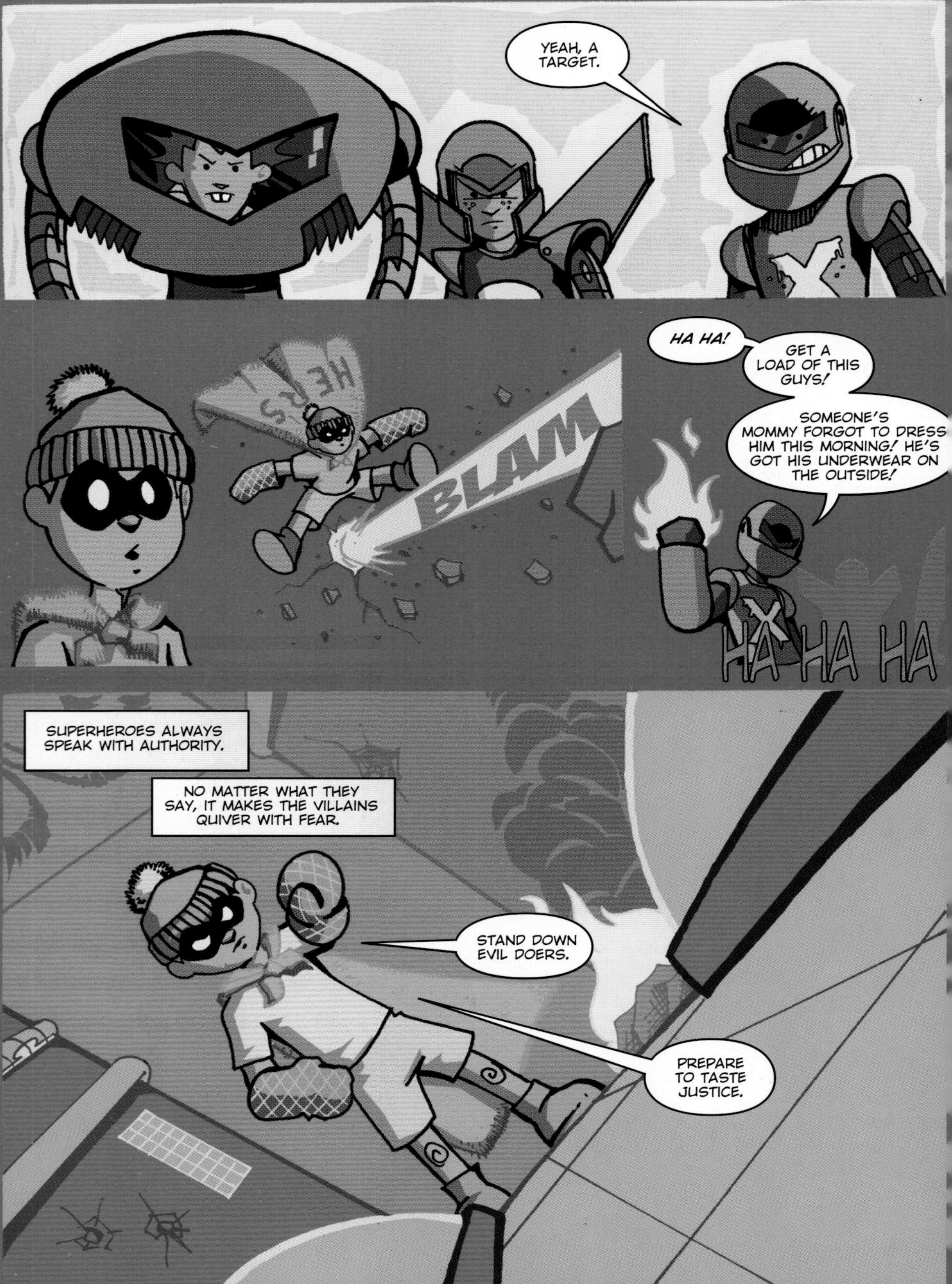
YEAH, A TARGET.
HERS
BLAM
HA HA!
GET A LOAD OF THIS GUYS!
SOMEONE'S MOMMY FORGOT TO DRESS HIM THIS MORNING! HE'S GOT HIS UNDERWEAR ON THE OUTSIDE!
HA HA HA
SUPERHEROES ALWAYS SPEAK WITH AUTHORITY.
NO MATTER WHAT THEY SAY, IT MAKES THE VILLAINS QUIVER WITH FEAR.
STAND DOWN EVIL DOERS.
PREPARE TO TASTE JUSTICE.

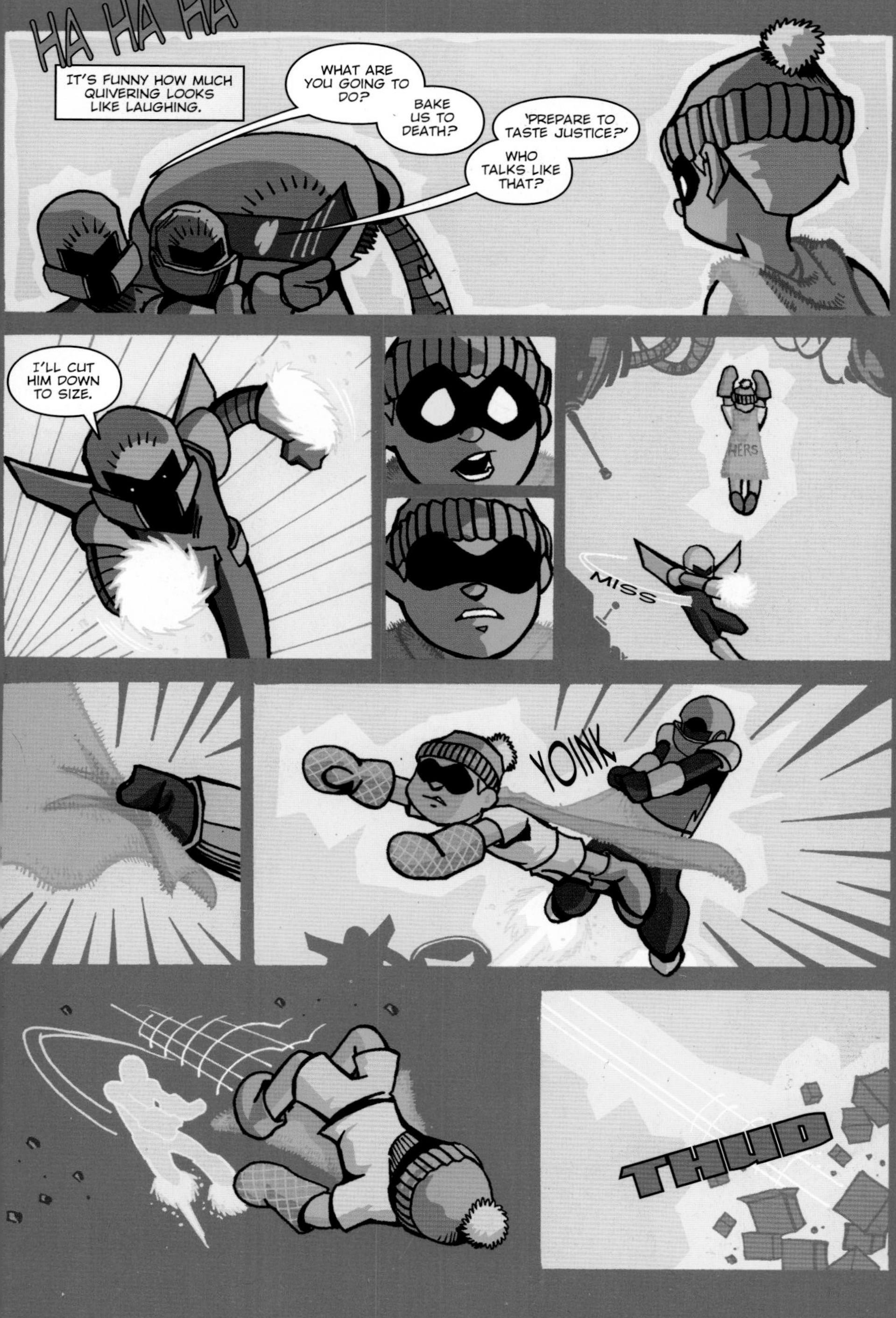
HA HA HA
IT'S FUNNY HOW MUCH QUIVERING LOOKS LIKE LAUGHING.
WHAT ARE YOU GOING TO DO?
BAKE US TO DEATH?
'PREPARE TO TASTE JUSTICE?'
WHO TALKS LIKE THAT?
I'LL CUT HIM DOWN TO SIZE.
HERS
MISS
YOINK
THUD

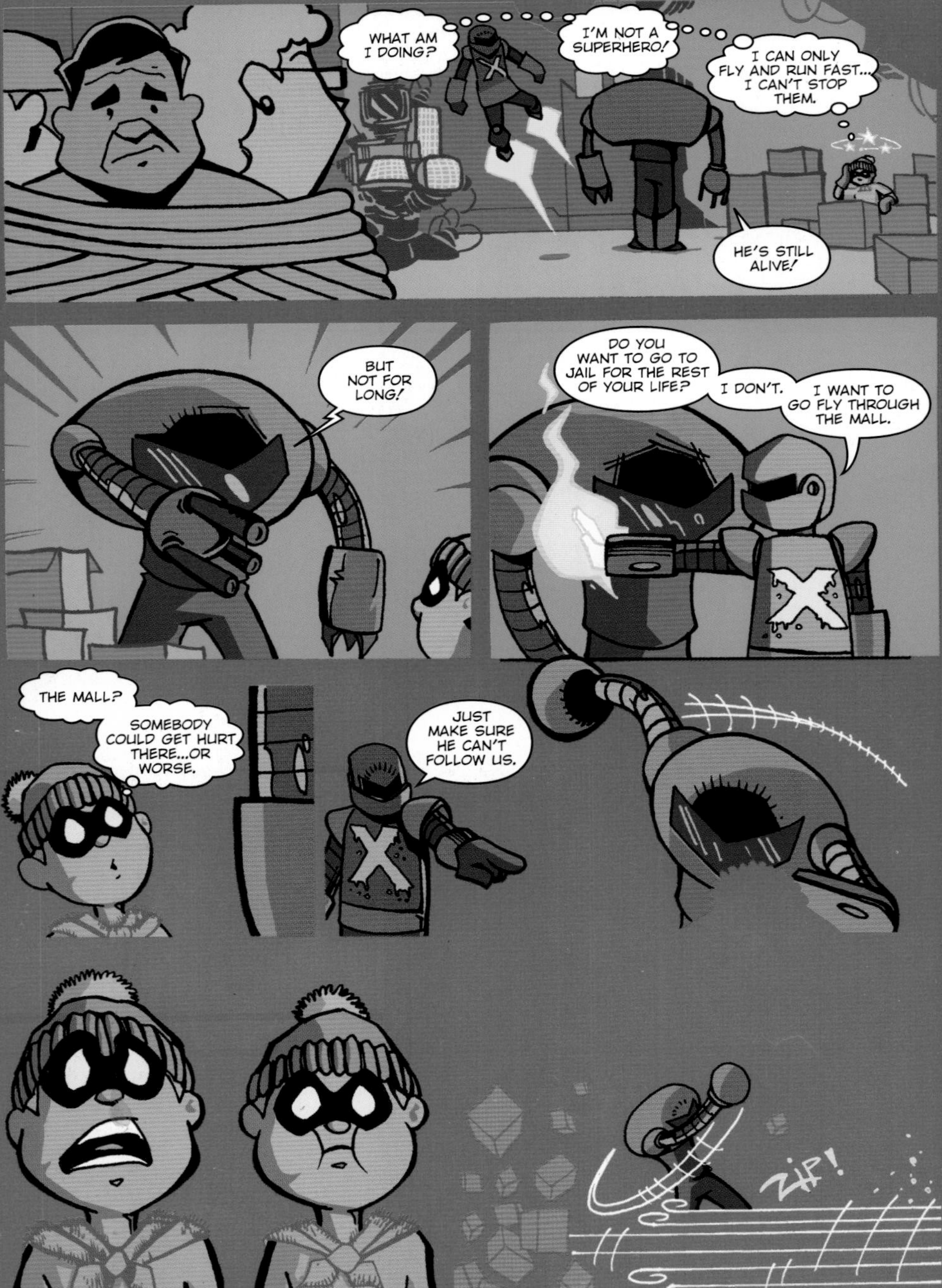
WHAT AM I DOING?
I'M NOT A SUPERHERO!
I CAN ONLY FLY AND RUN FAST... I CAN'T STOP THEM.
HE'S STILL ALIVE!
BUT NOT FOR LONG!
DO YOU WANT TO GO TO JAIL FOR THE REST OF YOUR LIFE?
I DON'T.
I WANT TO GO FLY THROUGH THE MALL.
THE MALL?
SOMEBODY COULD GET HURT THERE...OR WORSE.
JUST MAKE SURE HE CAN'T FOLLOW US.
ZIP!

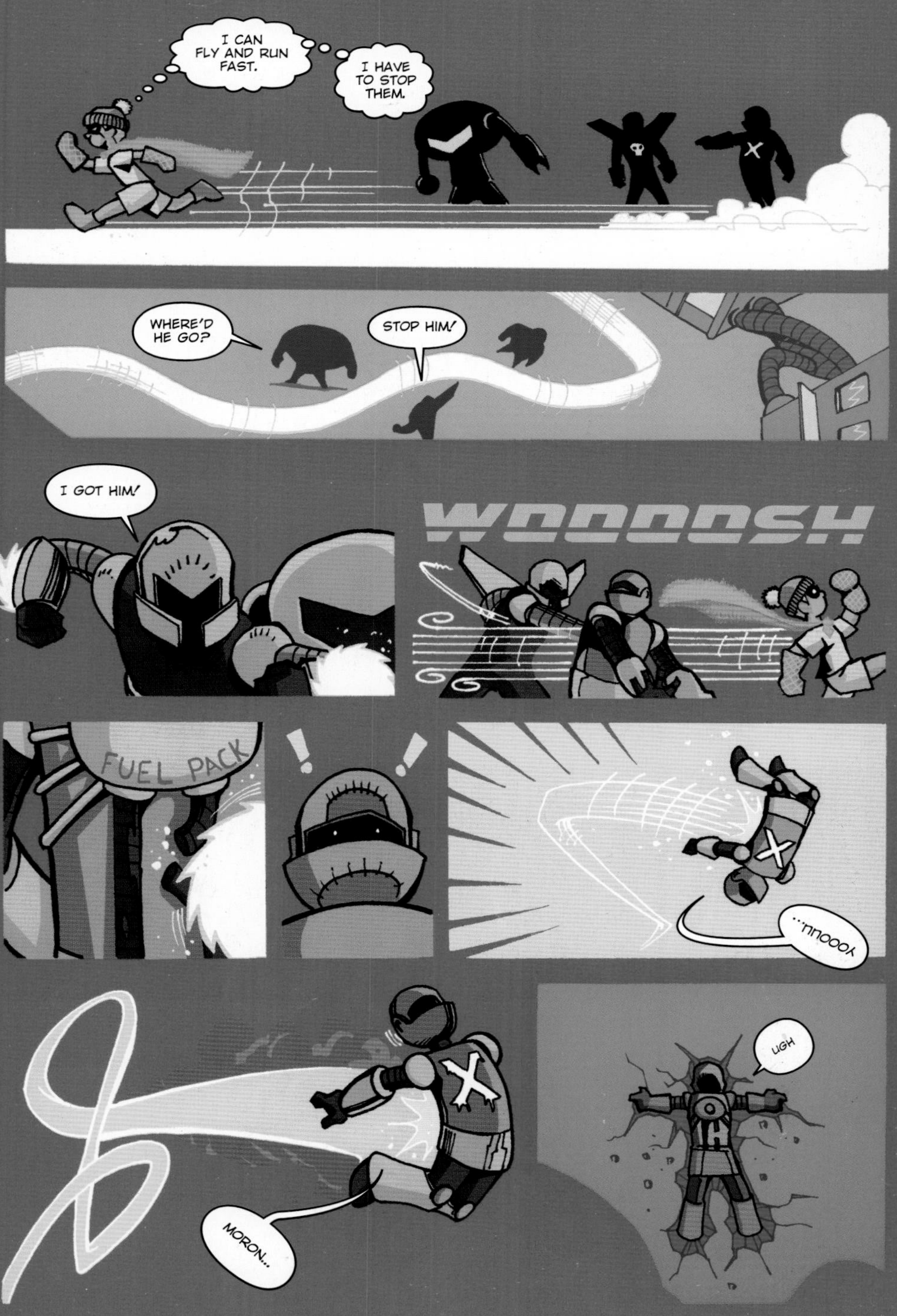
I CAN FLY AND RUN FAST.
I HAVE TO STOP THEM.
WHERE'D HE GO?
STOP HIM!
I GOT HIM!
WOOOOSH
FUEL PACK
!
!
YOOOUU...
MORON...
UGH

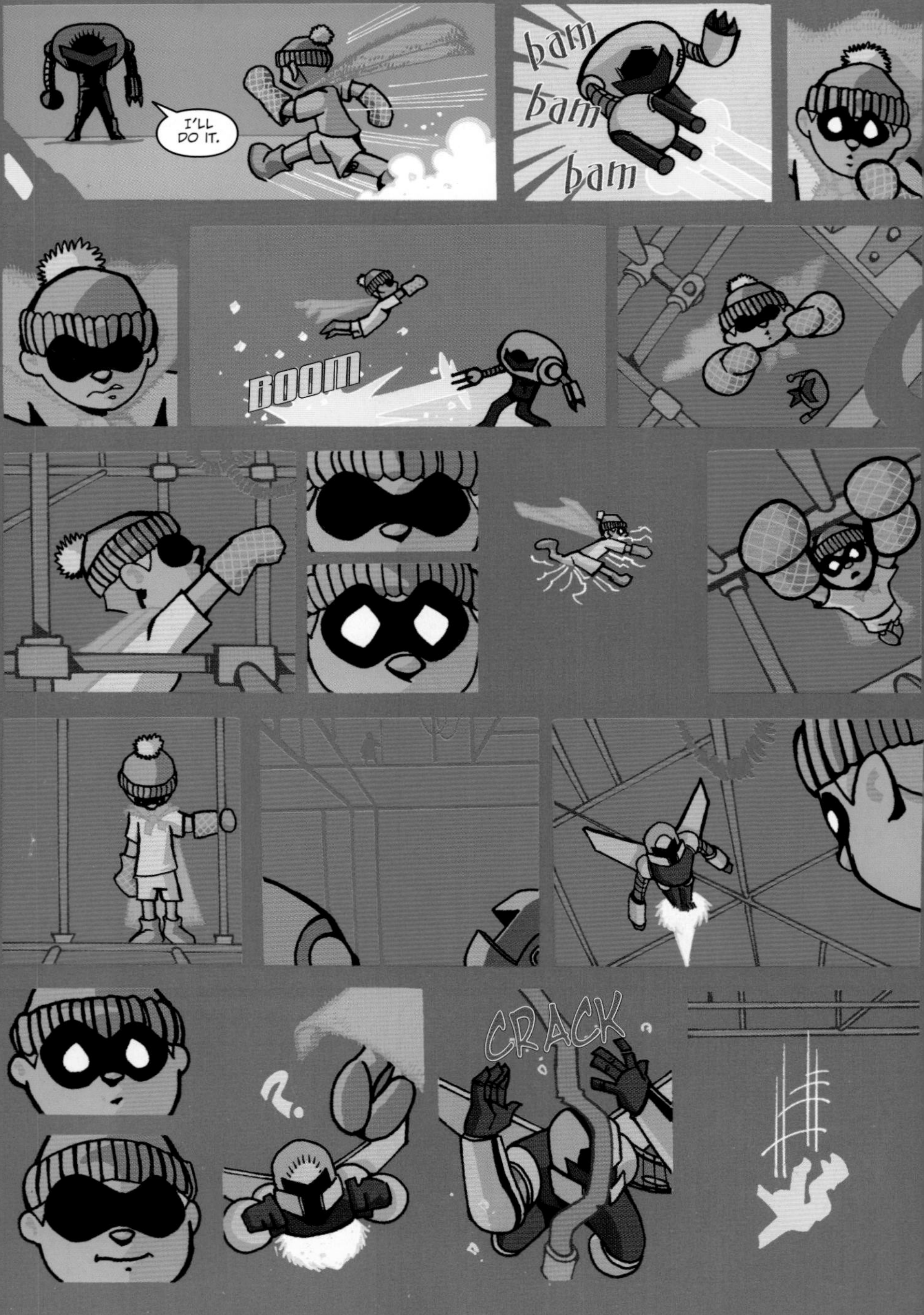
I'LL DO IT.
bam
bam
bam
BOOM
CRACK

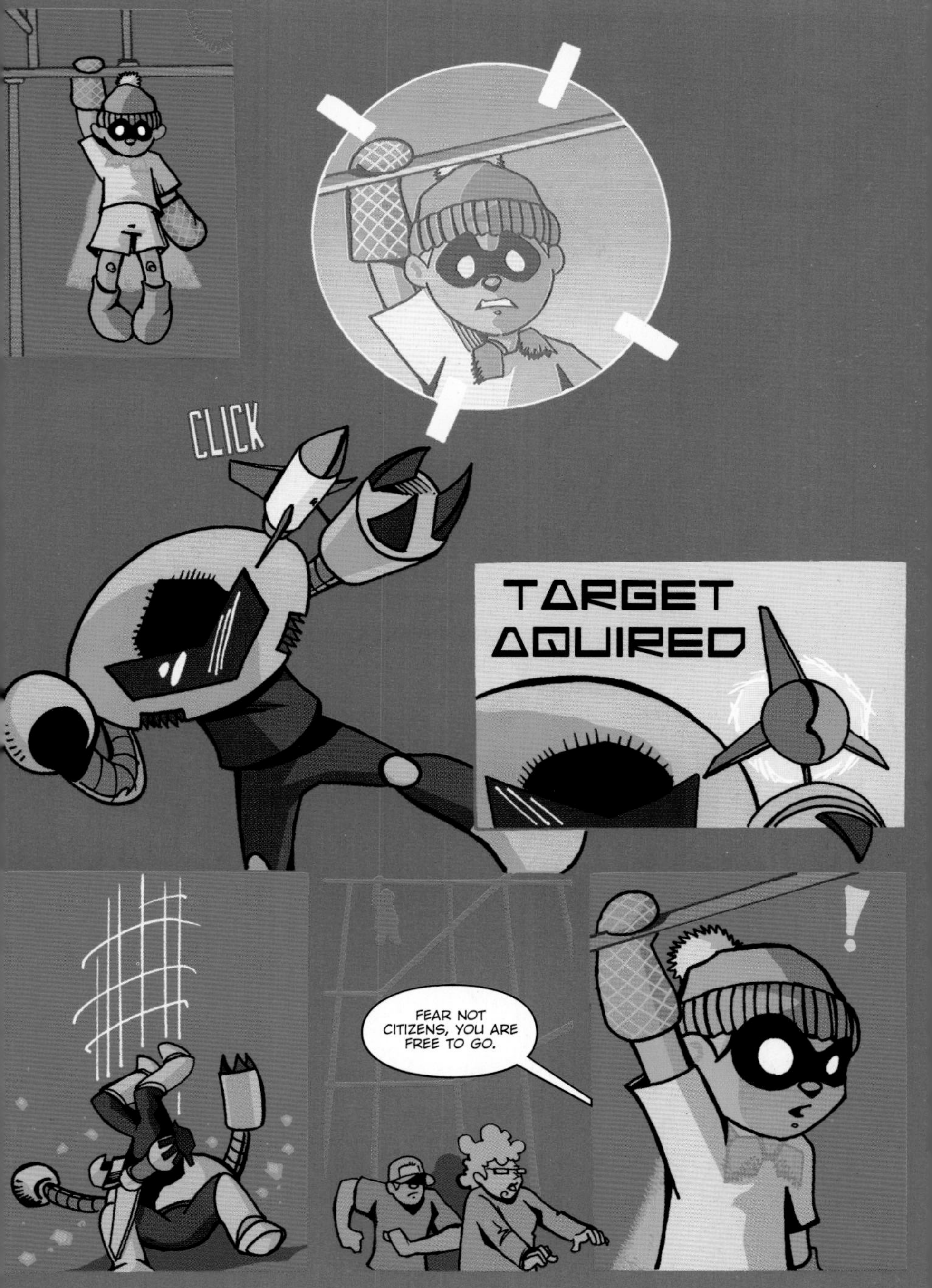
CLICK
TARGET AQUIRED
FEAR NOT CITIZENS, YOU ARE FREE TO GO.
!

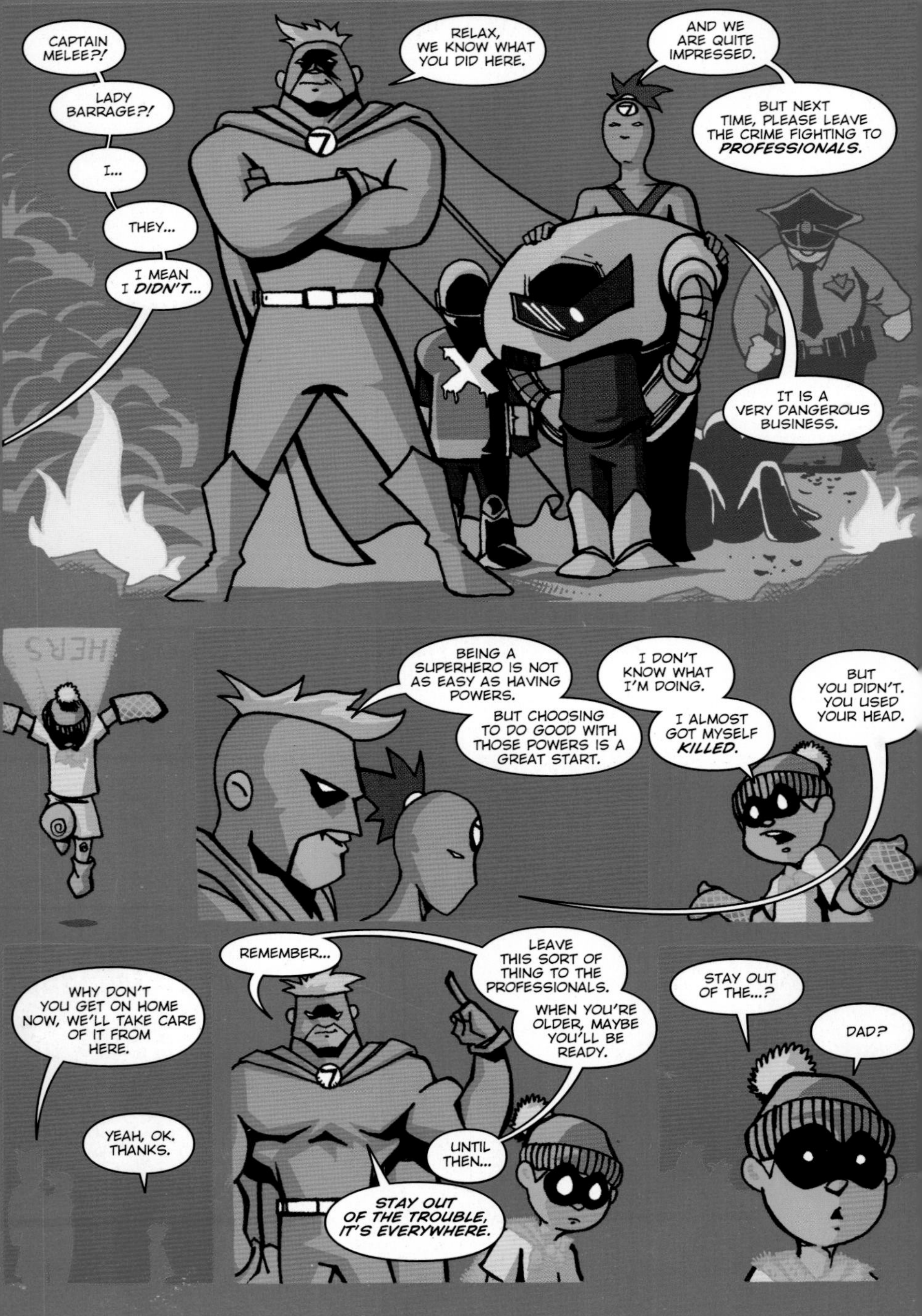
CAPTAIN MELEE?!
LADY BARRAGE?!
I...
THEY...
I MEAN I DIDN'T...
RELAX, WE KNOW WHAT YOU DID HERE.
AND WE ARE QUITE IMPRESSED.
BUT NEXT TIME, PLEASE LEAVE THE CRIME FIGHTING TO PROFESSIONALS.
IT IS A VERY DANGEROUS BUSINESS.
HERS
BEING A SUPERHERO IS NOT AS EASY AS HAVING POWERS.
BUT CHOOSING TO DO GOOD WITH THOSE POWERS IS A GREAT START.
I DON'T KNOW WHAT I'M DOING.
I ALMOST GOT MYSELF KILLED.
BUT YOU DIDN'T. YOU USED YOUR HEAD.
WHY DON'T YOU GET ON HOME NOW, WE'LL TAKE CARE OF IT FROM HERE.
YEAH, OK. THANKS.
REMEMBER...
LEAVE THIS SORT OF THING TO THE PROFESSIONALS.
WHEN YOU'RE OLDER, MAYBE YOU'LL BE READY.
UNTIL THEN...
STAY OUT OF THE TROUBLE, IT'S EVERYWHERE.
STAY OUT OF THE...?
DAD?

KYLE!

ARE YOU WATCHING THE NEWS?!

...AND THEN I LET ALL THE HOSTAGES GO.

TURN IT ON CHANNEL 3!

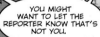

THE THREE BOYS WERE APPREHENDED BY TWO OF KENSVILLE'S VERY OWN NOBLE SEVEN: CAPTAIN MELEE AND LADY BARRAGE.

SHUT IT.

YOU MIGHT WANT TO LET THE REPORTER KNOW THAT'S NOT YOU.

AND WHILE YOU ARE THERE, YOU SHOULD LET THEM KNOW YOU HAVE THE INSIDE SCOOP ON A KID GOING CRAZY.

BEEP

COLD   COLD   COLD

ZAP

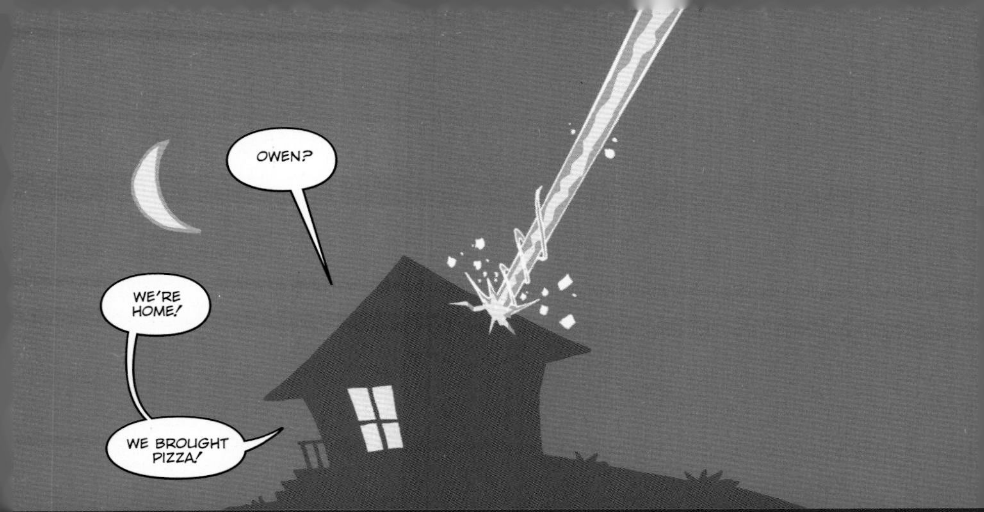
OWEN?
WE'RE HOME!
WE BROUGHT PIZZA!

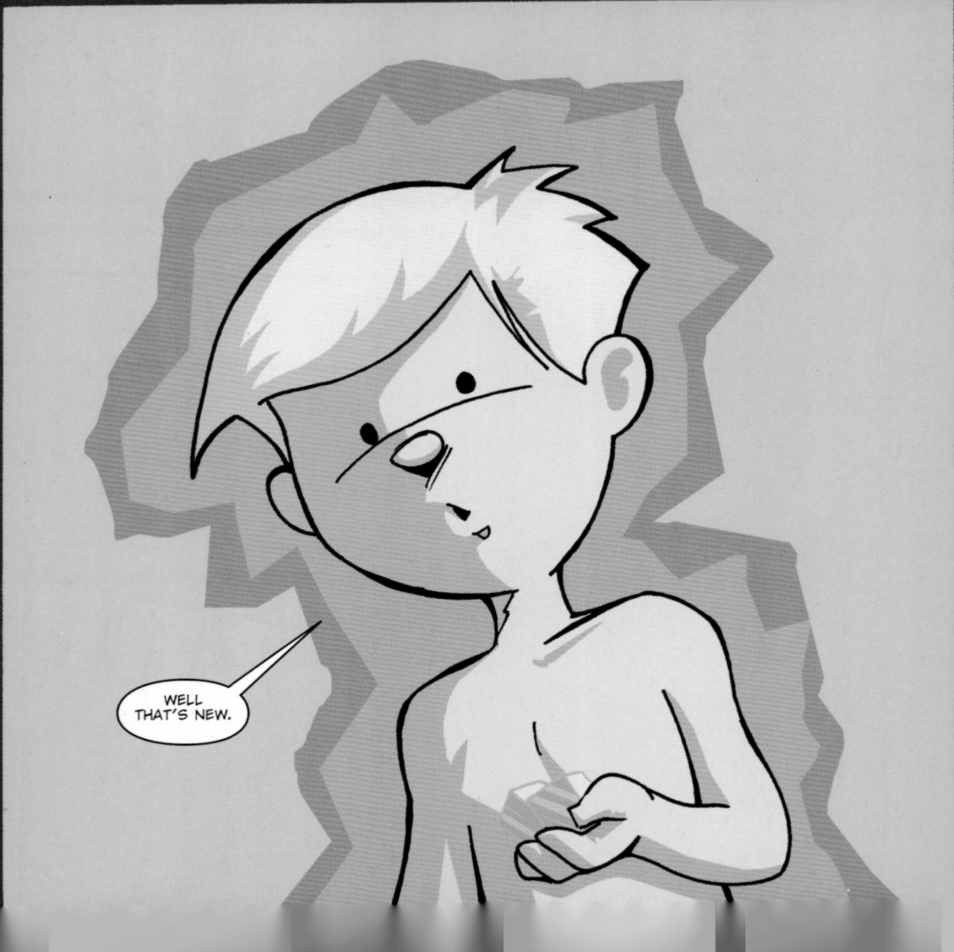
WELL THAT'S NEW.

chapter 2
THE ASTONISH KID

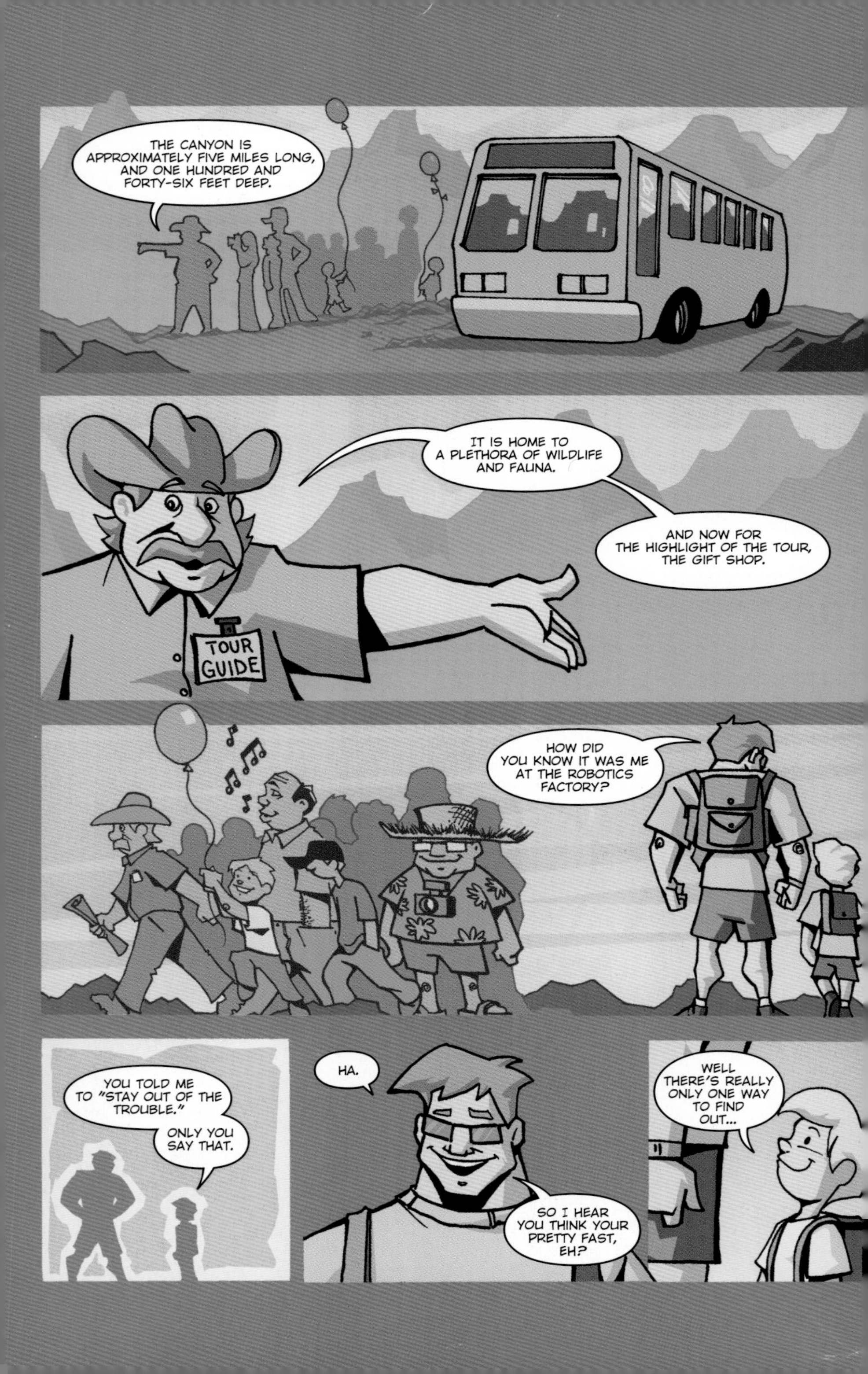
THE CANYON IS APPROXIMATELY FIVE MILES LONG, AND ONE HUNDRED AND FORTY-SIX FEET DEEP.
IT IS HOME TO A PLETHORA OF WILDLIFE AND FAUNA.
AND NOW FOR THE HIGHLIGHT OF THE TOUR, THE GIFT SHOP.
TOUR GUIDE
HOW DID YOU KNOW IT WAS ME AT THE ROBOTICS FACTORY?
YOU TOLD ME TO "STAY OUT OF THE TROUBLE."
ONLY YOU SAY THAT.
HA.
SO I HEAR YOU THINK YOUR PRETTY FAST, EH?
WELL THERE'S REALLY ONLY ONE WAY TO FIND OUT...

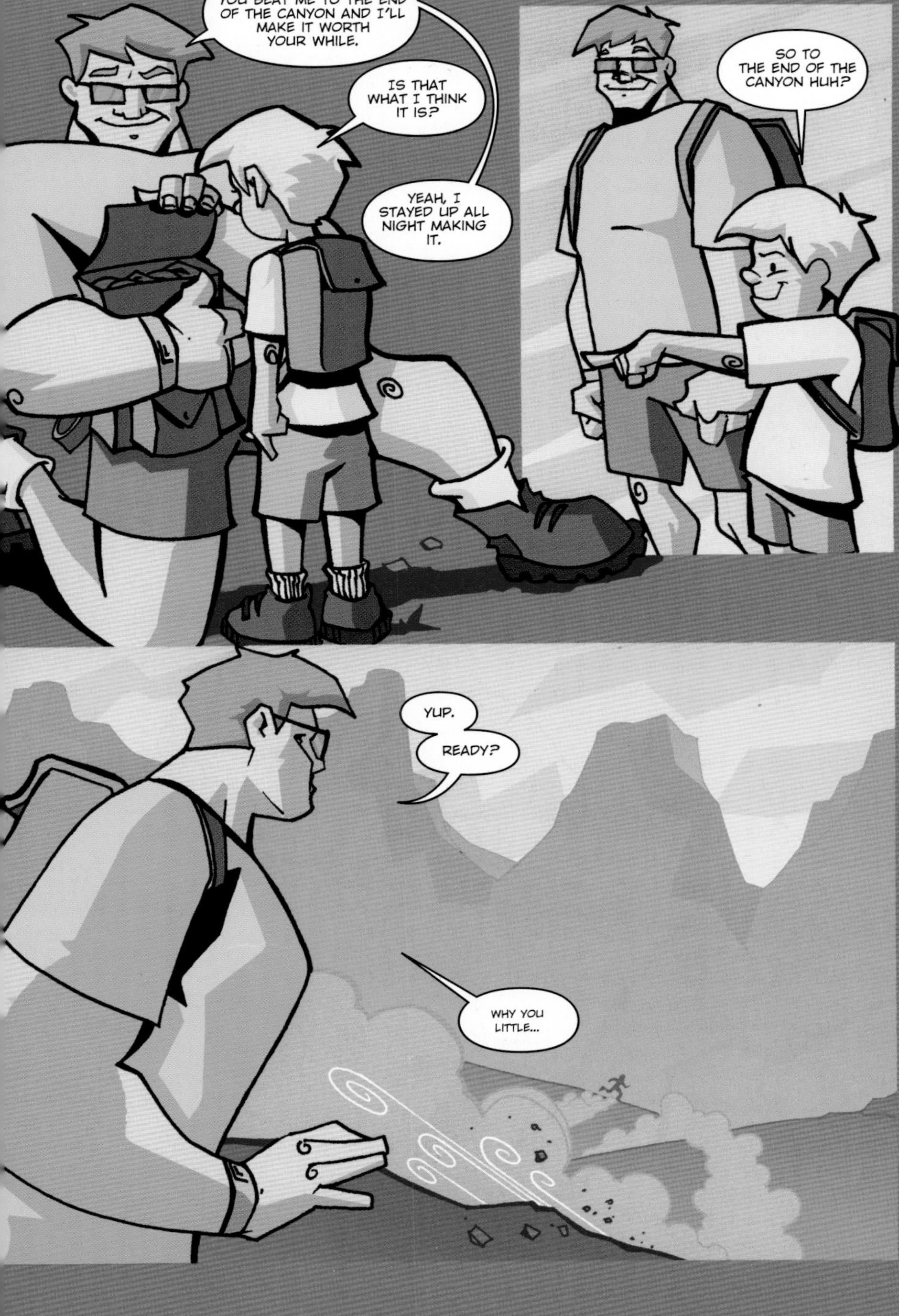
TELL YOU WHAT, YOU BEAT ME TO THE END OF THE CANYON AND I'LL MAKE IT WORTH YOUR WHILE.
IS THAT WHAT I THINK IT IS?
YEAH, I STAYED UP ALL NIGHT MAKING IT.
SO TO THE END OF THE CANYON HUH?
YUP.
READY?
WHY YOU LITTLE...

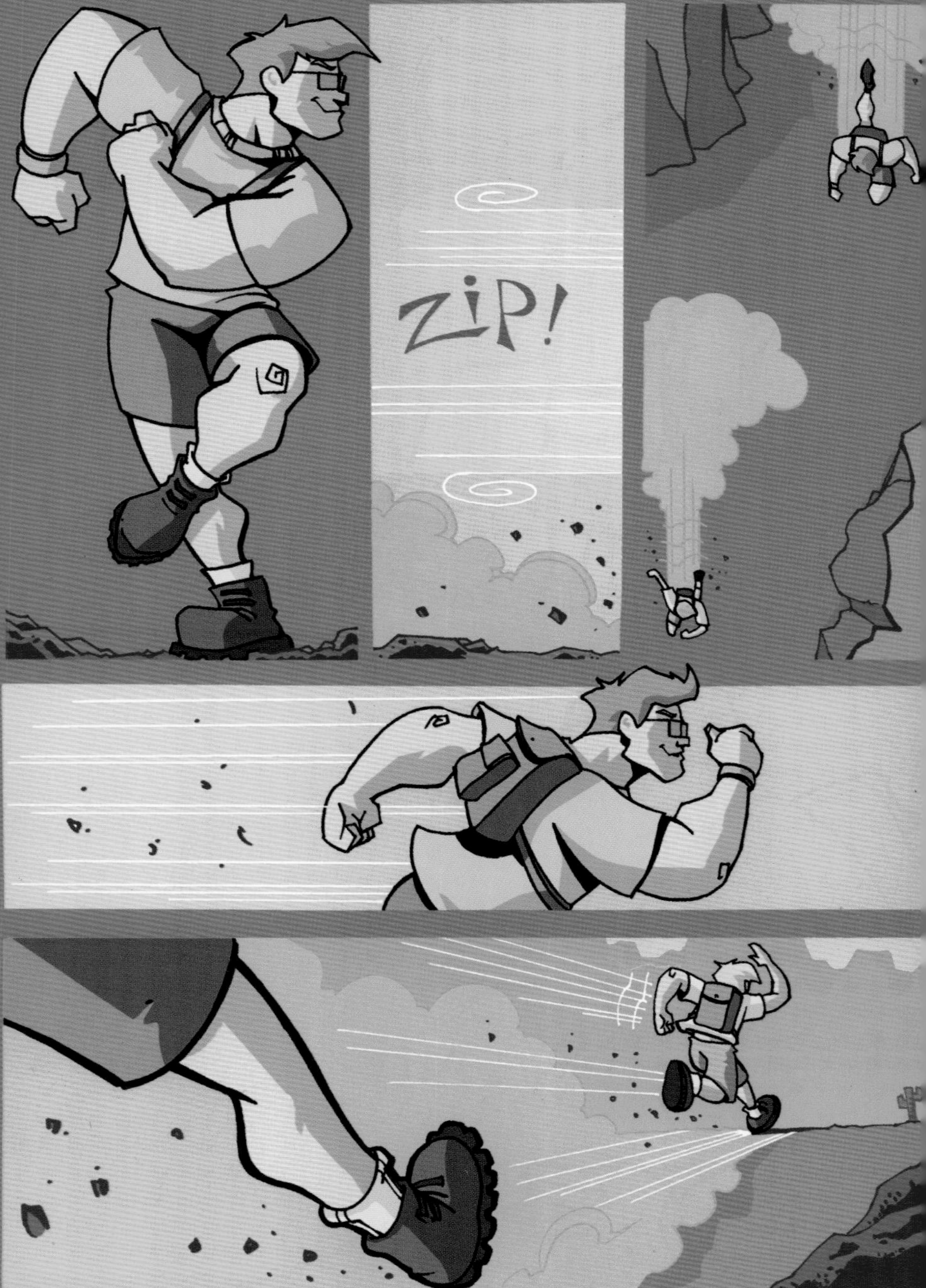
ZIP!

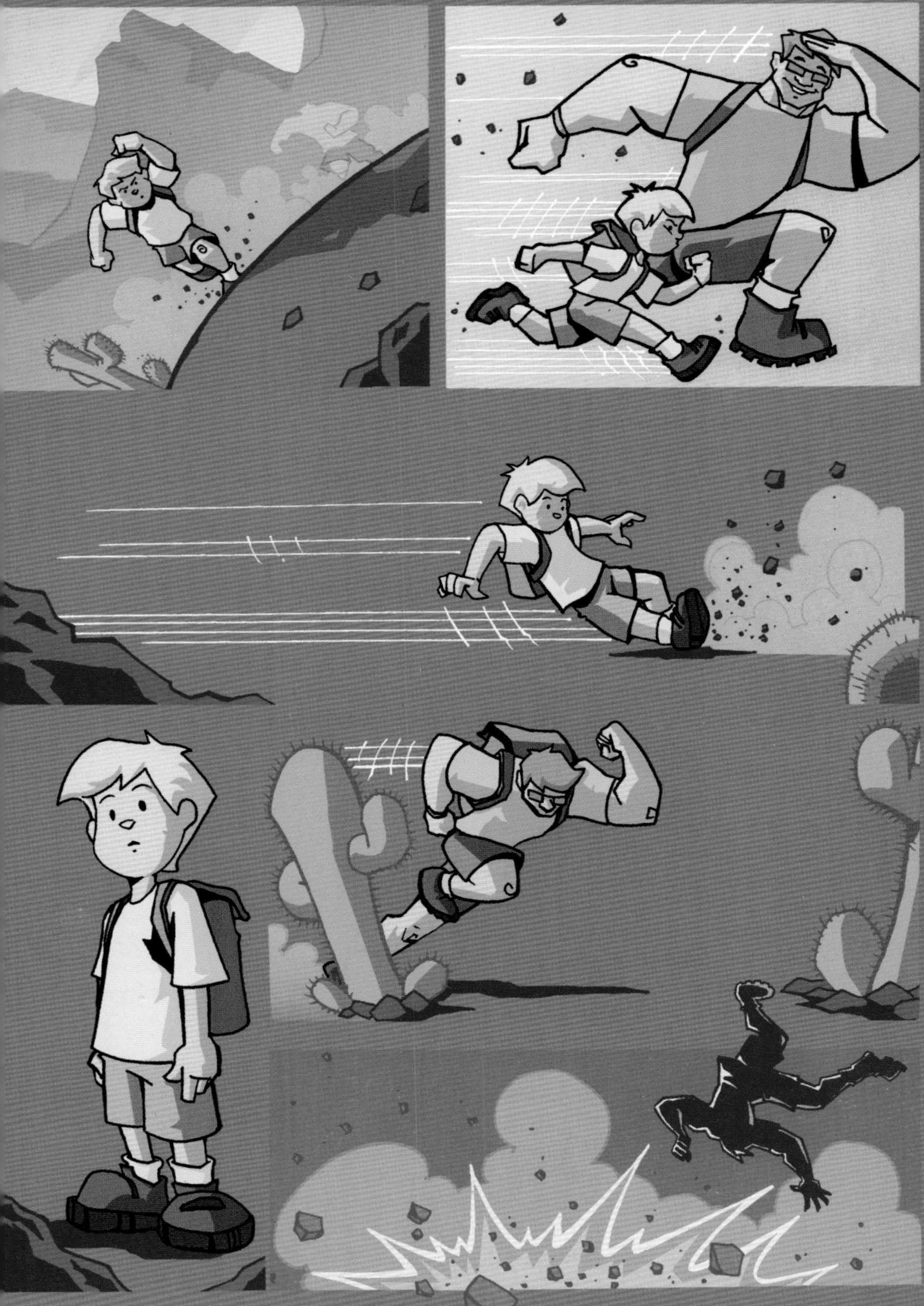

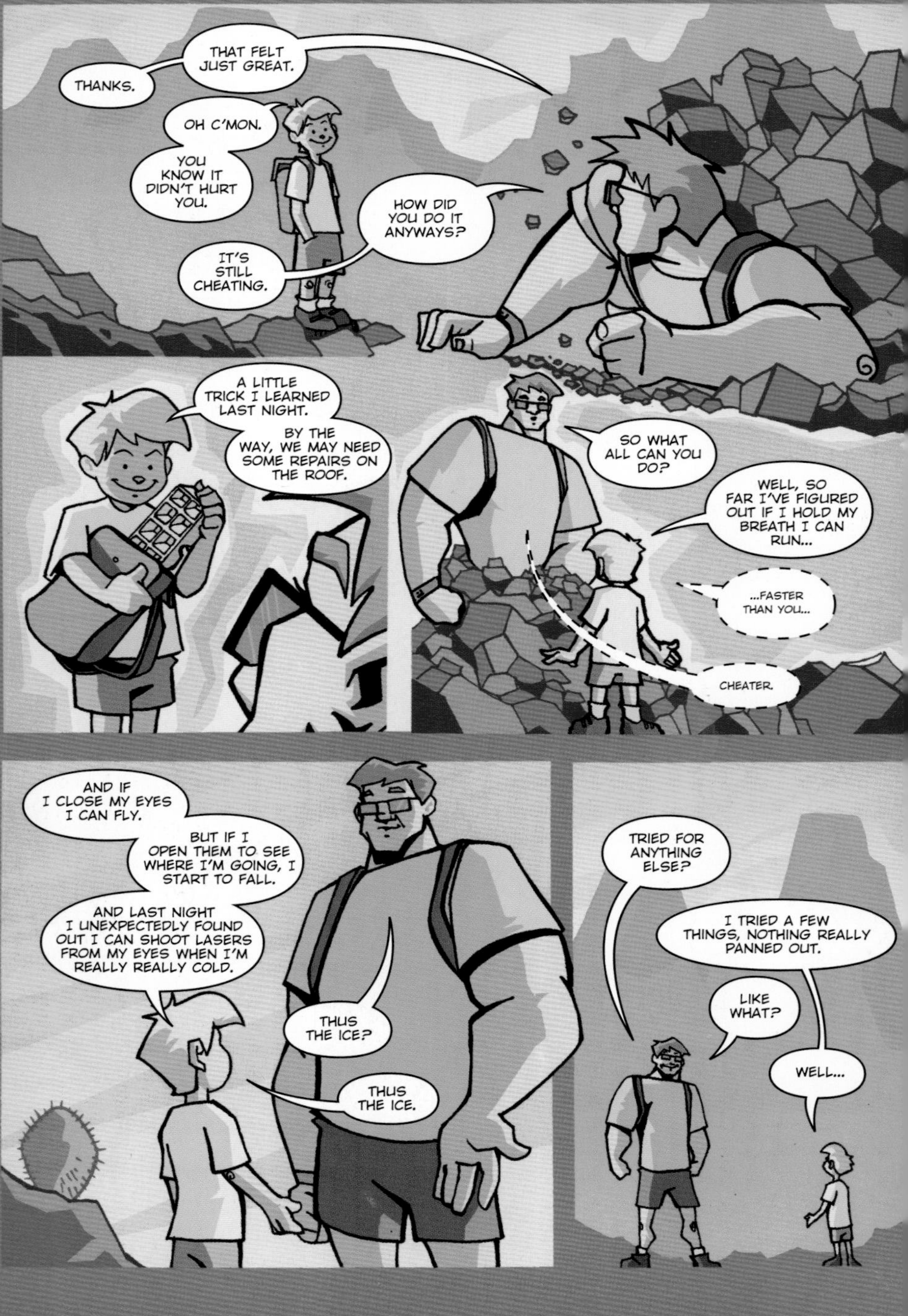
THANKS.
THAT FELT JUST GREAT.
OH C'MON.
YOU KNOW IT DIDN'T HURT YOU.
HOW DID YOU DO IT ANYWAYS?
IT'S STILL CHEATING.
A LITTLE TRICK I LEARNED LAST NIGHT.
BY THE WAY, WE MAY NEED SOME REPAIRS ON THE ROOF.
SO WHAT ALL CAN YOU DO?
WELL, SO FAR I'VE FIGURED OUT IF I HOLD MY BREATH I CAN RUN...
...FASTER THAN YOU...
CHEATER.
AND IF I CLOSE MY EYES I CAN FLY.
BUT IF I OPEN THEM TO SEE WHERE I'M GOING, I START TO FALL.
AND LAST NIGHT I UNEXPECTEDLY FOUND OUT I CAN SHOOT LASERS FROM MY EYES WHEN I'M REALLY REALLY COLD.
THUS THE ICE?
THUS THE ICE.
TRIED FOR ANYTHING ELSE?
I TRIED A FEW THINGS, NOTHING REALLY PANNED OUT.
LIKE WHAT?
WELL...

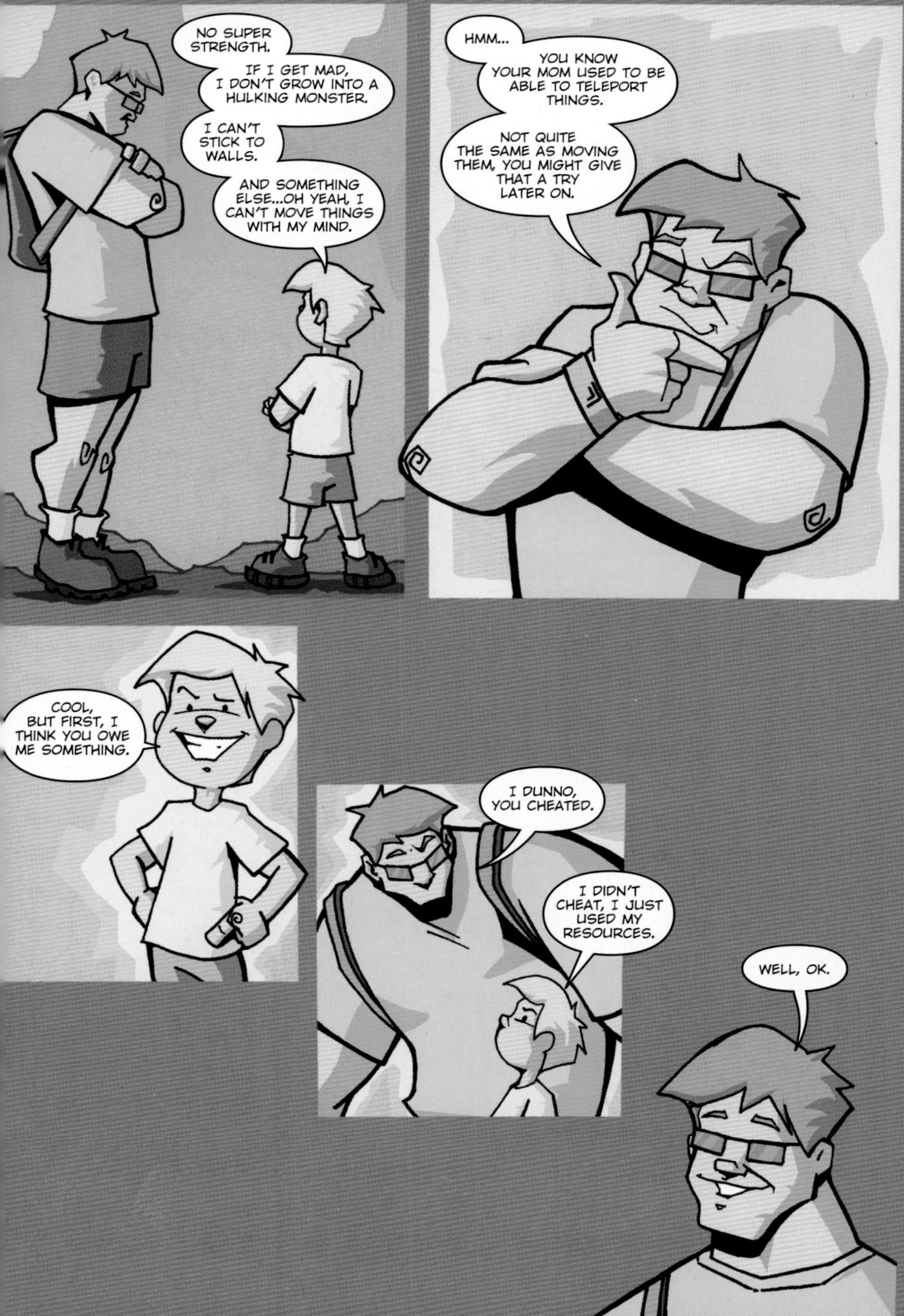
NO SUPER STRENGTH.
IF I GET MAD, I DON'T GROW INTO A HULKING MONSTER.
I CAN'T STICK TO WALLS.
AND SOMETHING ELSE...OH YEAH, I CAN'T MOVE THINGS WITH MY MIND.
HMM...
YOU KNOW YOUR MOM USED TO BE ABLE TO TELEPORT THINGS.
NOT QUITE THE SAME AS MOVING THEM, YOU MIGHT GIVE THAT A TRY LATER ON.
COOL, BUT FIRST, I THINK YOU OWE ME SOMETHING.
I DUNNO, YOU CHEATED.
I DIDN'T CHEAT, I JUST USED MY RESOURCES.
WELL, OK.

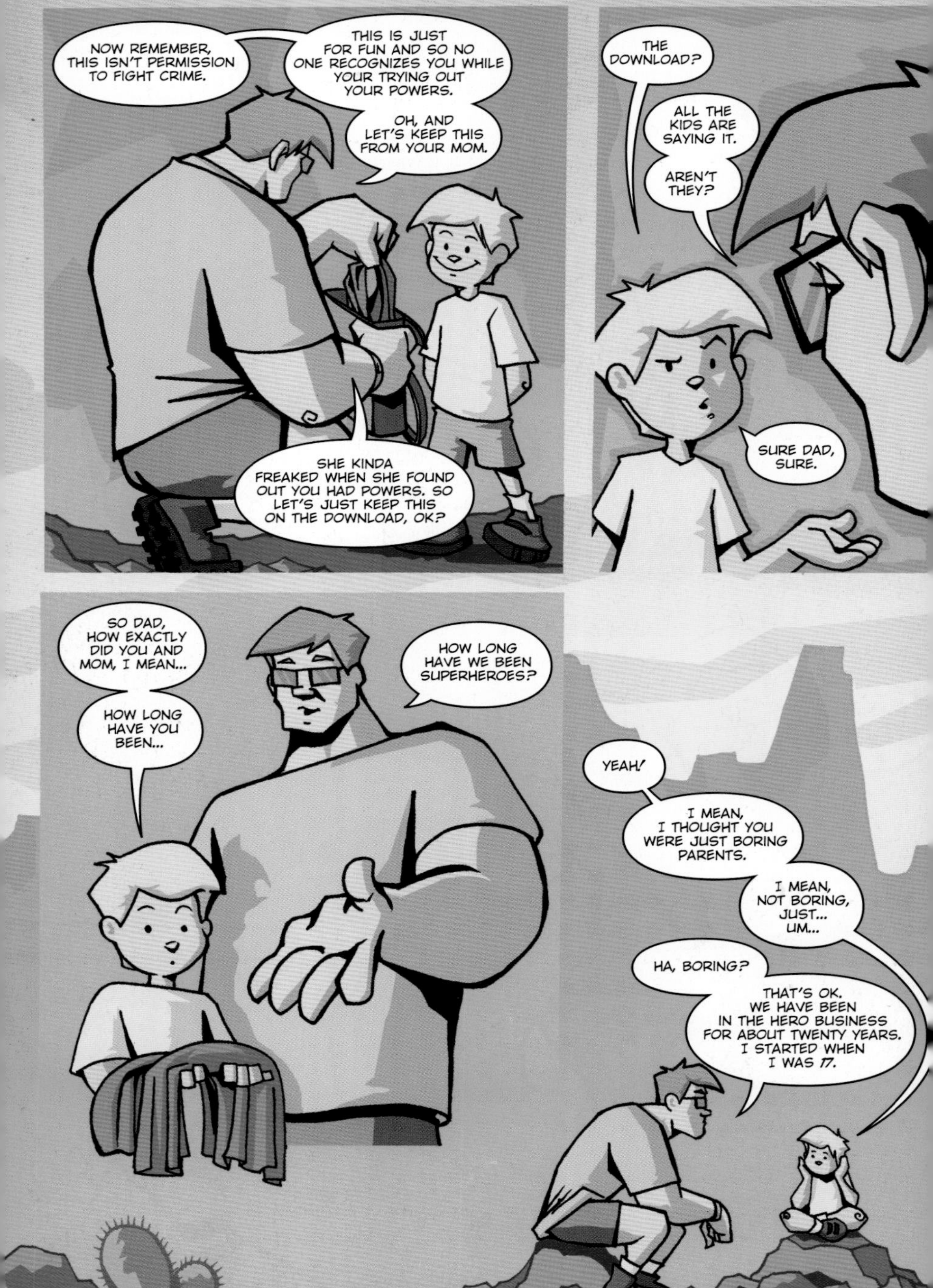

NOW REMEMBER, THIS ISN'T PERMISSION TO FIGHT CRIME.
THIS IS JUST FOR FUN AND SO NO ONE RECOGNIZES YOU WHILE YOUR TRYING OUT YOUR POWERS.
OH, AND LET'S KEEP THIS FROM YOUR MOM.
SHE KINDA FREAKED WHEN SHE FOUND OUT YOU HAD POWERS. SO LET'S JUST KEEP THIS ON THE DOWNLOAD, OK?
THE DOWNLOAD?
ALL THE KIDS ARE SAYING IT.
AREN'T THEY?
SURE DAD, SURE.
SO DAD, HOW EXACTLY DID YOU AND MOM, I MEAN...
HOW LONG HAVE YOU BEEN...
HOW LONG HAVE WE BEEN SUPERHEROES?
YEAH!
I MEAN, I THOUGHT YOU WERE JUST BORING PARENTS.
I MEAN, NOT BORING, JUST... UM...
HA, BORING?
THAT'S OK. WE HAVE BEEN IN THE HERO BUSINESS FOR ABOUT TWENTY YEARS. I STARTED WHEN I WAS 17.

I WASN'T BORN WITH SUPERPOWERS.

I WAS JUST A KID IN HIGH SCHOOL.
I WAS THE QUARTERBACK, PROM KING.
I WAS DATING THE HEAD CHEERLEADER.

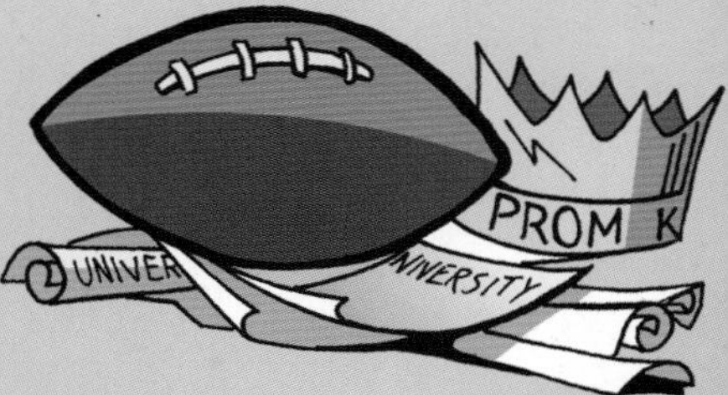
PROM K
UNIVER
NIVERSITY

I THOUGHT I HAD IT ALL TOGETHER.
I HAD A SCHOLARSHIP ALL SET UP
TO PLAY BALL.

THEN I BLEW OUT MY KNEE.

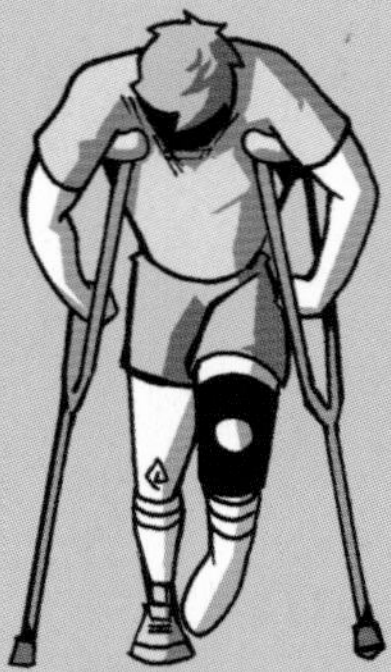

WHILE I WAS HEALING I STARTED REALIZING
THAT WITHOUT FOOTBALL, I REALLY
DIDN'T HAVE ANYTHING AT ALL. I LOST MY
SCHOLARSHIP. MY GIRLFRIEND LEFT ME. MY
FRIENDS WEREN'T REALLY FRIENDS.

IT WAS TOUGH.

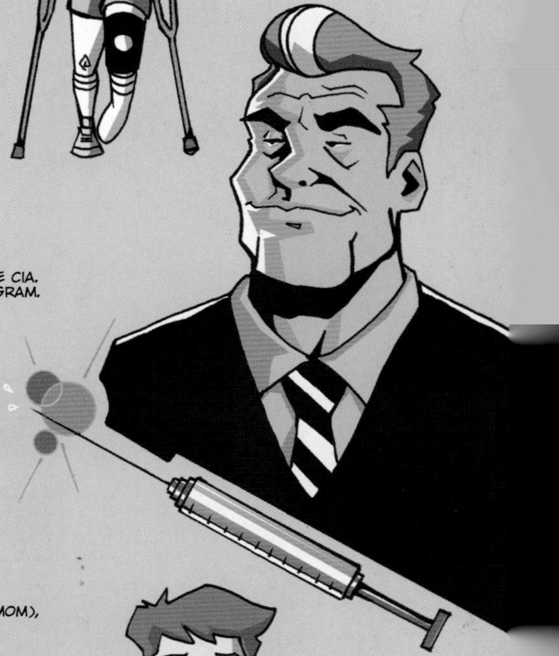

THEN I MET STAN.

STAN WAS A RECRUITER FOR THE CIA.
HE WANTED ME FOR A NEW PROGRAM.

SINCE SCHOOL WAS OUT, I JOINED UP.

THE NEW PROGRAM HE PUT ME IN INVOLVED
A SERUM TO HEAL MY LEG FASTER.

THERE WERE THREE OF US
THAT TOOK THE SERUM.

MYSELF,
A BEAUTIFUL GIRL NAMED SHELBY (YOUR MOM),
AND AN OLDER KID NAMED LEONARD.

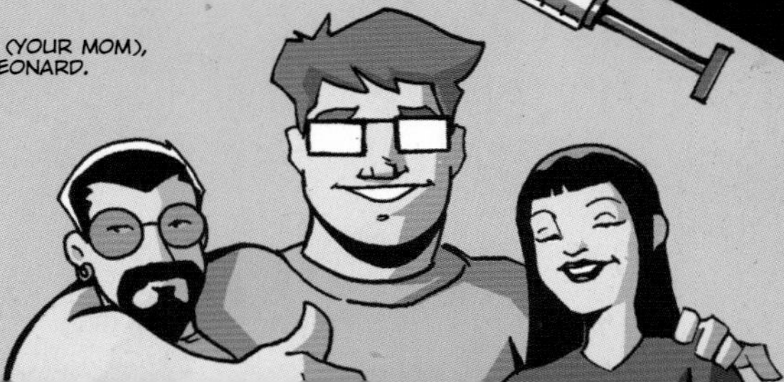

LEONARD WAS A WEIRD GUY, KIND OF A LONER.
HE LOST HIS LEG IN THE WAR.

YOUR MOM HAD ASTHMA SO BAD,
SHE COULD BARELY GO OUTSIDE.
SHE'D BEEN HOME-SCHOOLED AND
RAISED INSIDE MOST OF HER LIFE.

WE LIVED AND TRAINED TOGETHER.

AT FIRST WITH OUR DISABILITIES, IT
WAS HARD AND I WAS A KID. I
HAD TOO MUCH ATTITUDE.

ALMOST LEFT SEVERAL TIMES.

YOUR MOM AND LEONARD WERE DATING
BACK THEN, SO I REALLY DIDN'T
HAVE ANYONE TO TURN TO.

THEN, AFTER TWO MONTHS OF TRAINING, THEY
TOLD US THE SERUM WAS READY TO TRY. WE
EACH WERE LAID ON HOSPITAL BEDS WHILE THEY
INJECTED THE SERUM INTO OUR ARMS.

RIGHT AWAY I KNEW SOMETHING WAS WRONG.
MY ARM BURNED TERRIBLY AND THEN MY LEG
FELT LIKE IT HAD BEEN CRUSHED AND SET ON FIRE.

I COULD HEAR YOUR MOM STRUGGLING
TO BREATH, AND LEONARD.

I'LL NEVER FORGET HIS SCREAMS.

I PASSED OUT SOON AFTER.

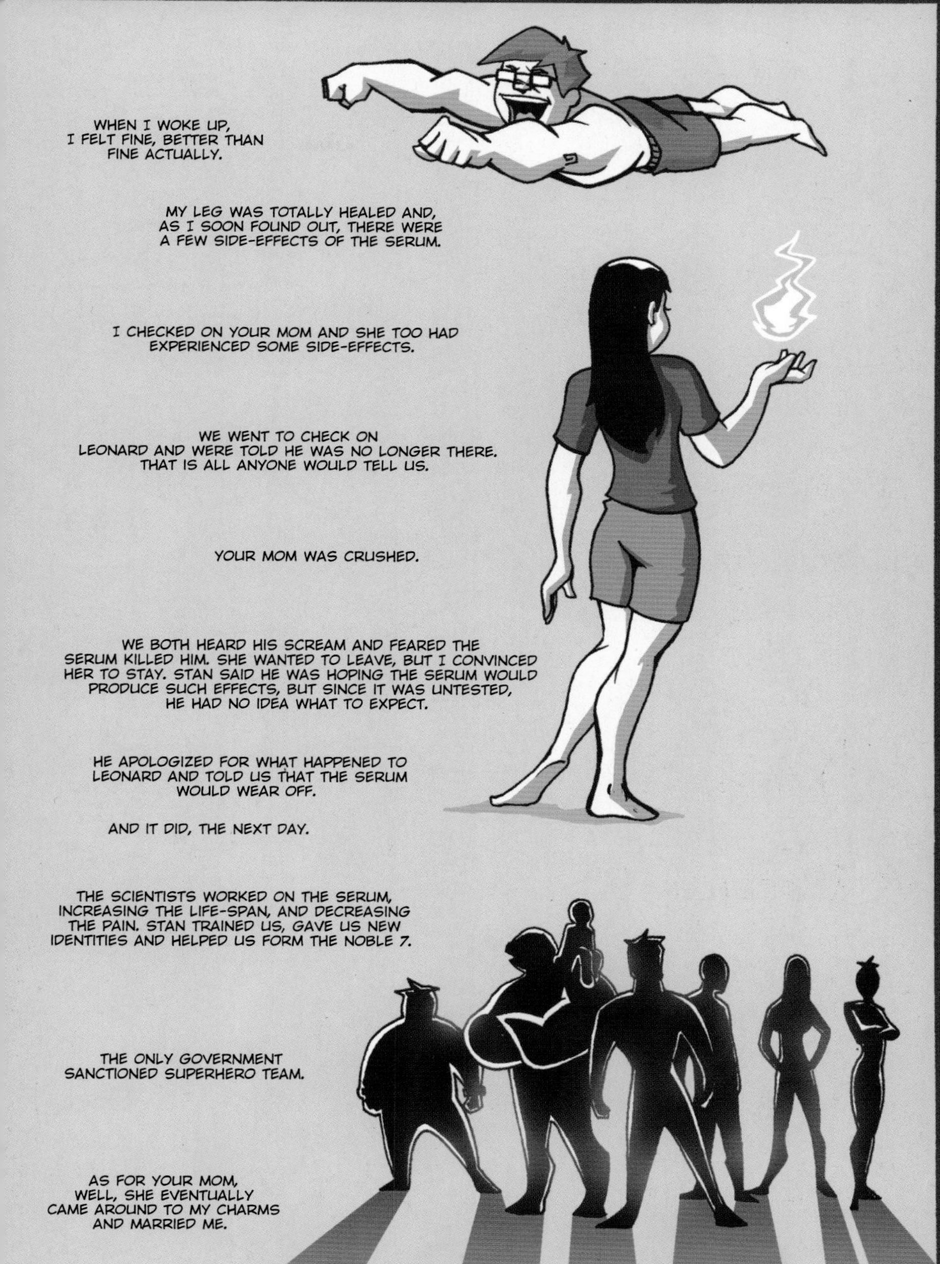
WHEN I WOKE UP, I FELT FINE, BETTER THAN FINE ACTUALLY.
MY LEG WAS TOTALLY HEALED AND, AS I SOON FOUND OUT, THERE WERE A FEW SIDE-EFFECTS OF THE SERUM.
I CHECKED ON YOUR MOM AND SHE TOO HAD EXPERIENCED SOME SIDE-EFFECTS.
WE WENT TO CHECK ON LEONARD AND WERE TOLD HE WAS NO LONGER THERE. THAT IS ALL ANYONE WOULD TELL US.
YOUR MOM WAS CRUSHED.
WE BOTH HEARD HIS SCREAM AND FEARED THE SERUM KILLED HIM. SHE WANTED TO LEAVE, BUT I CONVINCED HER TO STAY. STAN SAID HE WAS HOPING THE SERUM WOULD PRODUCE SUCH EFFECTS, BUT SINCE IT WAS UNTESTED, HE HAD NO IDEA WHAT TO EXPECT.
HE APOLOGIZED FOR WHAT HAPPENED TO LEONARD AND TOLD US THAT THE SERUM WOULD WEAR OFF.
AND IT DID, THE NEXT DAY.
THE SCIENTISTS WORKED ON THE SERUM, INCREASING THE LIFE-SPAN, AND DECREASING THE PAIN. STAN TRAINED US, GAVE US NEW IDENTITIES AND HELPED US FORM THE NOBLE 7.
THE ONLY GOVERNMENT SANCTIONED SUPERHERO TEAM.
AS FOR YOUR MOM, WELL, SHE EVENTUALLY CAME AROUND TO MY CHARMS AND MARRIED ME.

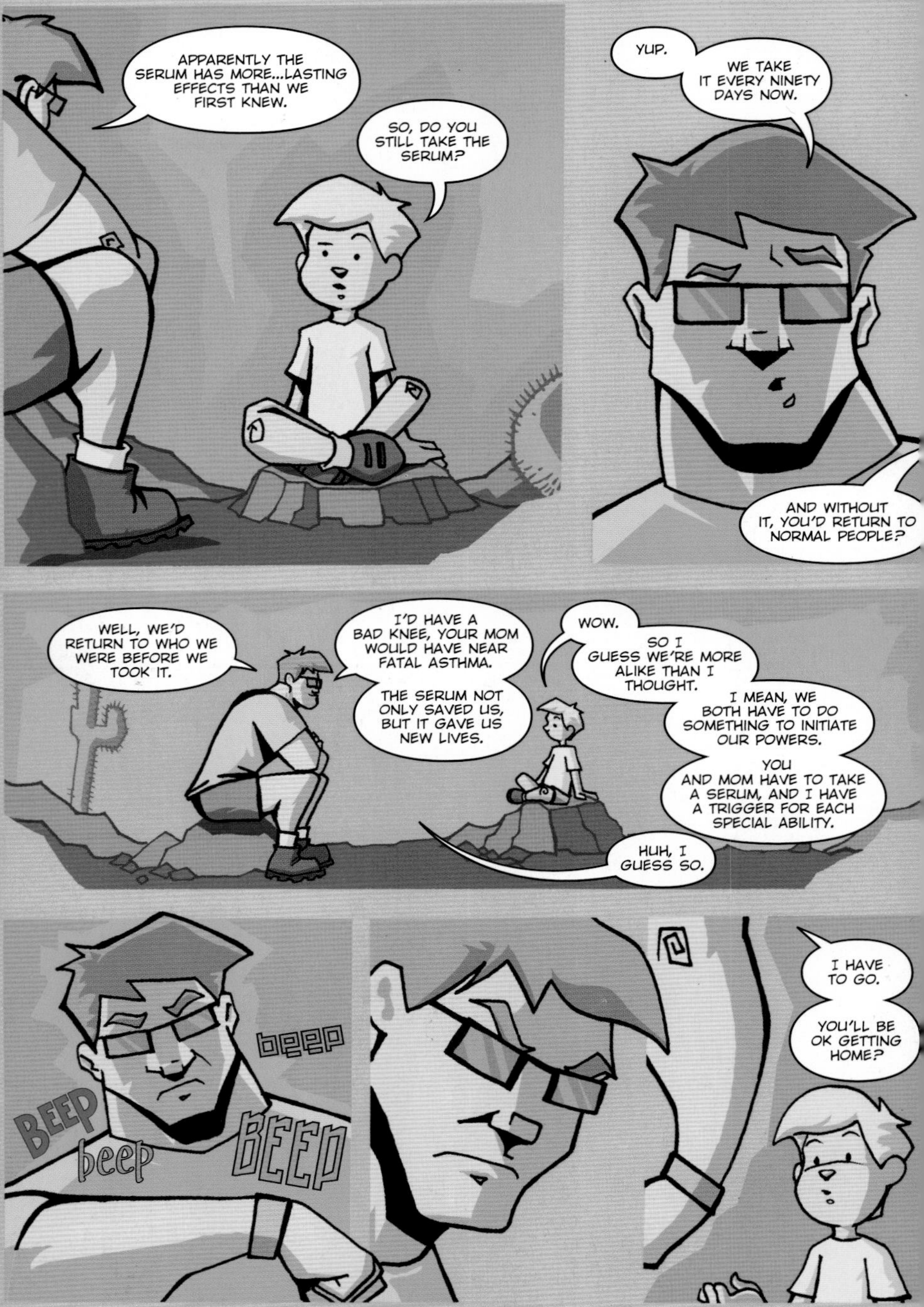

APPARENTLY THE SERUM HAS MORE...LASTING EFFECTS THAN WE FIRST KNEW.
SO, DO YOU STILL TAKE THE SERUM?
YUP.
WE TAKE IT EVERY NINETY DAYS NOW.
AND WITHOUT IT, YOU'D RETURN TO NORMAL PEOPLE?
WELL, WE'D RETURN TO WHO WE WERE BEFORE WE TOOK IT.
I'D HAVE A BAD KNEE, YOUR MOM WOULD HAVE NEAR FATAL ASTHMA.
THE SERUM NOT ONLY SAVED US, BUT IT GAVE US NEW LIVES.
WOW.
SO I GUESS WE'RE MORE ALIKE THAN I THOUGHT.
I MEAN, WE BOTH HAVE TO DO SOMETHING TO INITIATE OUR POWERS.
YOU AND MOM HAVE TO TAKE A SERUM, AND I HAVE A TRIGGER FOR EACH SPECIAL ABILITY.
HUH, I GUESS SO.
beep
BEEP
beep
BEEP
I HAVE TO GO.
YOU'LL BE OK GETTING HOME?

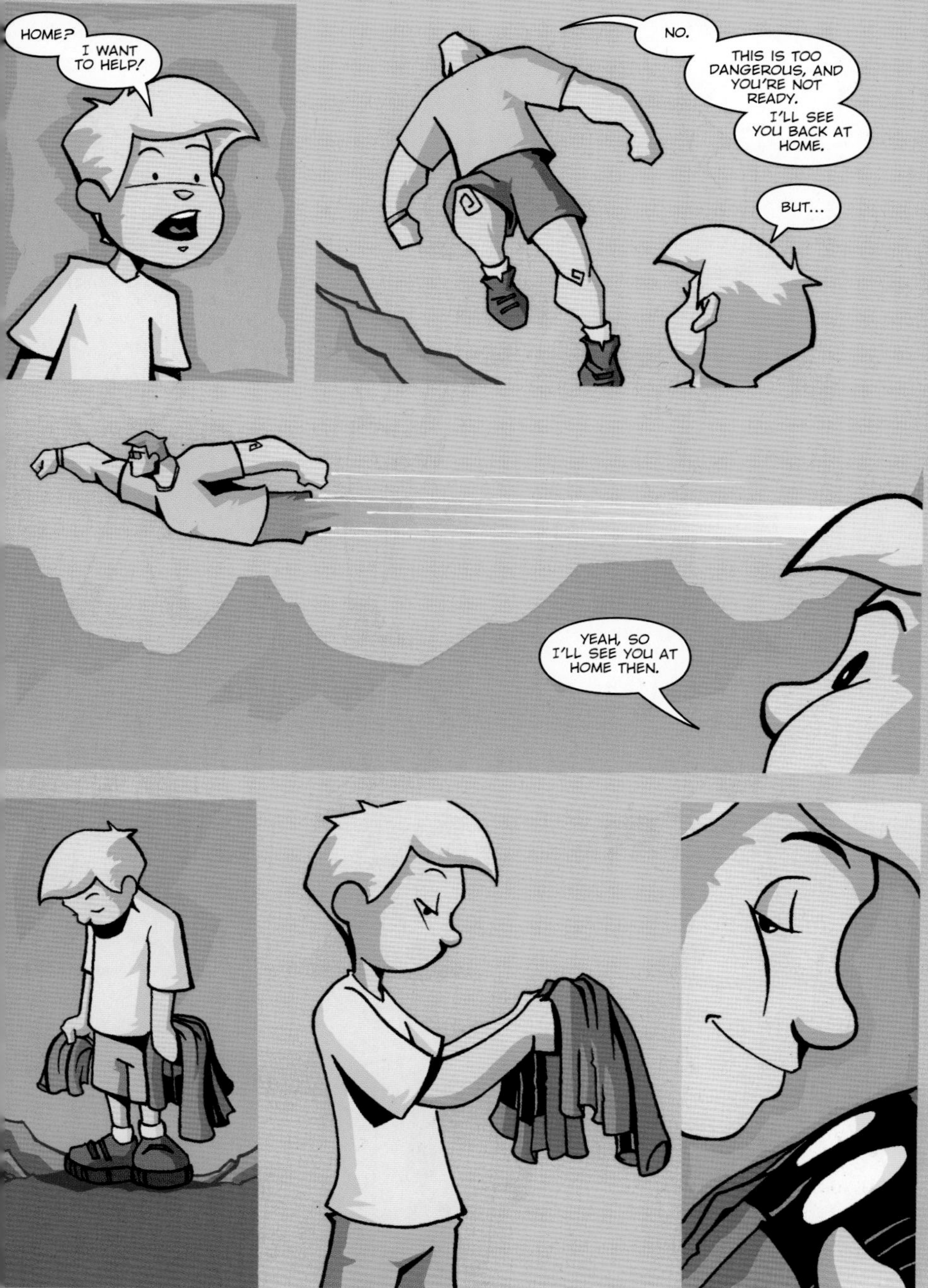
HOME? I WANT TO HELP!
NO.
THIS IS TOO DANGEROUS, AND YOU'RE NOT READY.
I'LL SEE YOU BACK AT HOME.
BUT...
YEAH, SO I'LL SEE YOU AT HOME THEN.

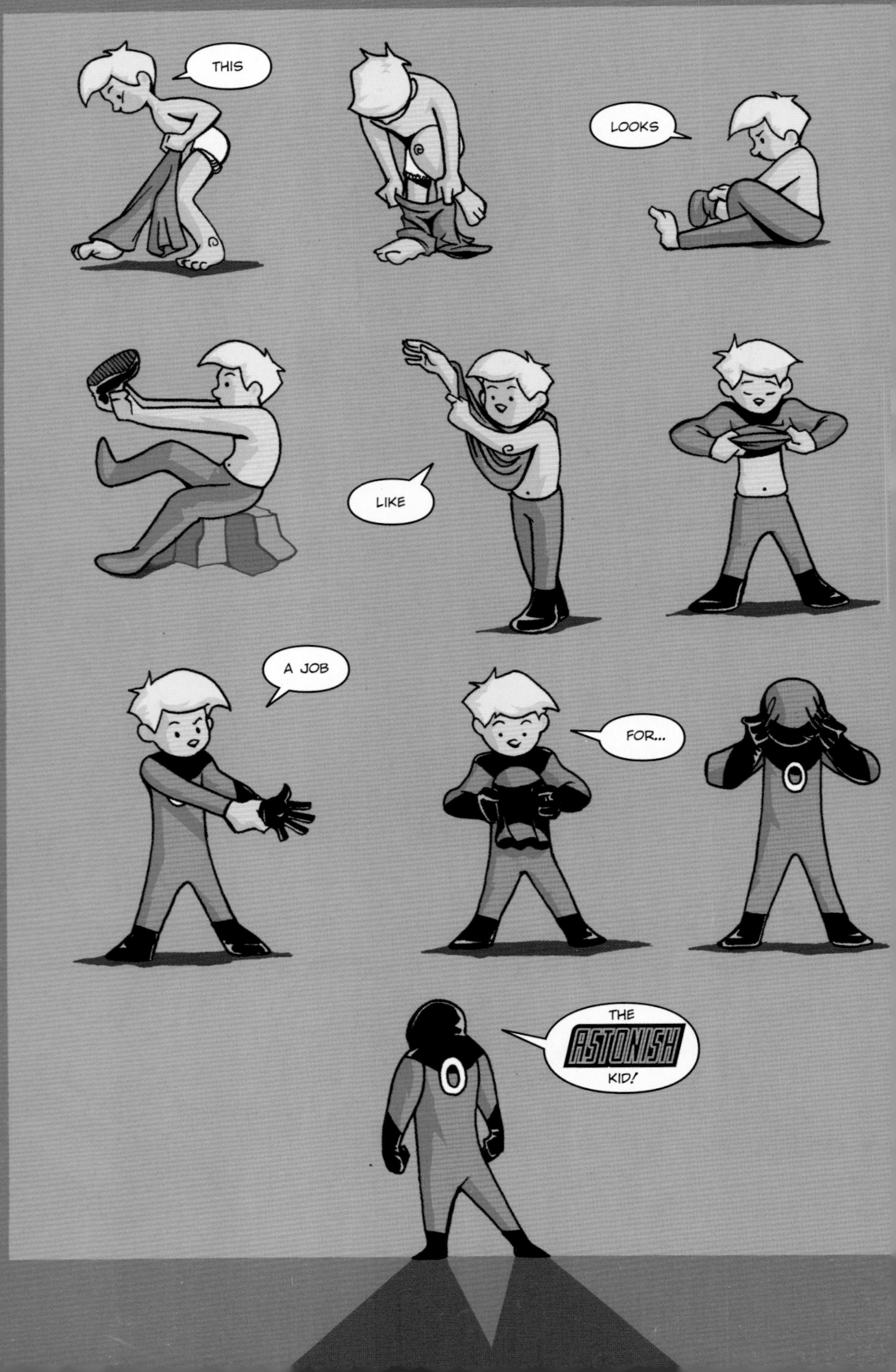
THIS
LOOKS
LIKE
A JOB
FOR...
THE
ASTONISH
KID!

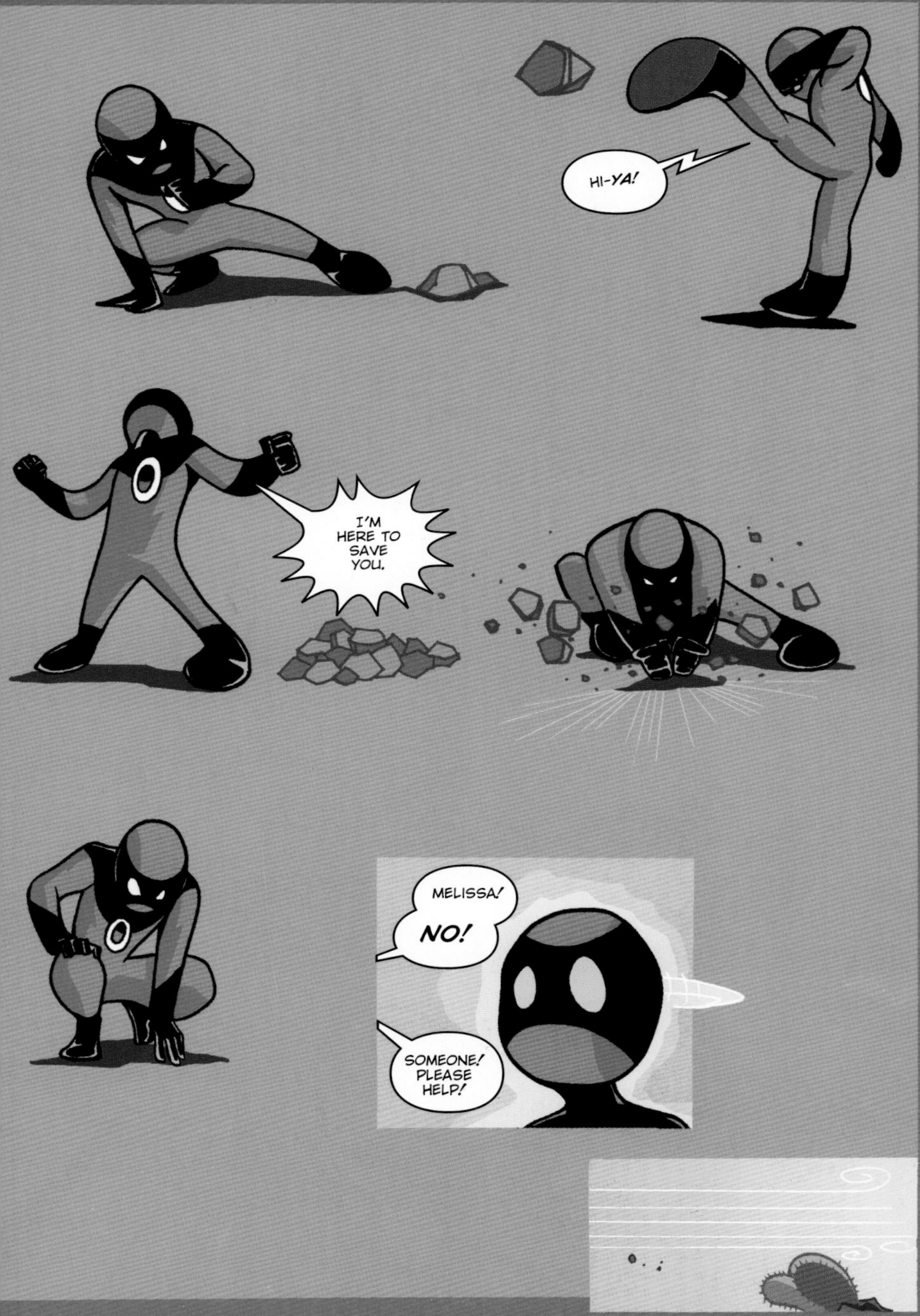
HI-YA!
I'M HERE TO SAVE YOU.
MELISSA!
NO!
SOMEONE! PLEASE HELP!

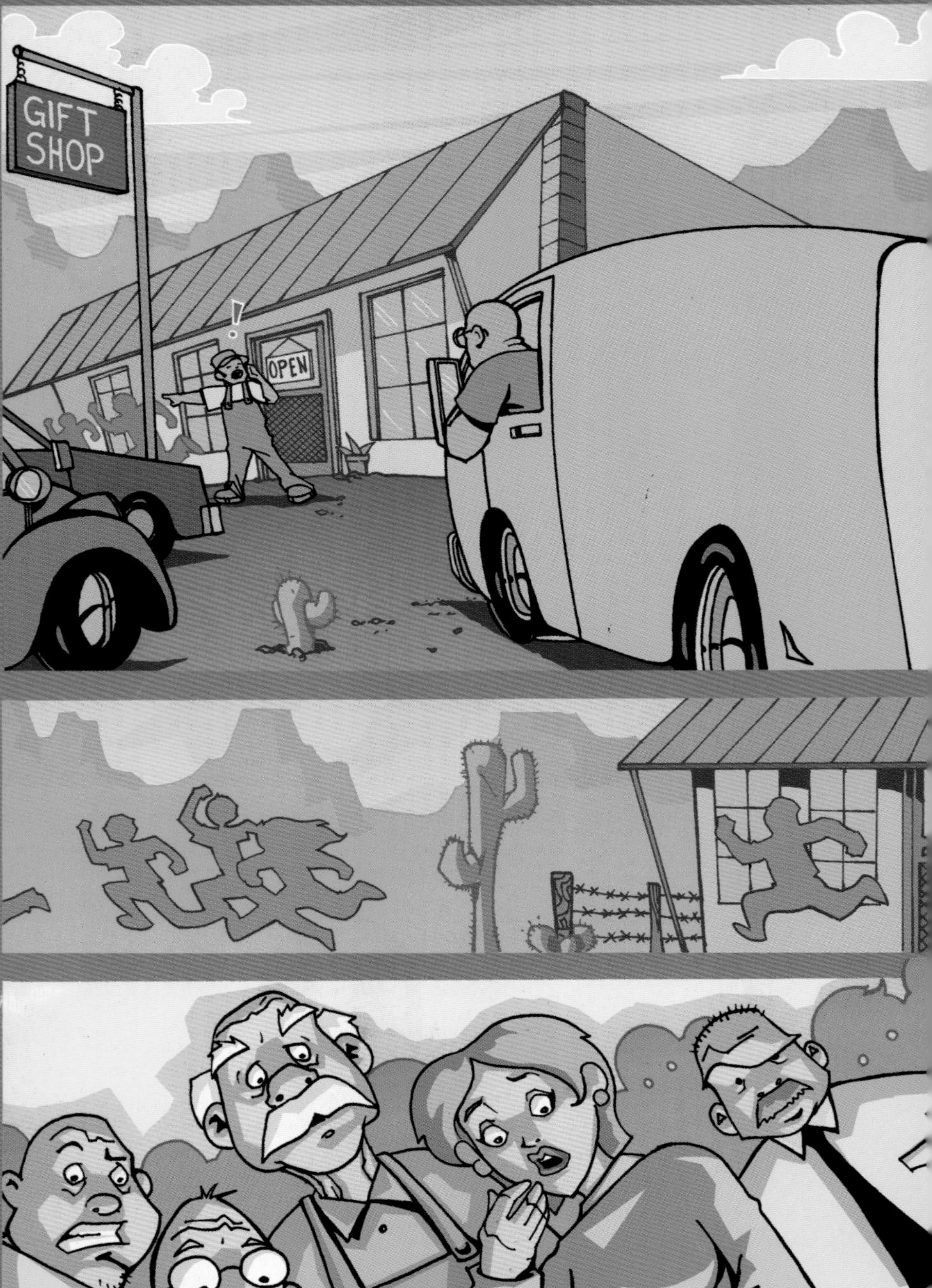
GIFT SHOP
OPEN

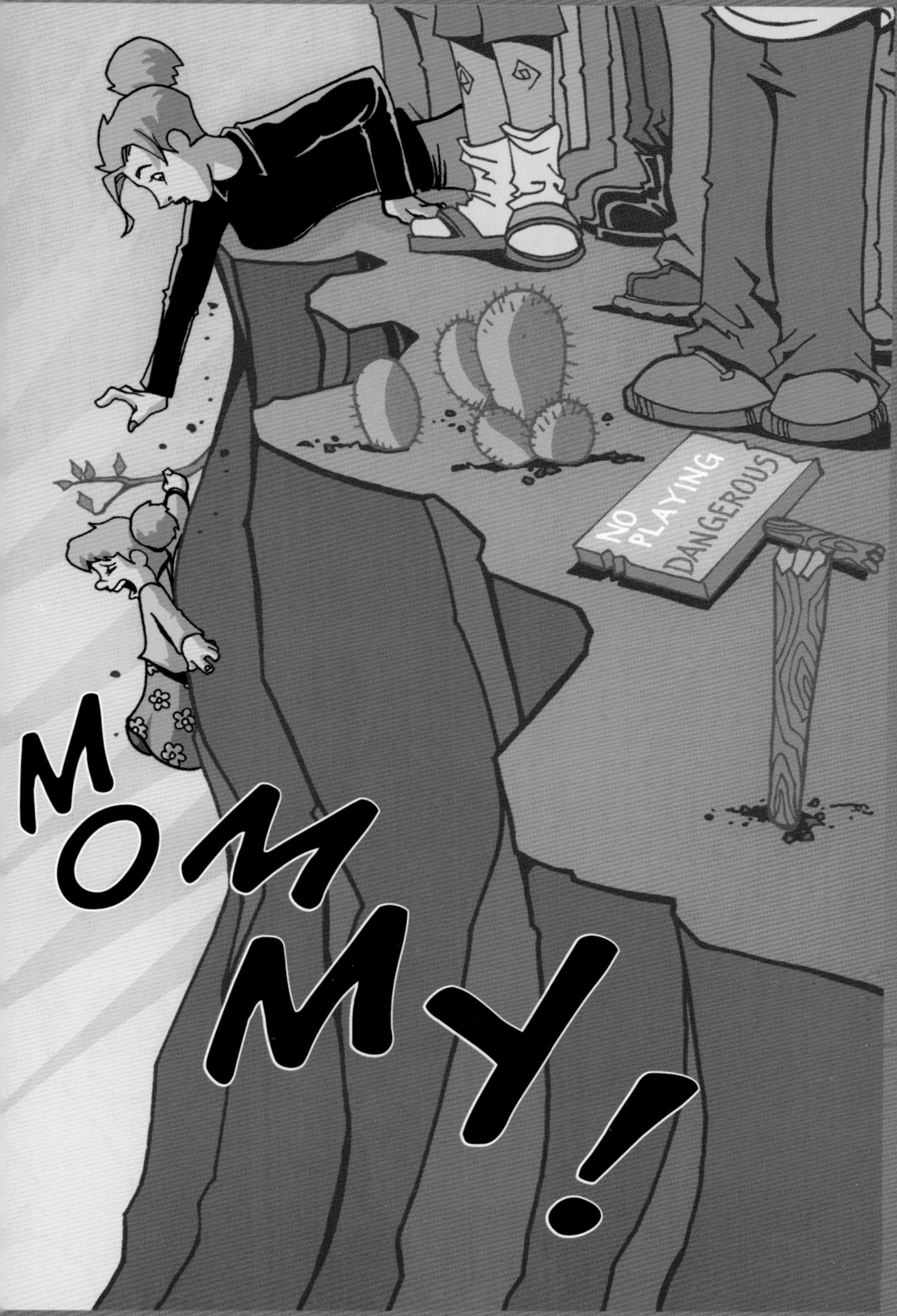
NO PLAYING
DANGEROUS
MOMMY!

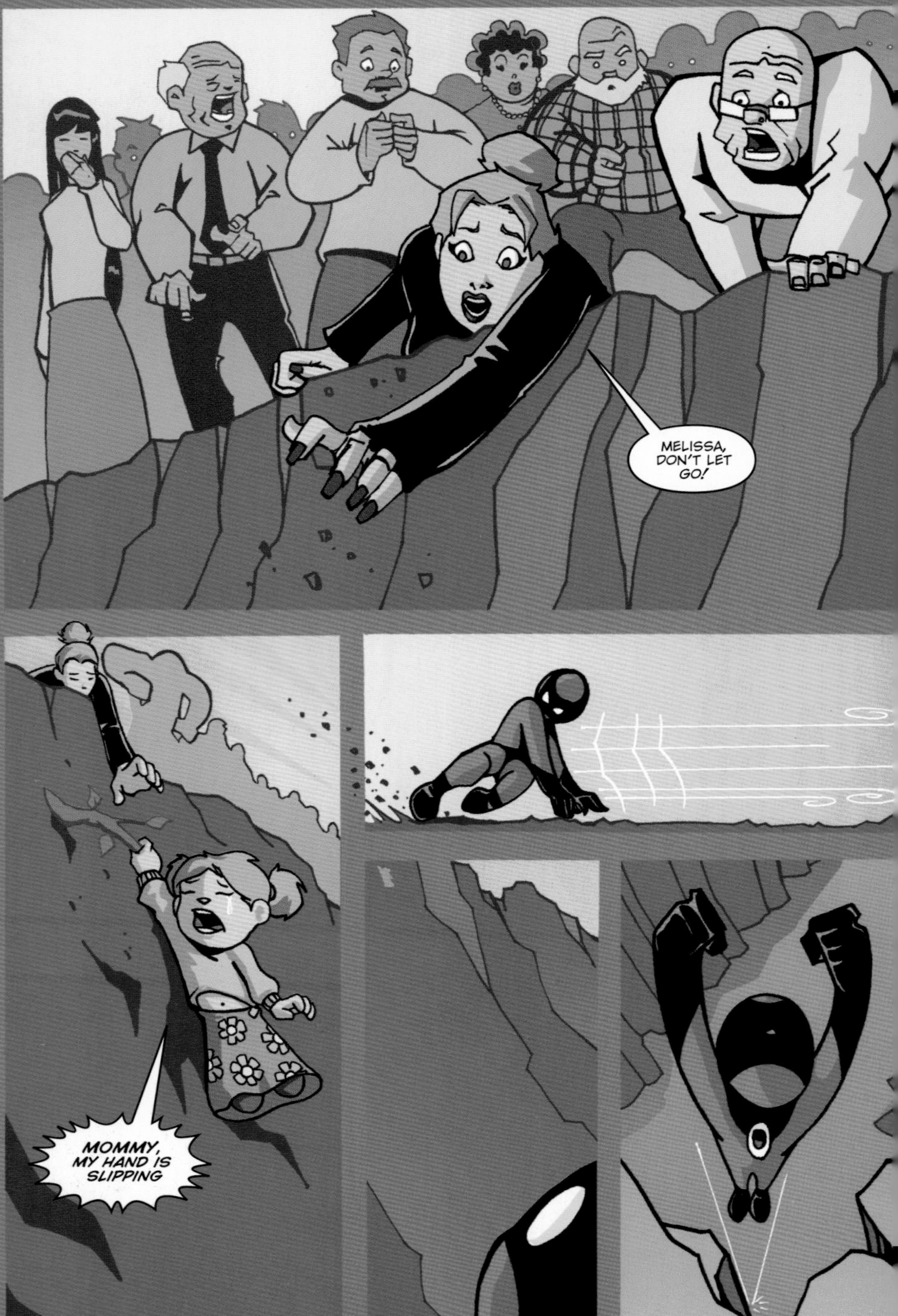
MELISSA, DON'T LET GO!
MOMMY, MY HAND IS SLIPPING

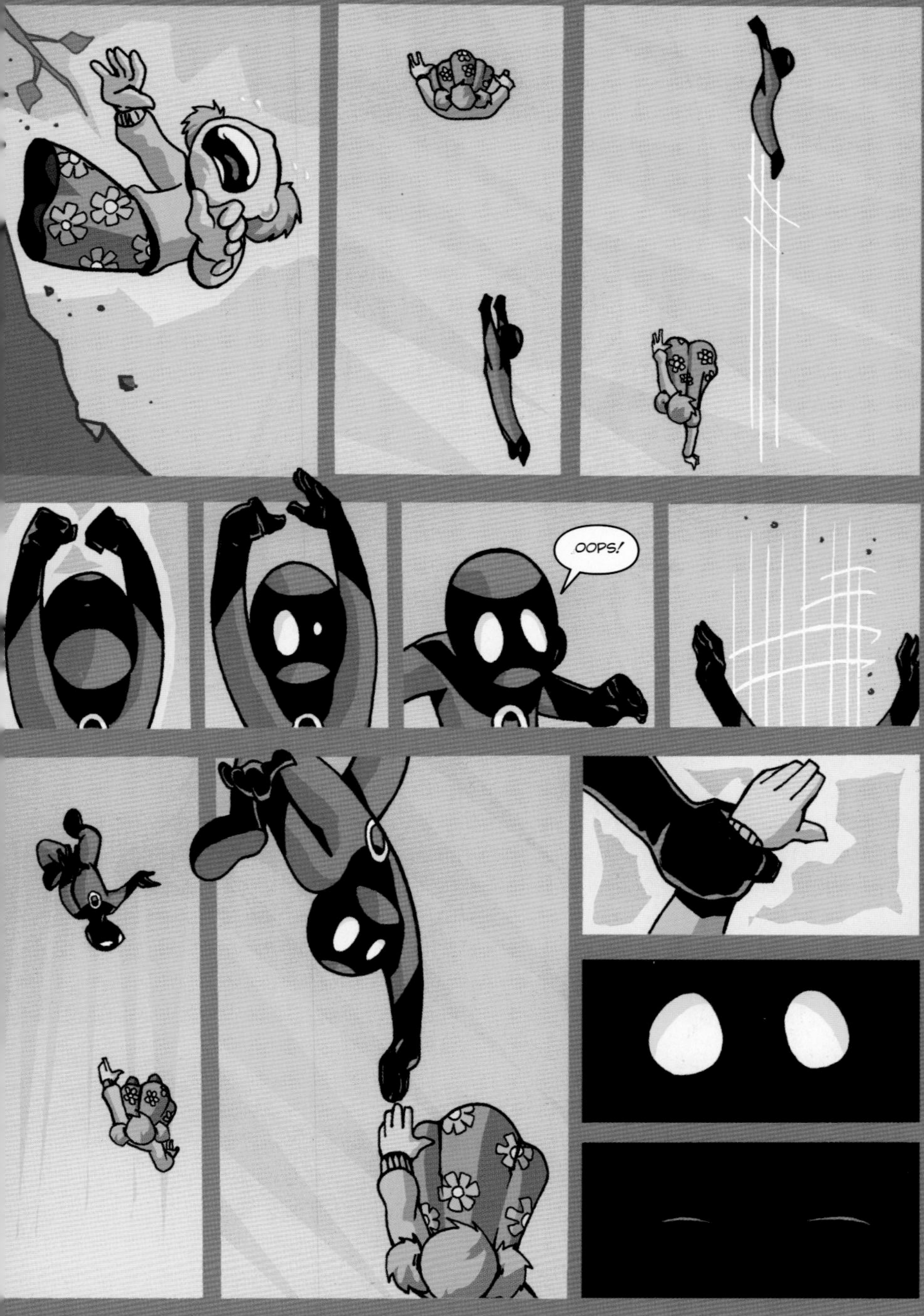
OOPS!

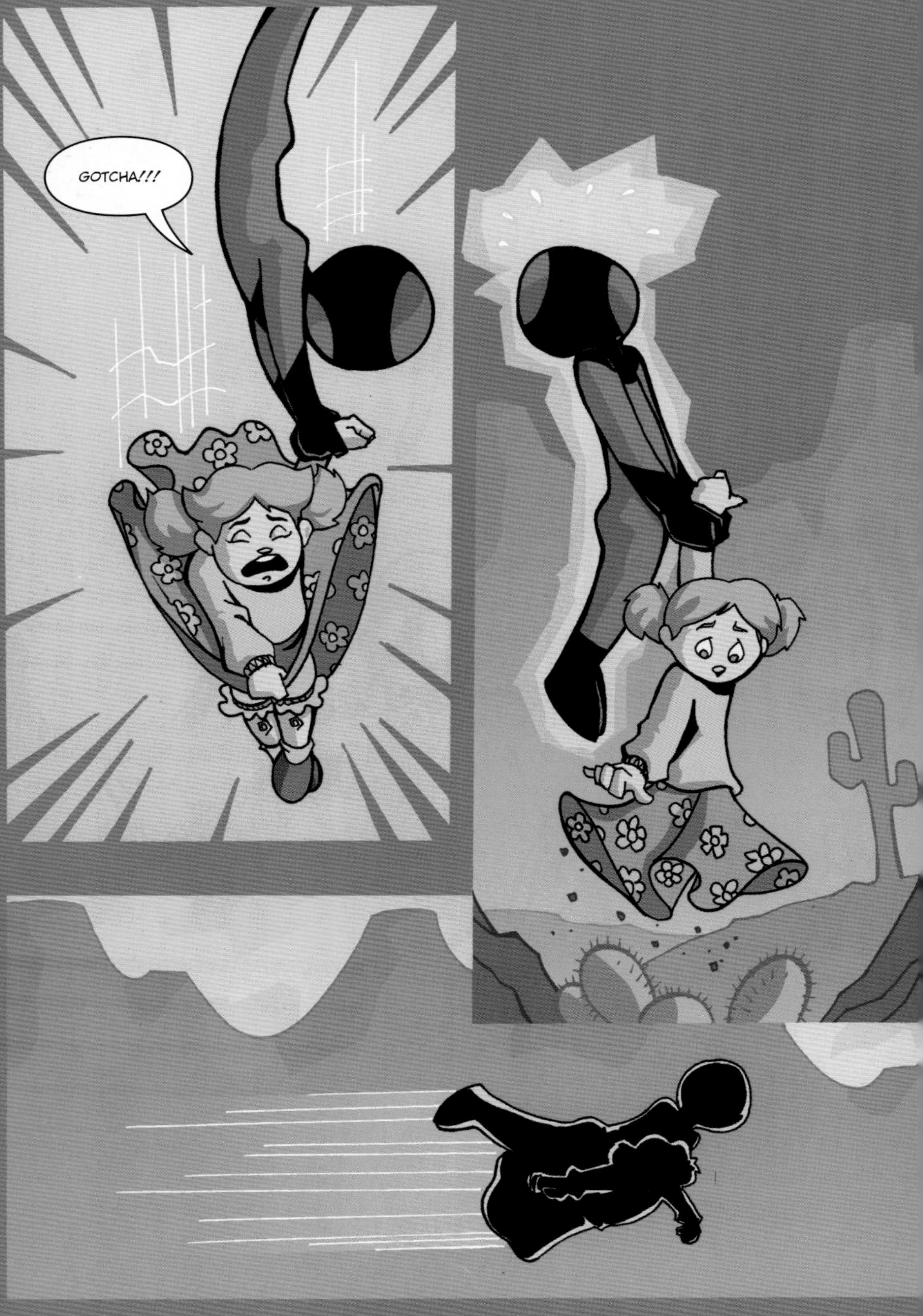
GOTCHA!!!

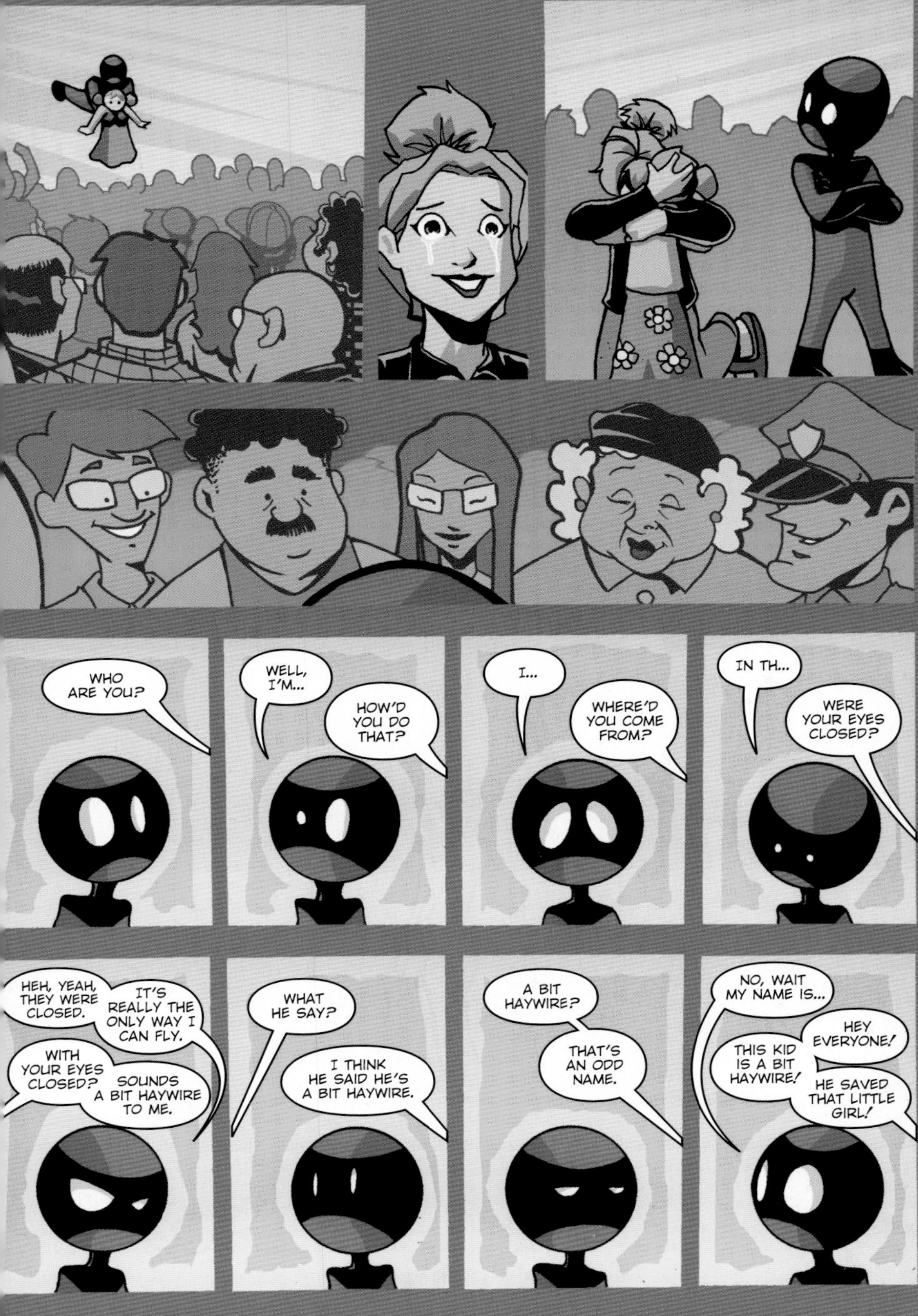
WHO ARE YOU?
WELL, I'M...
HOW'D YOU DO THAT?
I...
WHERE'D YOU COME FROM?
IN TH...
WERE YOUR EYES CLOSED?
HEH, YEAH, THEY WERE CLOSED.
IT'S REALLY THE ONLY WAY I CAN FLY.
WITH YOUR EYES CLOSED?
SOUNDS A BIT HAYWIRE TO ME.
WHAT HE SAY?
I THINK HE SAID HE'S A BIT HAYWIRE.
A BIT HAYWIRE?
THAT'S AN ODD NAME.
NO, WAIT MY NAME IS...
HEY EVERYONE!
THIS KID IS A BIT HAYWIRE!
HE SAVED THAT LITTLE GIRL!

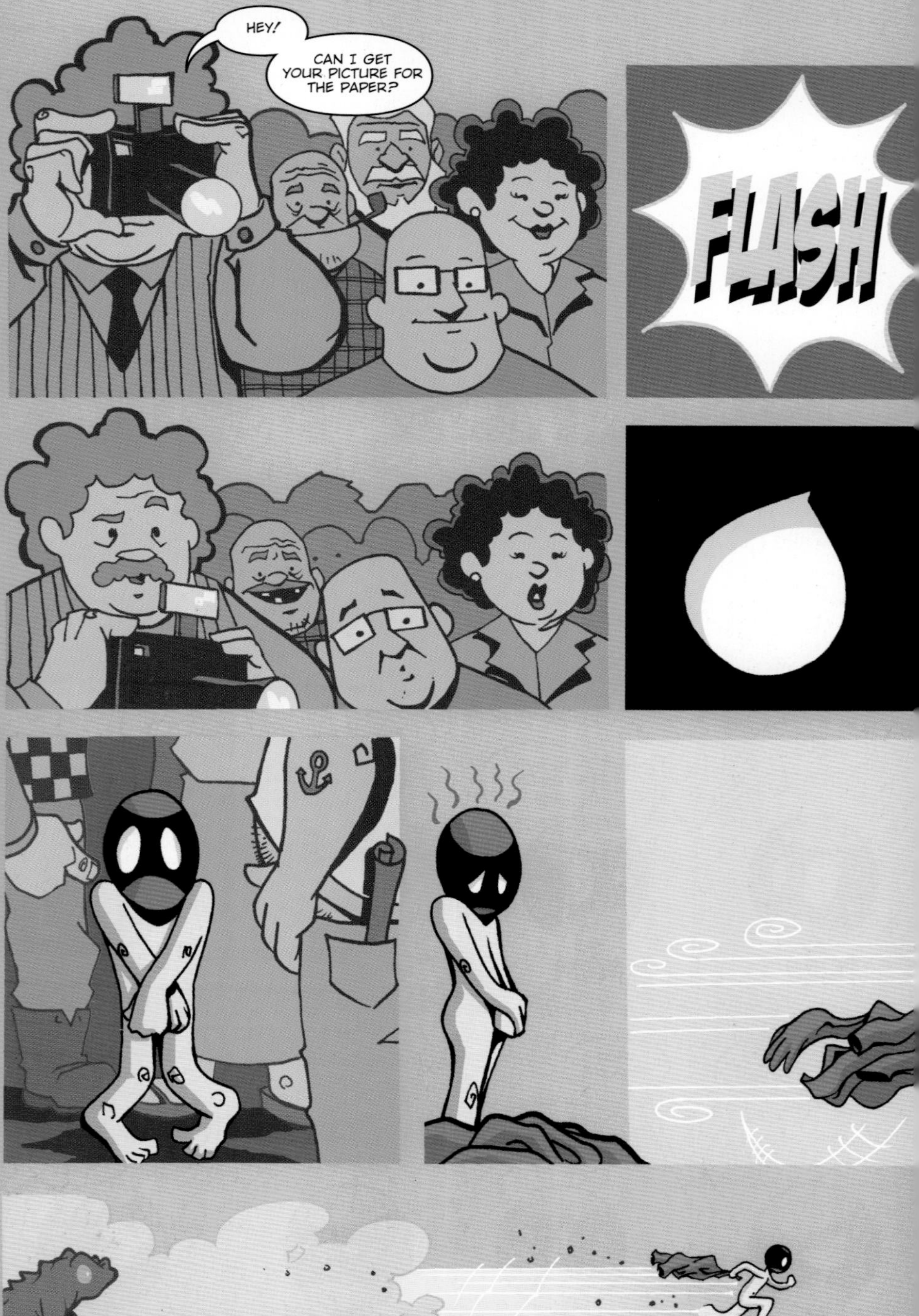
HEY!
CAN I GET YOUR PICTURE FOR THE PAPER?
FLASH

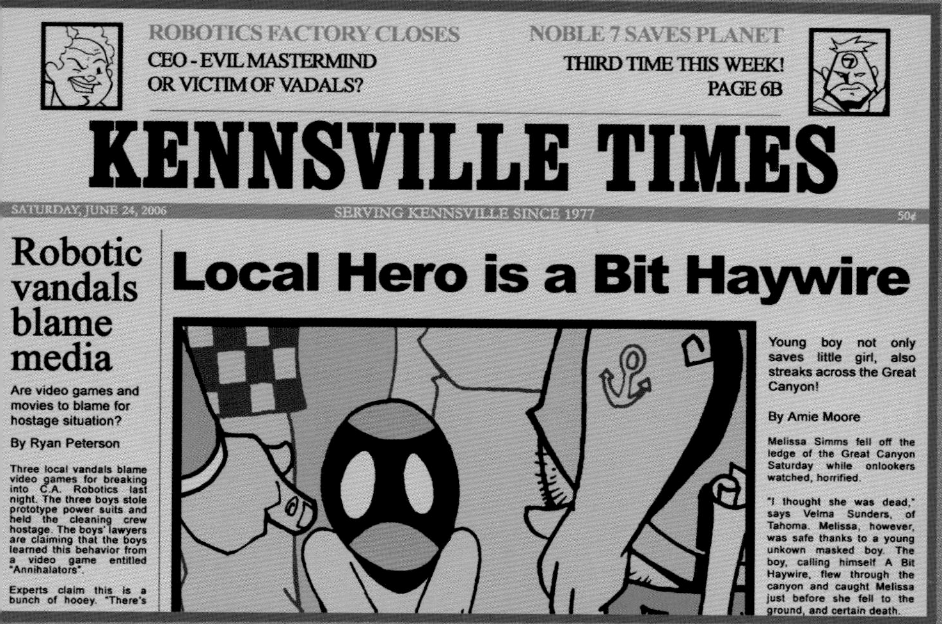
ROBOTICS FACTORY CLOSES
CEO - EVIL MASTERMIND
OR VICTIM OF VADALS?
NOBLE 7 SAVES PLANET
THIRD TIME THIS WEEK!
PAGE 6B
KENNSVILLE TIMES
SATURDAY, JUNE 24, 2006
SERVING KENNSVILLE SINCE 1977
50¢
Robotic vandals blame media
Are video games and movies to blame for hostage situation?
By Ryan Peterson
Three local vandals blame video games for breaking into C.A. Robotics last night. The three boys stole prototype power suits and held the cleaning crew hostage. The boys' lawyers are claiming that the boys learned this behavior from a video game entitled "Annihalators".
Experts claim this is a bunch of hooey. "There's
Local Hero is a Bit Haywire
Young boy not only saves little girl, also streaks across the Great Canyon!
By Amie Moore
Melissa Simms fell off the ledge of the Great Canyon Saturday while onlookers watched, horrified.
"I thought she was dead," says Velma Sunders, of Tahoma. Melissa, however, was safe thanks to a young unkown masked boy. The boy, calling himself A Bit Haywire, flew through the canyon and caught Melissa just before she fell to the ground, and certain death.

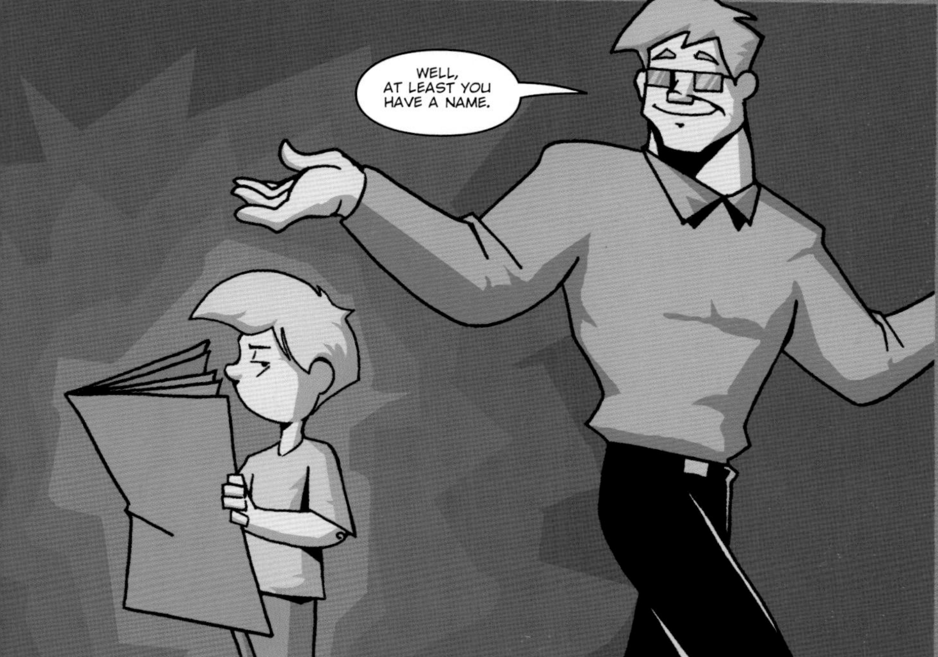
WELL, AT LEAST YOU HAVE A NAME.

chapter 3
COLD AND ALLERGY

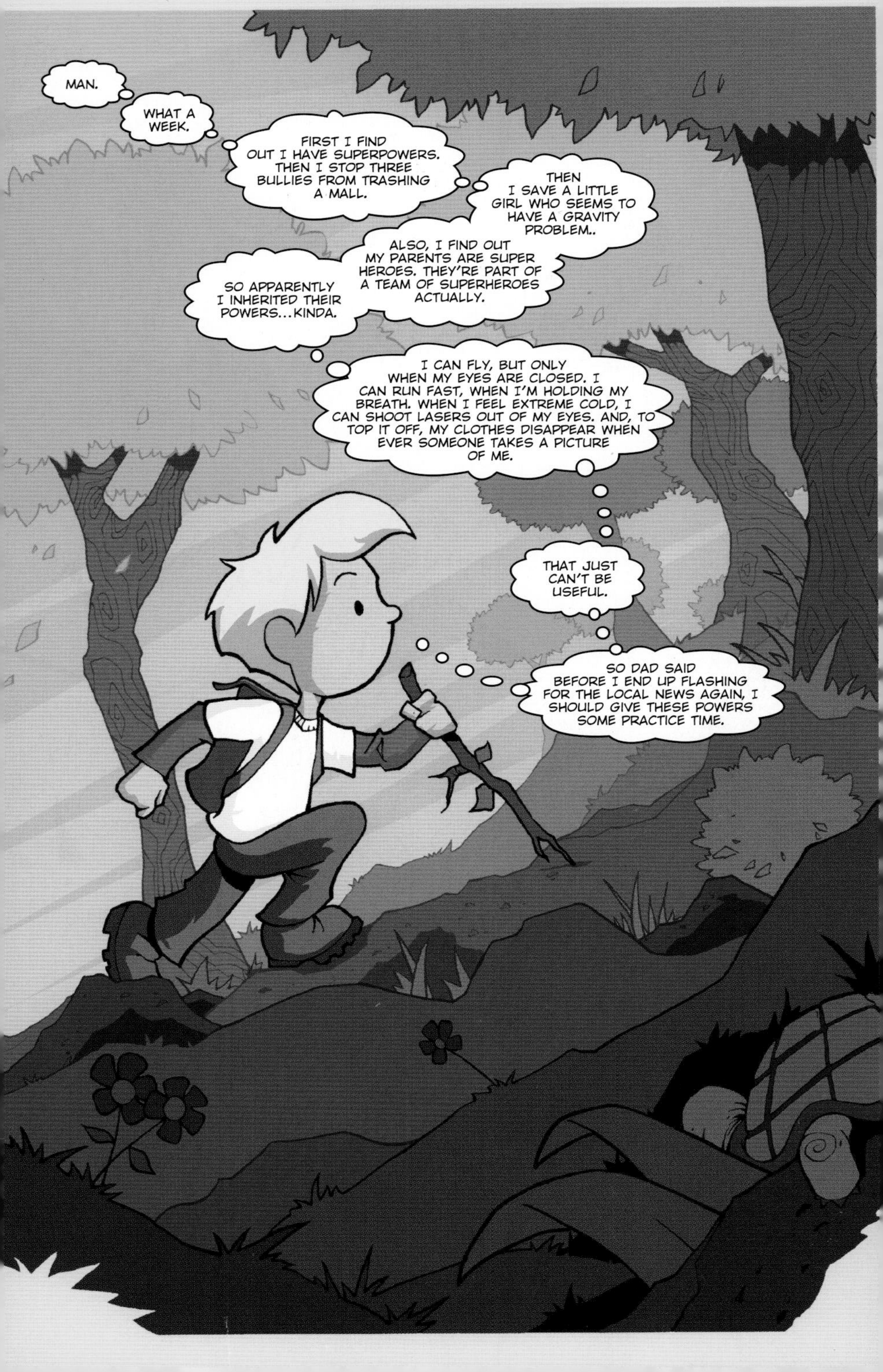
MAN.
WHAT A WEEK.
FIRST I FIND OUT I HAVE SUPERPOWERS. THEN I STOP THREE BULLIES FROM TRASHING A MALL.
THEN I SAVE A LITTLE GIRL WHO SEEMS TO HAVE A GRAVITY PROBLEM..
ALSO, I FIND OUT MY PARENTS ARE SUPER HEROES. THEY'RE PART OF A TEAM OF SUPERHEROES ACTUALLY.
SO APPARENTLY I INHERITED THEIR POWERS...KINDA.
I CAN FLY, BUT ONLY WHEN MY EYES ARE CLOSED. I CAN RUN FAST, WHEN I'M HOLDING MY BREATH. WHEN I FEEL EXTREME COLD, I CAN SHOOT LASERS OUT OF MY EYES. AND, TO TOP IT OFF, MY CLOTHES DISAPPEAR WHEN EVER SOMEONE TAKES A PICTURE OF ME.
THAT JUST CAN'T BE USEFUL.
SO DAD SAID BEFORE I END UP FLASHING FOR THE LOCAL NEWS AGAIN, I SHOULD GIVE THESE POWERS SOME PRACTICE TIME.

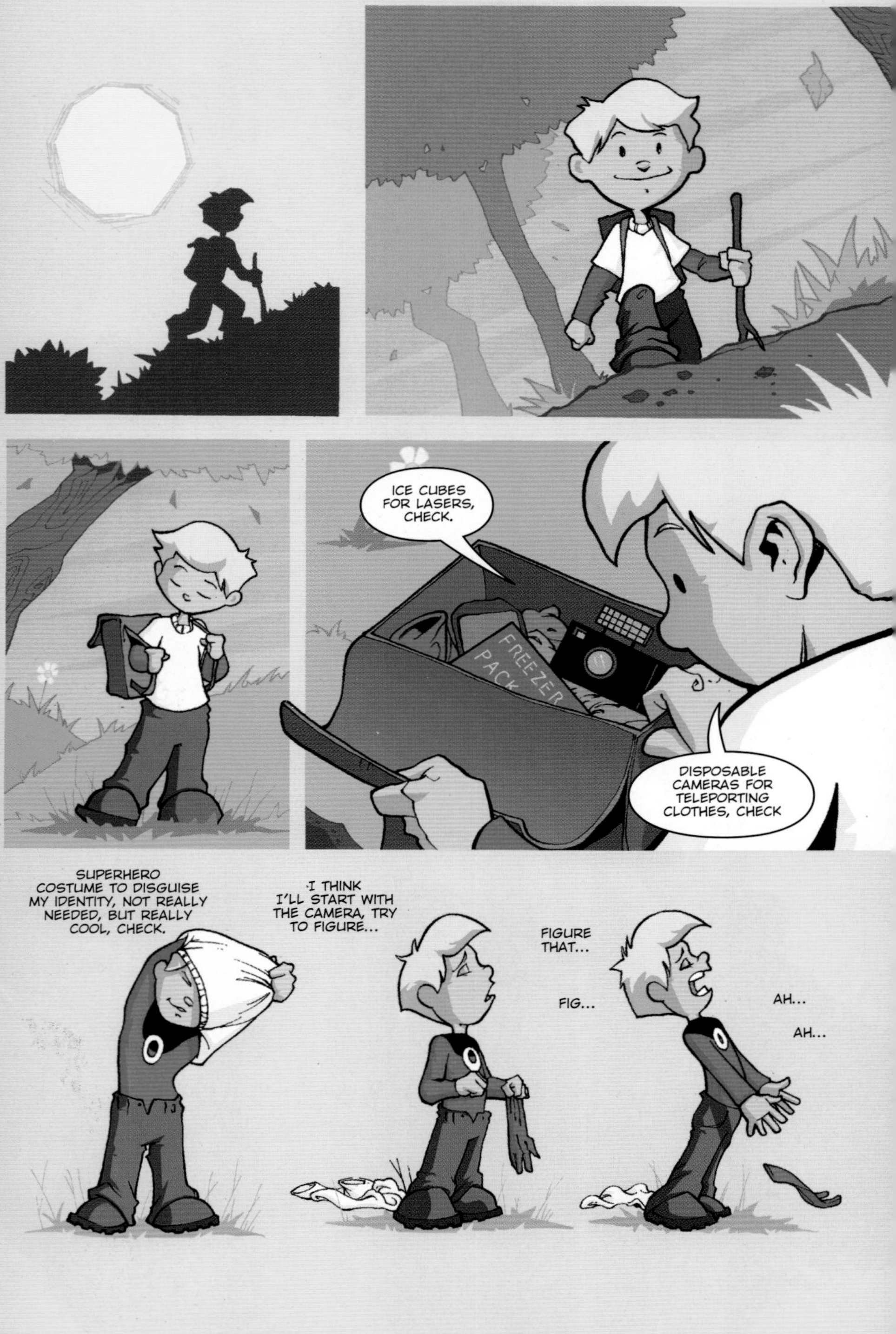
ICE CUBES FOR LASERS, CHECK.
FREEZER PACK
DISPOSABLE CAMERAS FOR TELEPORTING CLOTHES, CHECK
SUPERHERO COSTUME TO DISGUISE MY IDENTITY, NOT REALLY NEEDED, BUT REALLY COOL, CHECK.
I THINK I'LL START WITH THE CAMERA, TRY TO FIGURE...
FIGURE THAT...
FIG...
AH...
AH...

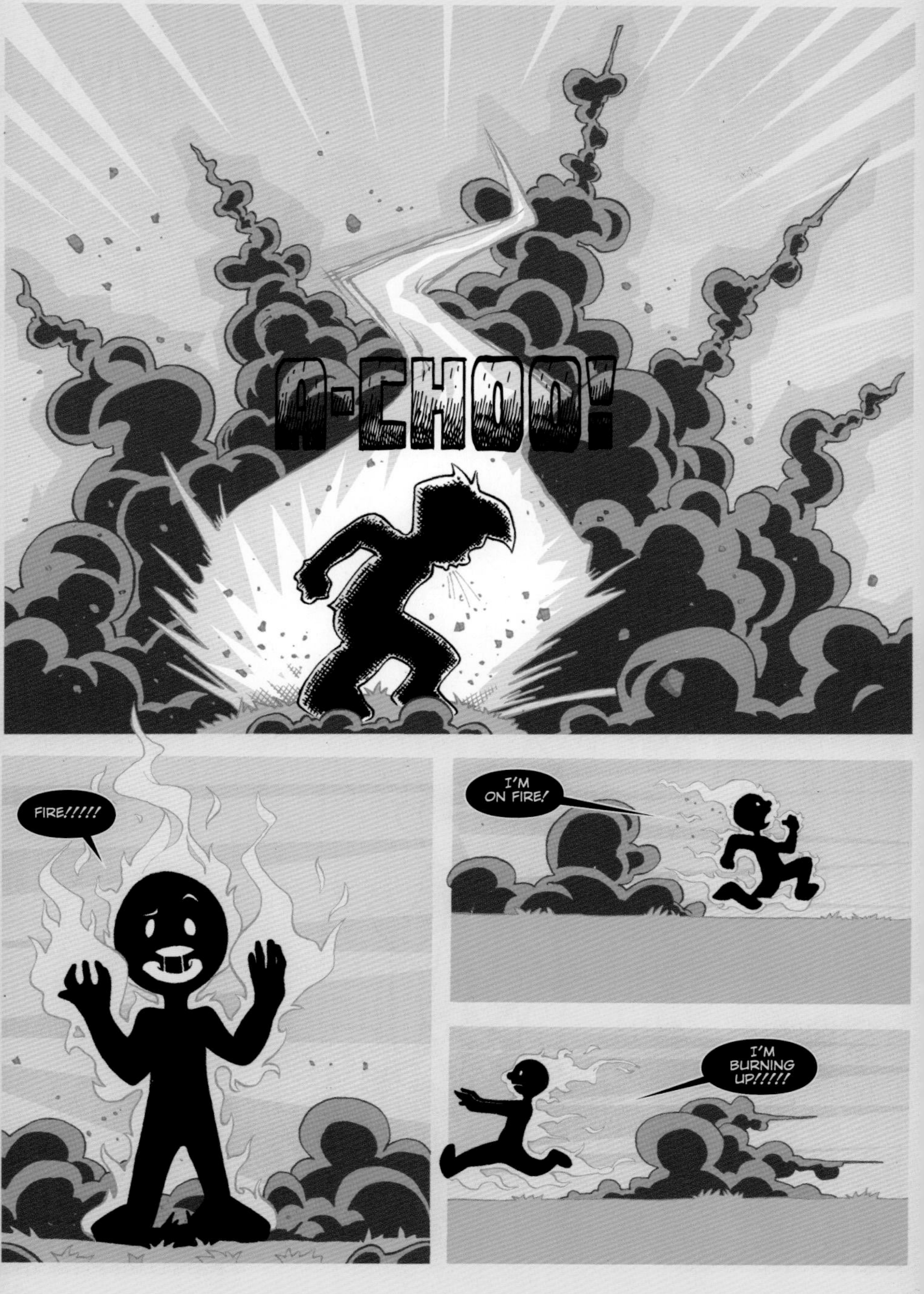
A-CHOO!
FIRE!!!!!
I'M ON FIRE!
I'M BURNING UP!!!!!

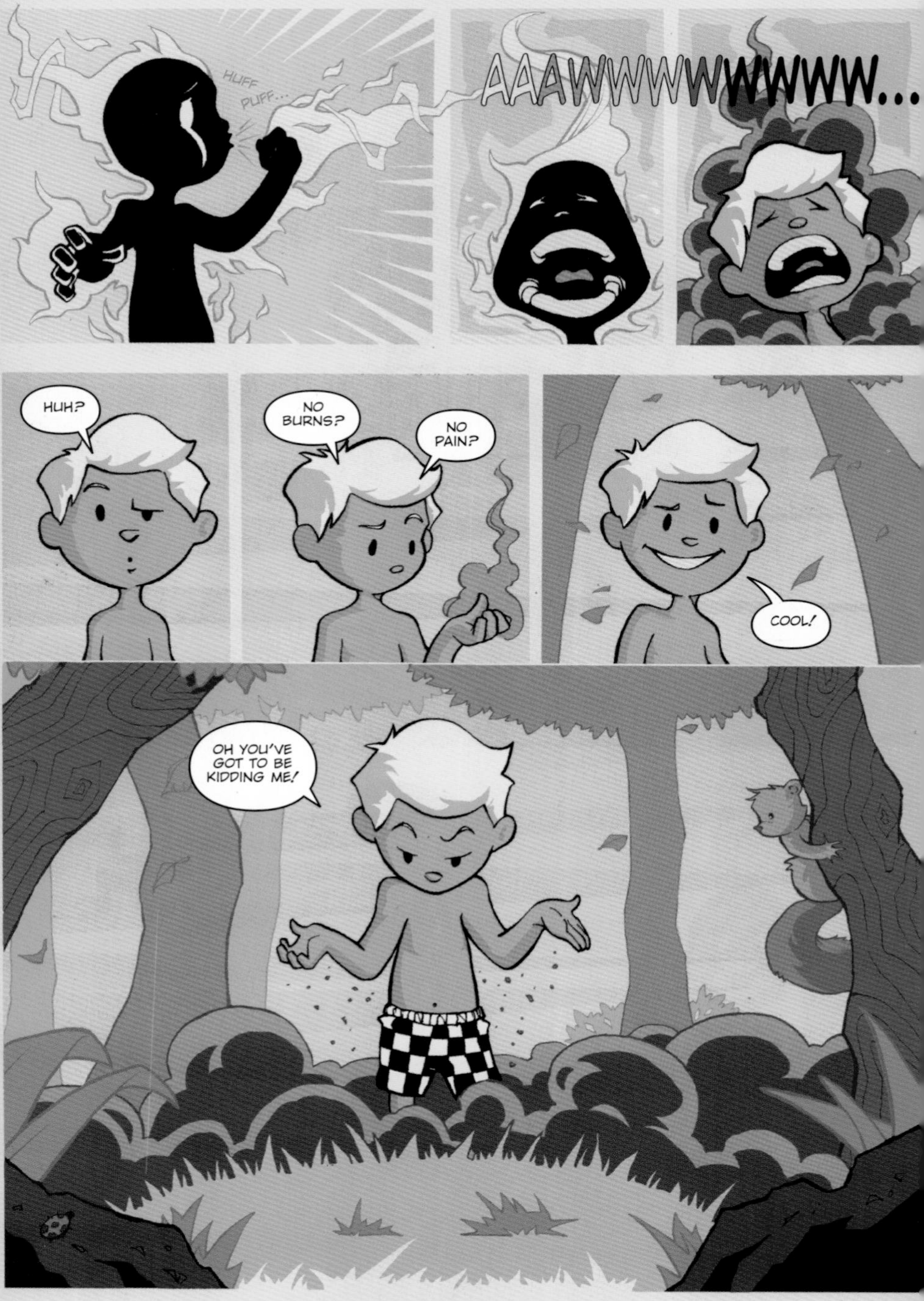
HUFF
PUFF...
AAAWWWWWWWWW...
HUH?
NO BURNS?
NO PAIN?
COOL!
OH YOU'VE GOT TO BE KIDDING ME!

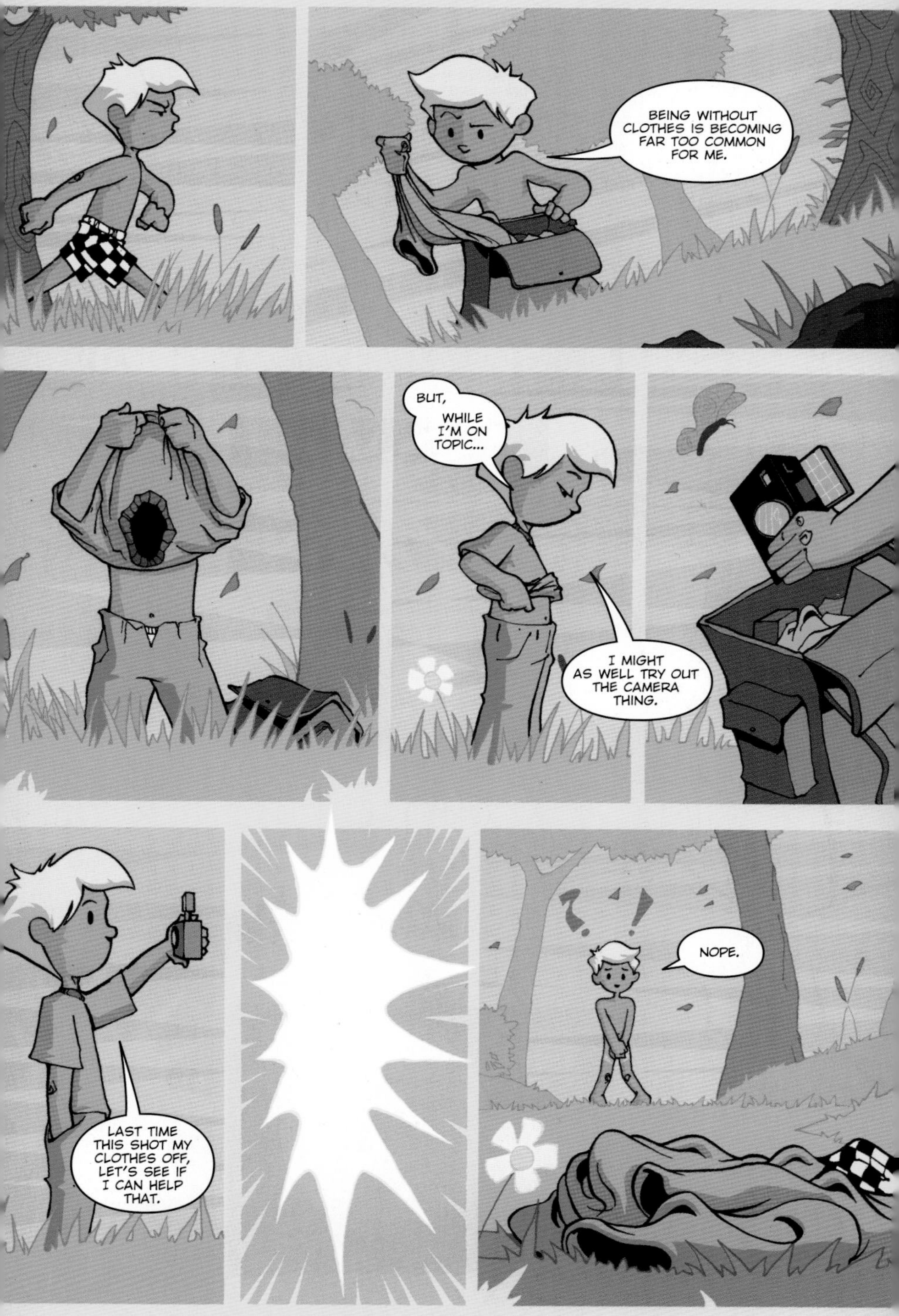
BEING WITHOUT CLOTHES IS BECOMING FAR TOO COMMON FOR ME.
BUT,
WHILE I'M ON TOPIC...
I MIGHT AS WELL TRY OUT THE CAMERA THING.
LAST TIME THIS SHOT MY CLOTHES OFF, LET'S SEE IF I CAN HELP THAT.
?!
NOPE.

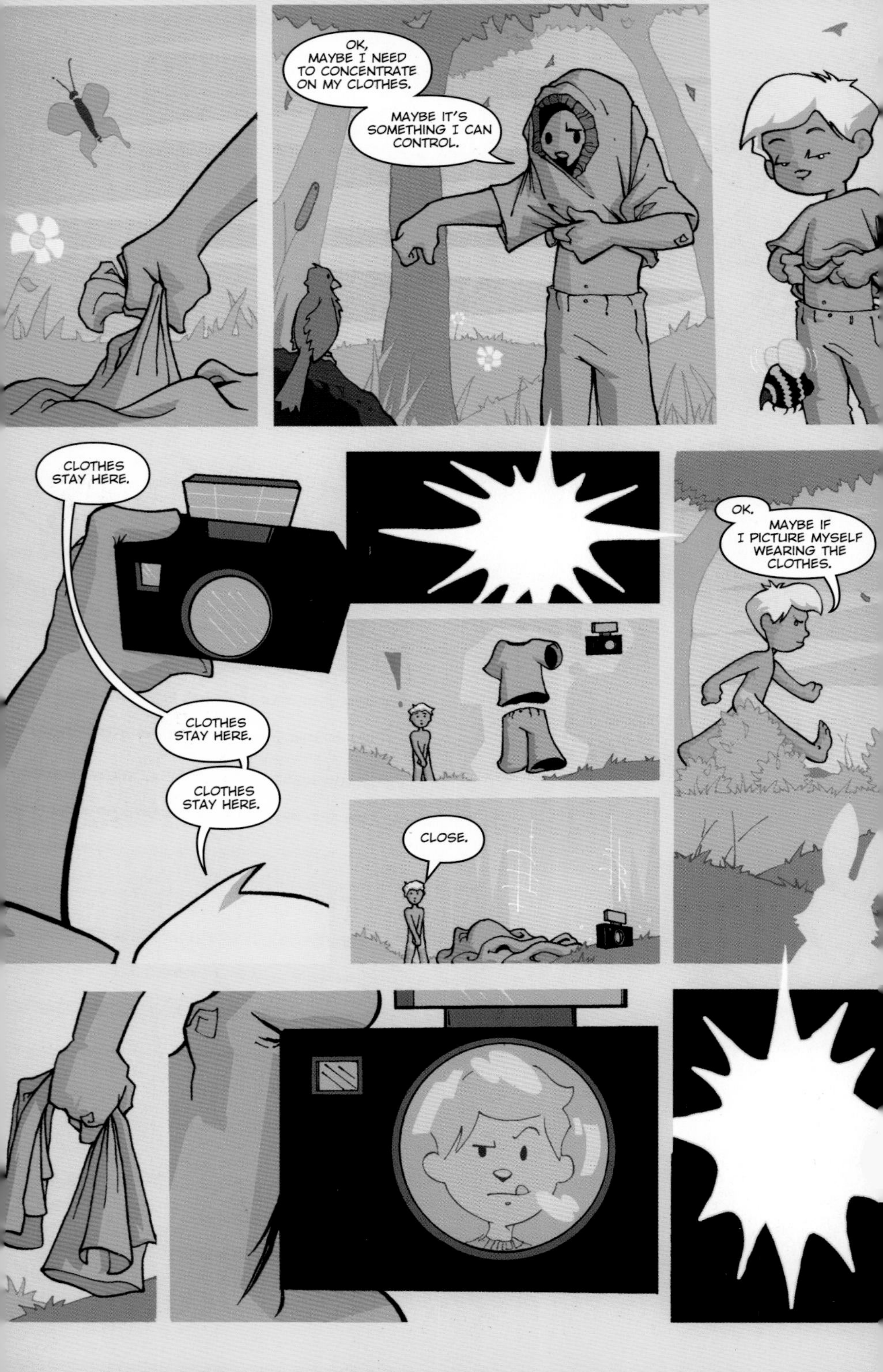
OK, MAYBE I NEED TO CONCENTRATE ON MY CLOTHES.
MAYBE IT'S SOMETHING I CAN CONTROL.
CLOTHES STAY HERE.
CLOTHES STAY HERE.
CLOTHES STAY HERE.
OK.
MAYBE IF I PICTURE MYSELF WEARING THE CLOTHES.
CLOSE.

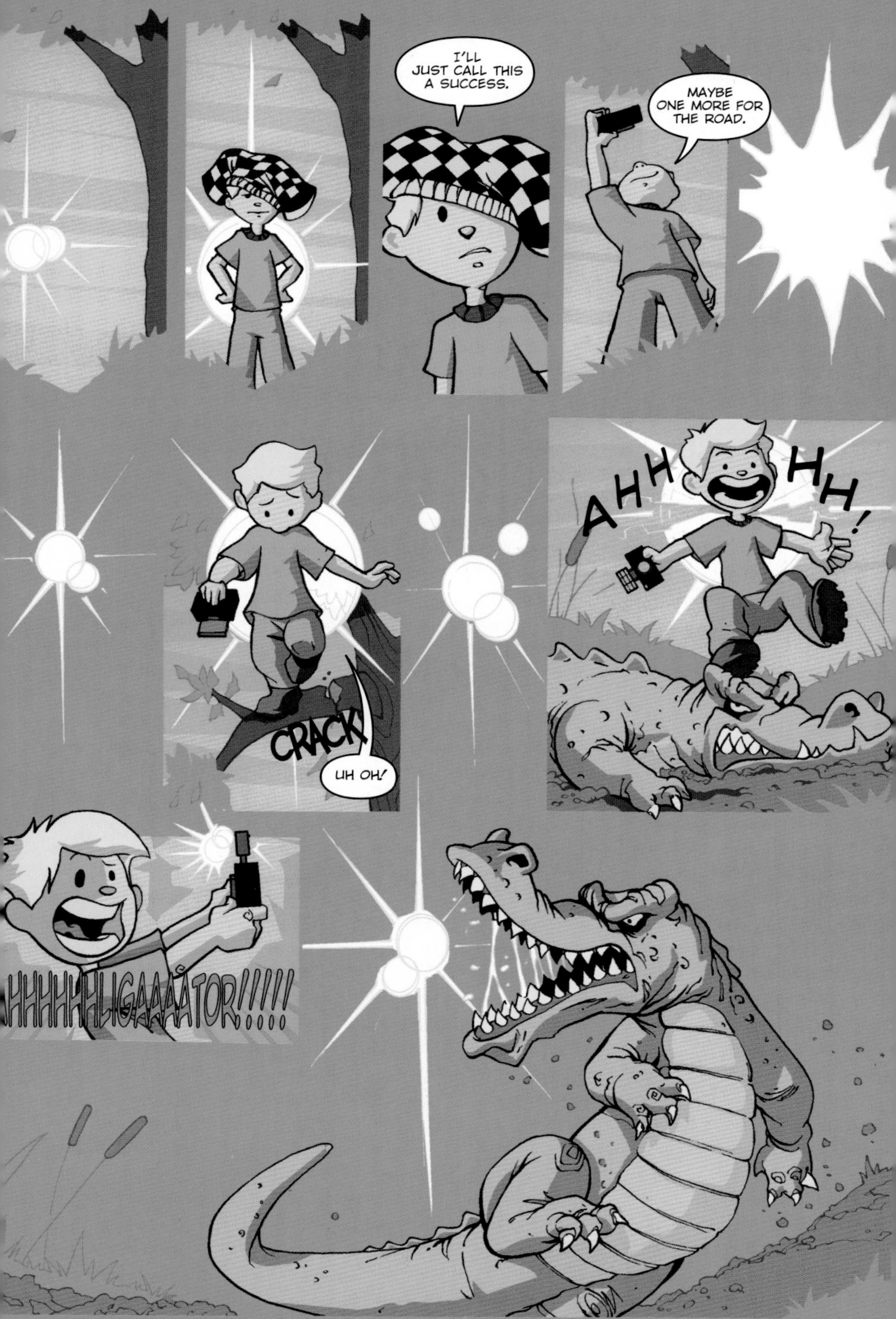
I'LL JUST CALL THIS A SUCCESS.
MAYBE ONE MORE FOR THE ROAD.
CRACK!
UH OH!
AHHHHH!
HHHHHHLIGAAAAATOR!!!!!

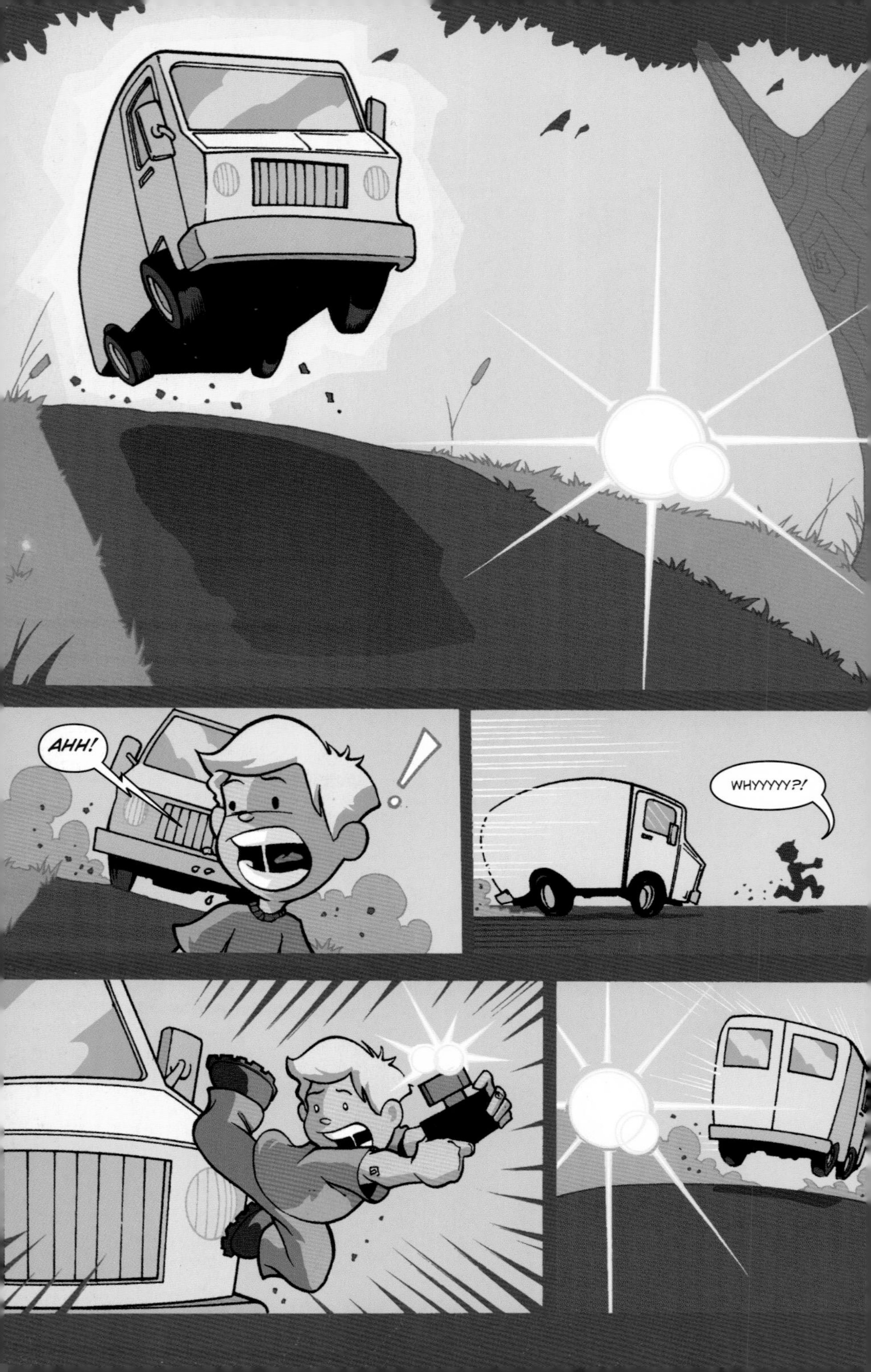
AHH!
WHYYYYY?!

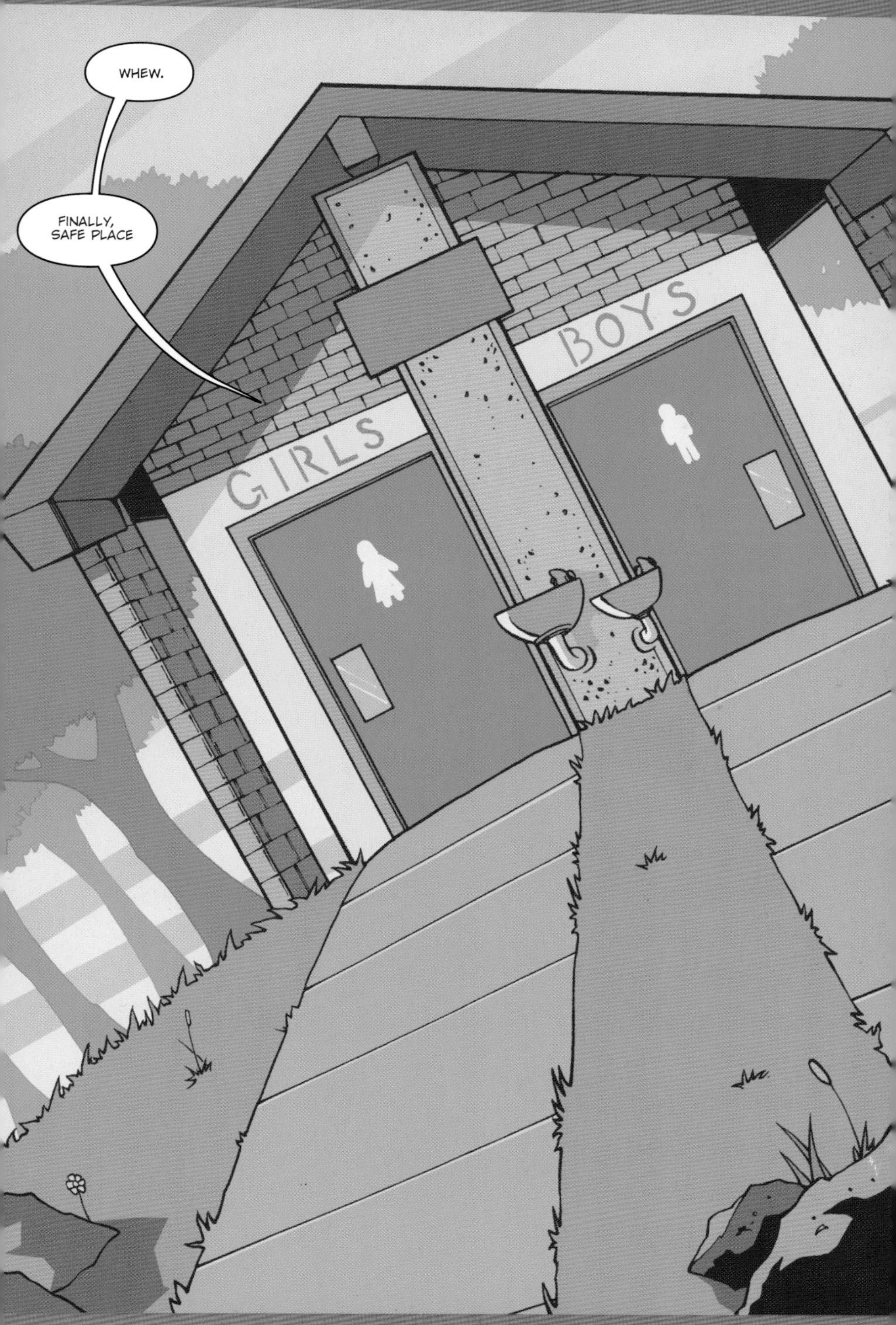
WHEW.
FINALLY, SAFE PLACE
GIRLS
BOYS

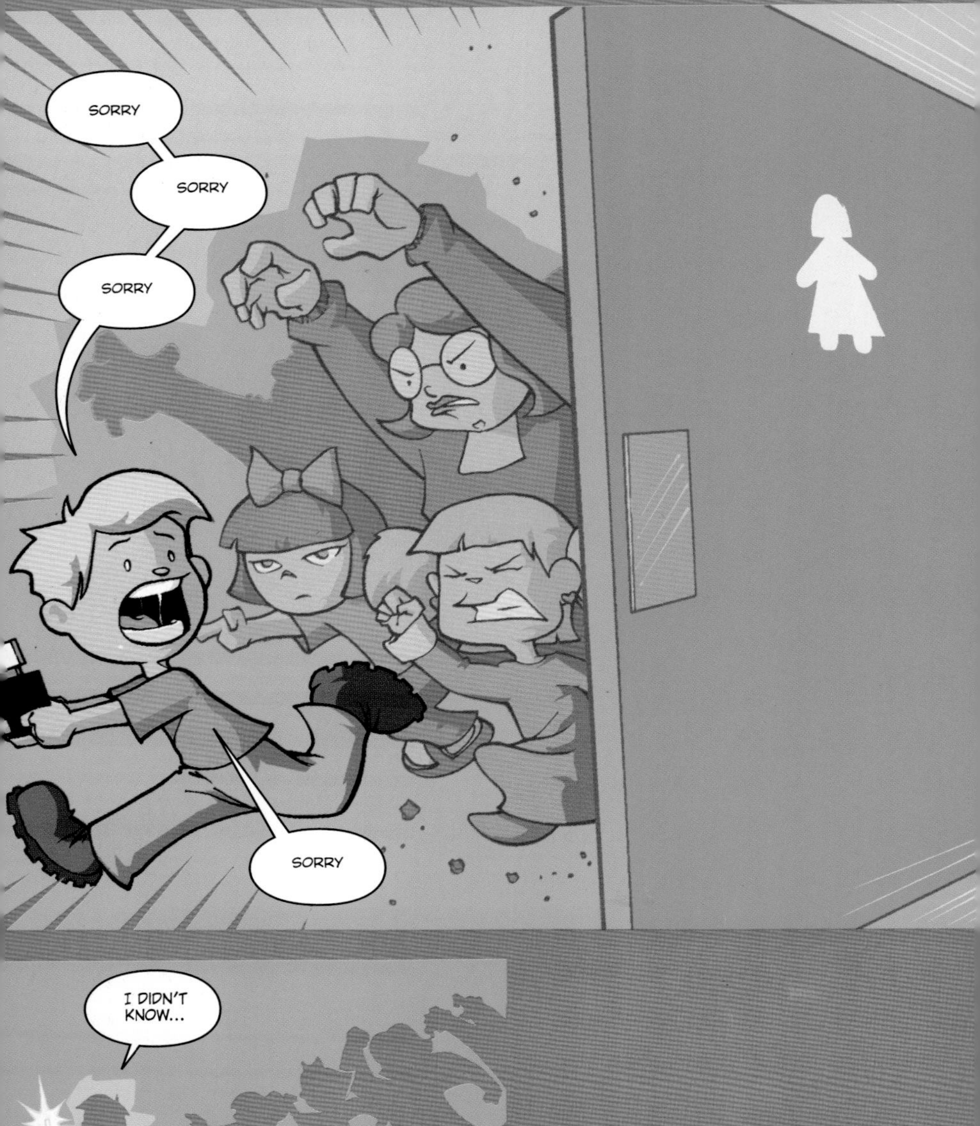
SORRY
SORRY
SORRY
SORRY

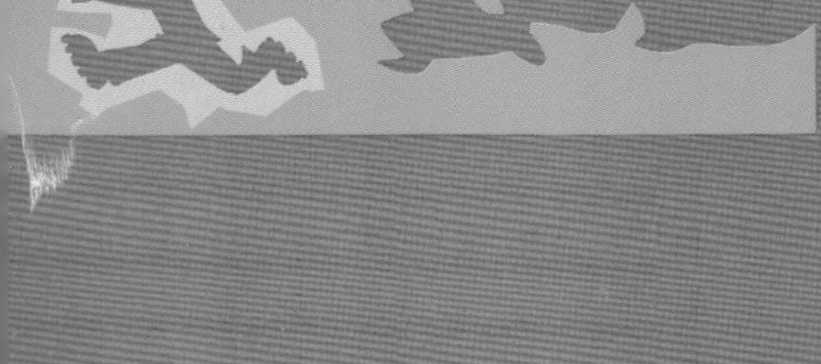
I DIDN'T KNOW...

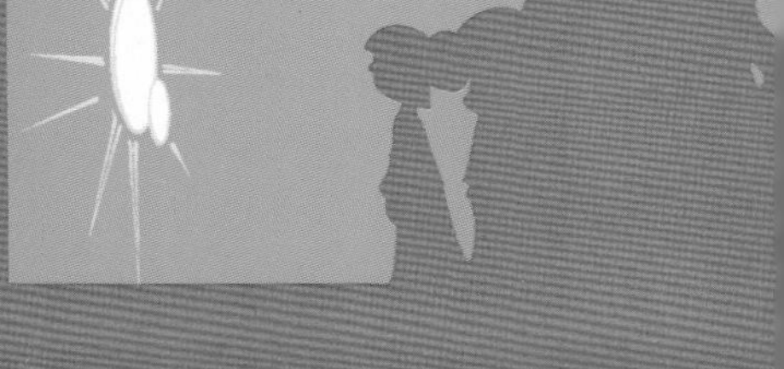
? ? ?

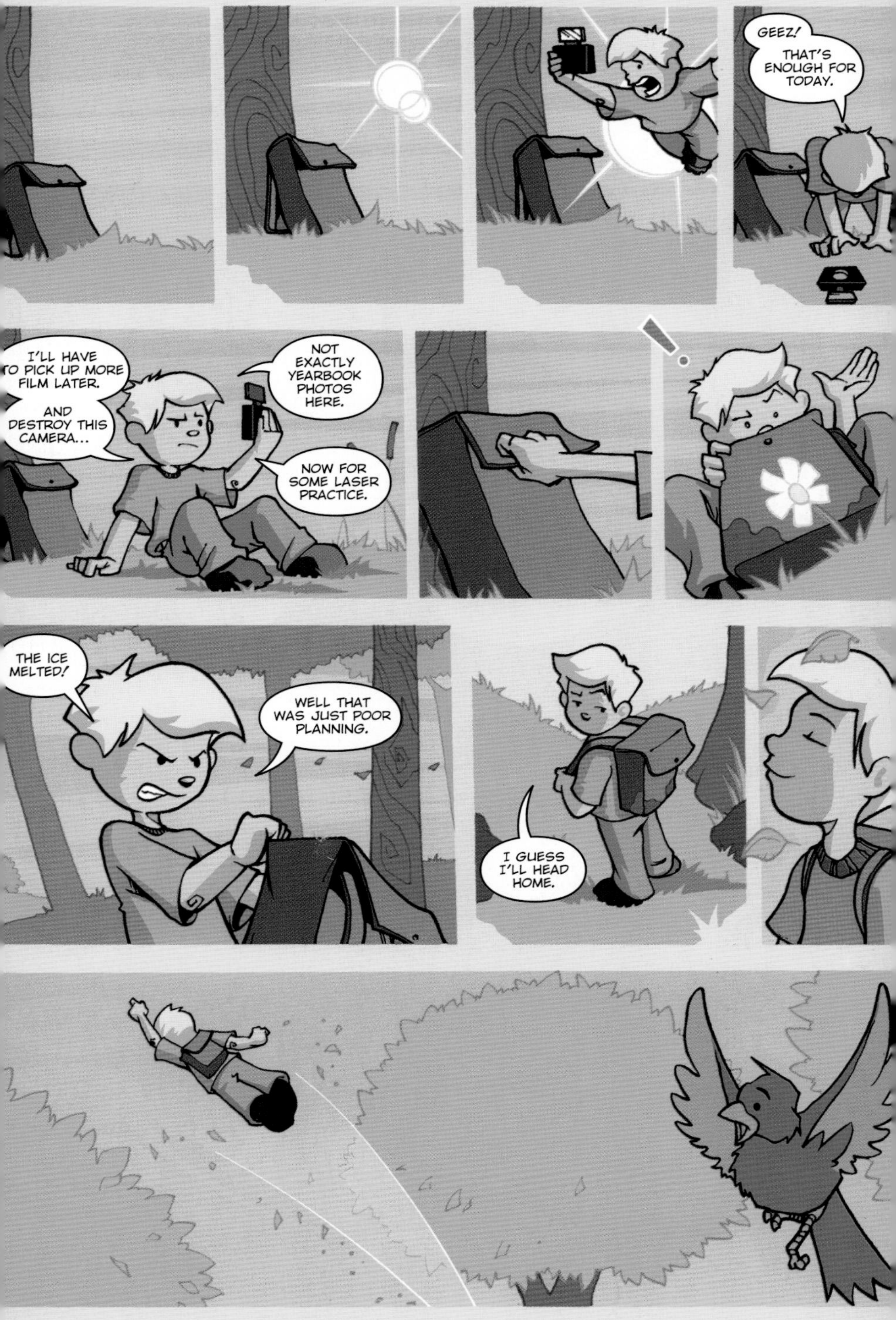
GEEZ!
THAT'S ENOUGH FOR TODAY.
I'LL HAVE TO PICK UP MORE FILM LATER.
AND DESTROY THIS CAMERA...
NOT EXACTLY YEARBOOK PHOTOS HERE.
NOW FOR SOME LASER PRACTICE.
!
THE ICE MELTED!
WELL THAT WAS JUST POOR PLANNING.
I GUESS I'LL HEAD HOME.

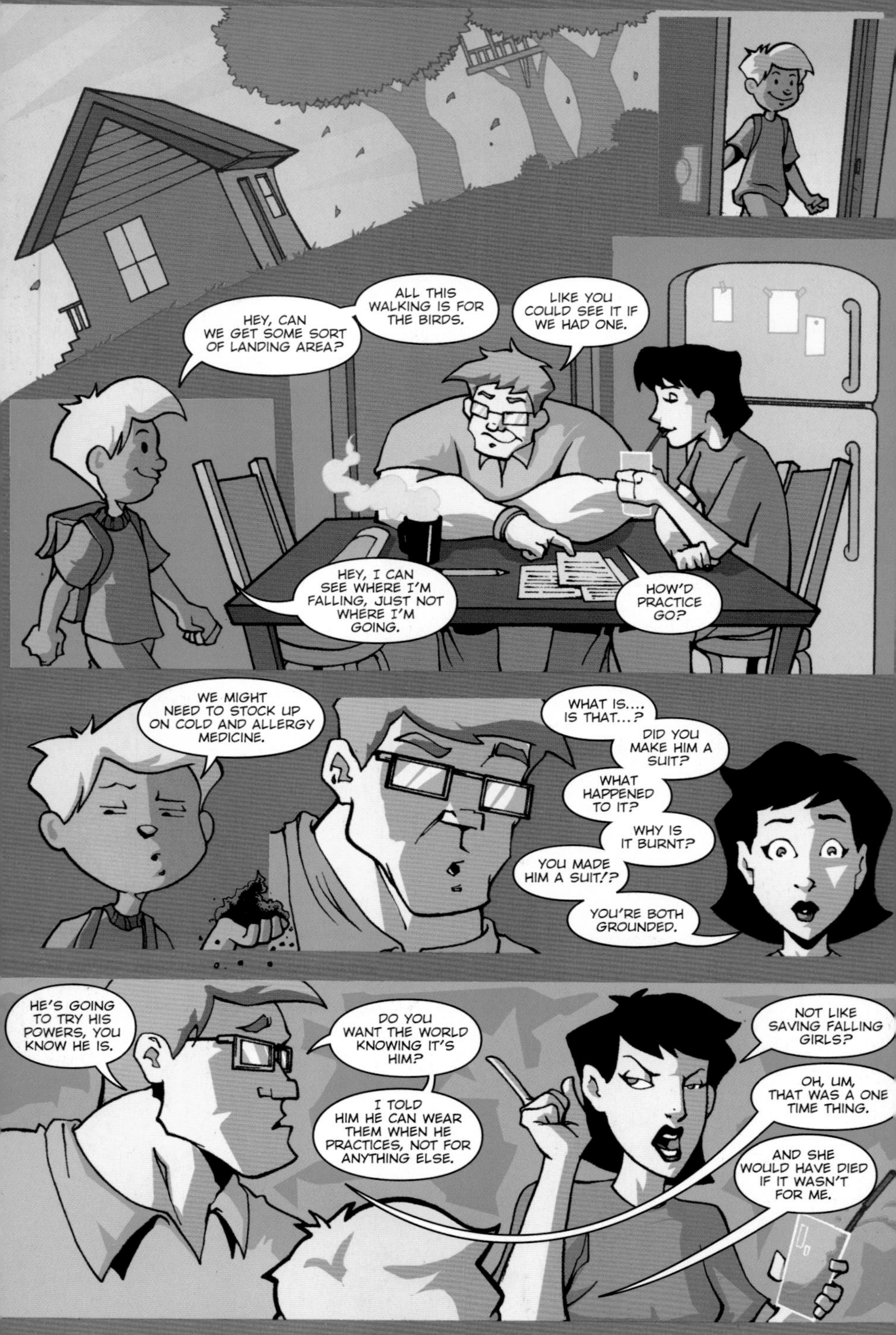
HEY, CAN WE GET SOME SORT OF LANDING AREA?
ALL THIS WALKING IS FOR THE BIRDS.
LIKE YOU COULD SEE IT IF WE HAD ONE.
HEY, I CAN SEE WHERE I'M FALLING, JUST NOT WHERE I'M GOING.
HOW'D PRACTICE GO?
WE MIGHT NEED TO STOCK UP ON COLD AND ALLERGY MEDICINE.
WHAT IS.... IS THAT...?
DID YOU MAKE HIM A SUIT?
WHAT HAPPENED TO IT?
WHY IS IT BURNT?
YOU MADE HIM A SUIT!?
YOU'RE BOTH GROUNDED.
HE'S GOING TO TRY HIS POWERS, YOU KNOW HE IS.
DO YOU WANT THE WORLD KNOWING IT'S HIM?
I TOLD HIM HE CAN WEAR THEM WHEN HE PRACTICES, NOT FOR ANYTHING ELSE.
NOT LIKE SAVING FALLING GIRLS?
OH, UM, THAT WAS A ONE TIME THING.
AND SHE WOULD HAVE DIED IF IT WASN'T FOR ME.

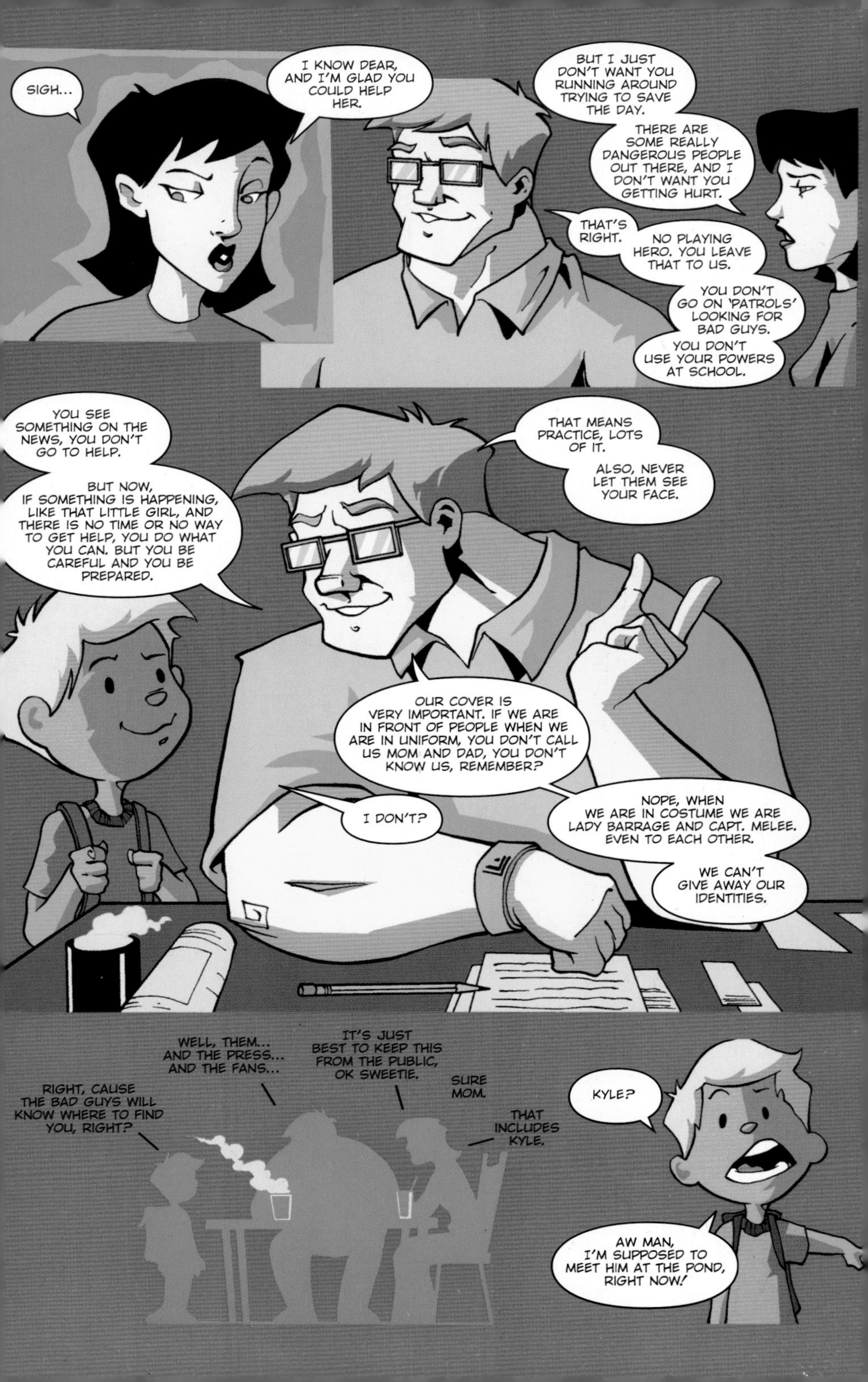
SIGH...
I KNOW DEAR, AND I'M GLAD YOU COULD HELP HER.
BUT I JUST DON'T WANT YOU RUNNING AROUND TRYING TO SAVE THE DAY.
THERE ARE SOME REALLY DANGEROUS PEOPLE OUT THERE, AND I DON'T WANT YOU GETTING HURT.
THAT'S RIGHT.
NO PLAYING HERO. YOU LEAVE THAT TO US.
YOU DON'T GO ON 'PATROLS' LOOKING FOR BAD GUYS.
YOU DON'T USE YOUR POWERS AT SCHOOL.
YOU SEE SOMETHING ON THE NEWS, YOU DON'T GO TO HELP.
BUT NOW, IF SOMETHING IS HAPPENING, LIKE THAT LITTLE GIRL, AND THERE IS NO TIME OR NO WAY TO GET HELP, YOU DO WHAT YOU CAN. BUT YOU BE CAREFUL AND YOU BE PREPARED.
THAT MEANS PRACTICE, LOTS OF IT.
ALSO, NEVER LET THEM SEE YOUR FACE.
OUR COVER IS VERY IMPORTANT. IF WE ARE IN FRONT OF PEOPLE WHEN WE ARE IN UNIFORM, YOU DON'T CALL US MOM AND DAD, YOU DON'T KNOW US, REMEMBER?
I DON'T?
NOPE, WHEN WE ARE IN COSTUME WE ARE LADY BARRAGE AND CAPT. MELEE. EVEN TO EACH OTHER.
WE CAN'T GIVE AWAY OUR IDENTITIES.
RIGHT, CAUSE THE BAD GUYS WILL KNOW WHERE TO FIND YOU, RIGHT?
WELL, THEM... AND THE PRESS... AND THE FANS...
IT'S JUST BEST TO KEEP THIS FROM THE PUBLIC, OK SWEETIE.
SURE MOM.
THAT INCLUDES KYLE.
KYLE?
AW MAN, I'M SUPPOSED TO MEET HIM AT THE POND, RIGHT NOW!

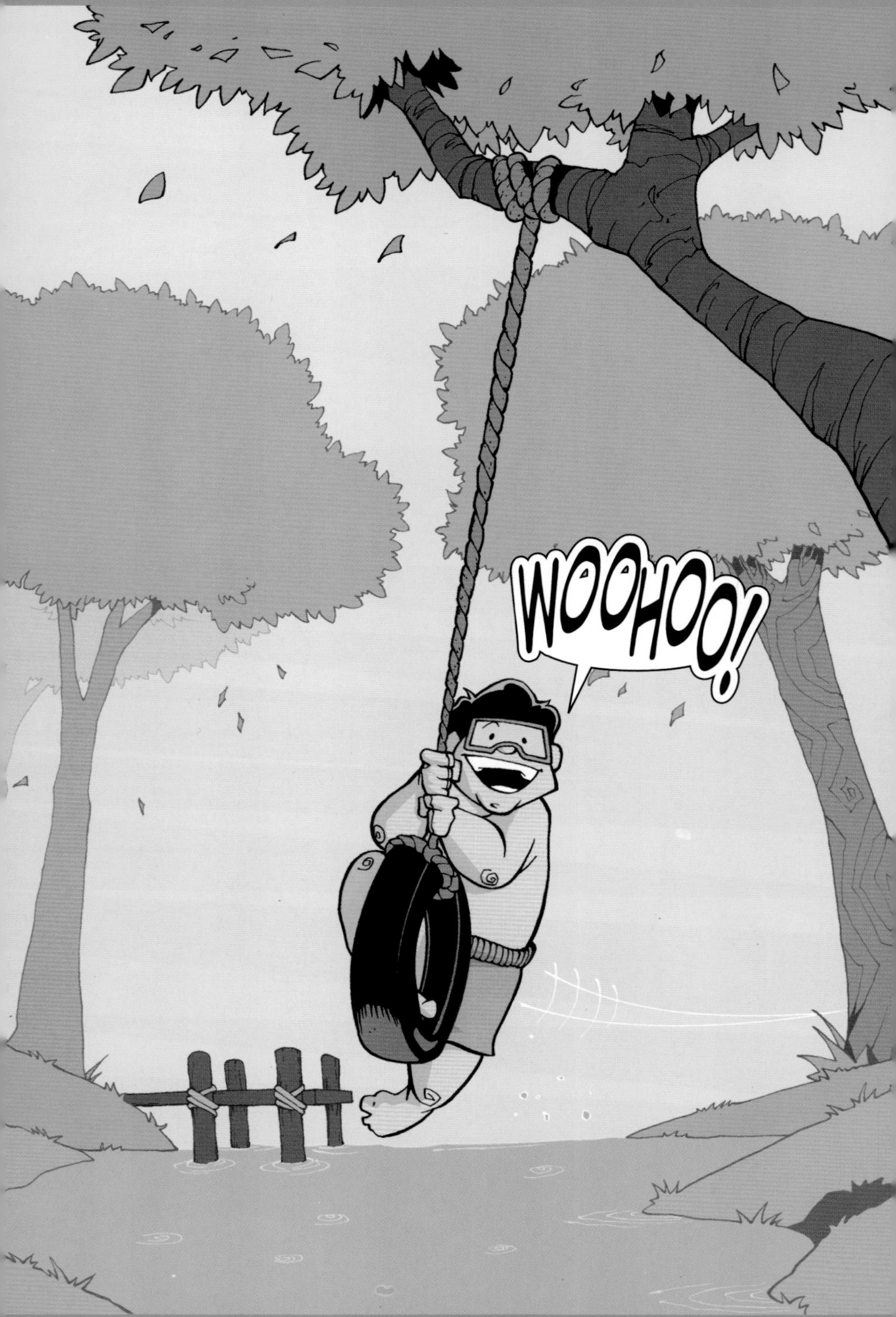
WOOHOO!

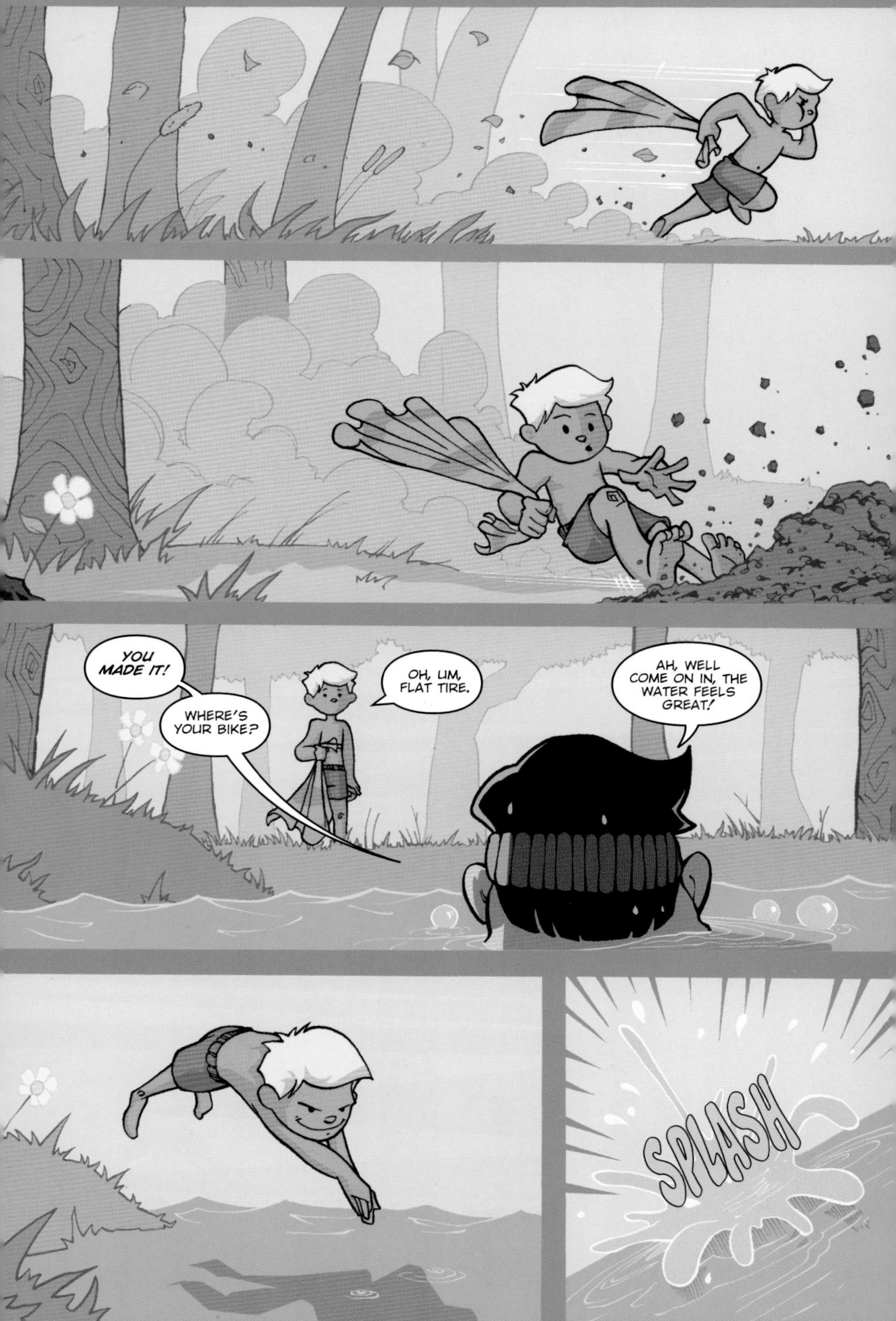
YOU MADE IT!
WHERE'S YOUR BIKE?
OH, UM, FLAT TIRE.
AH, WELL COME ON IN, THE WATER FEELS GREAT!
SPLASH

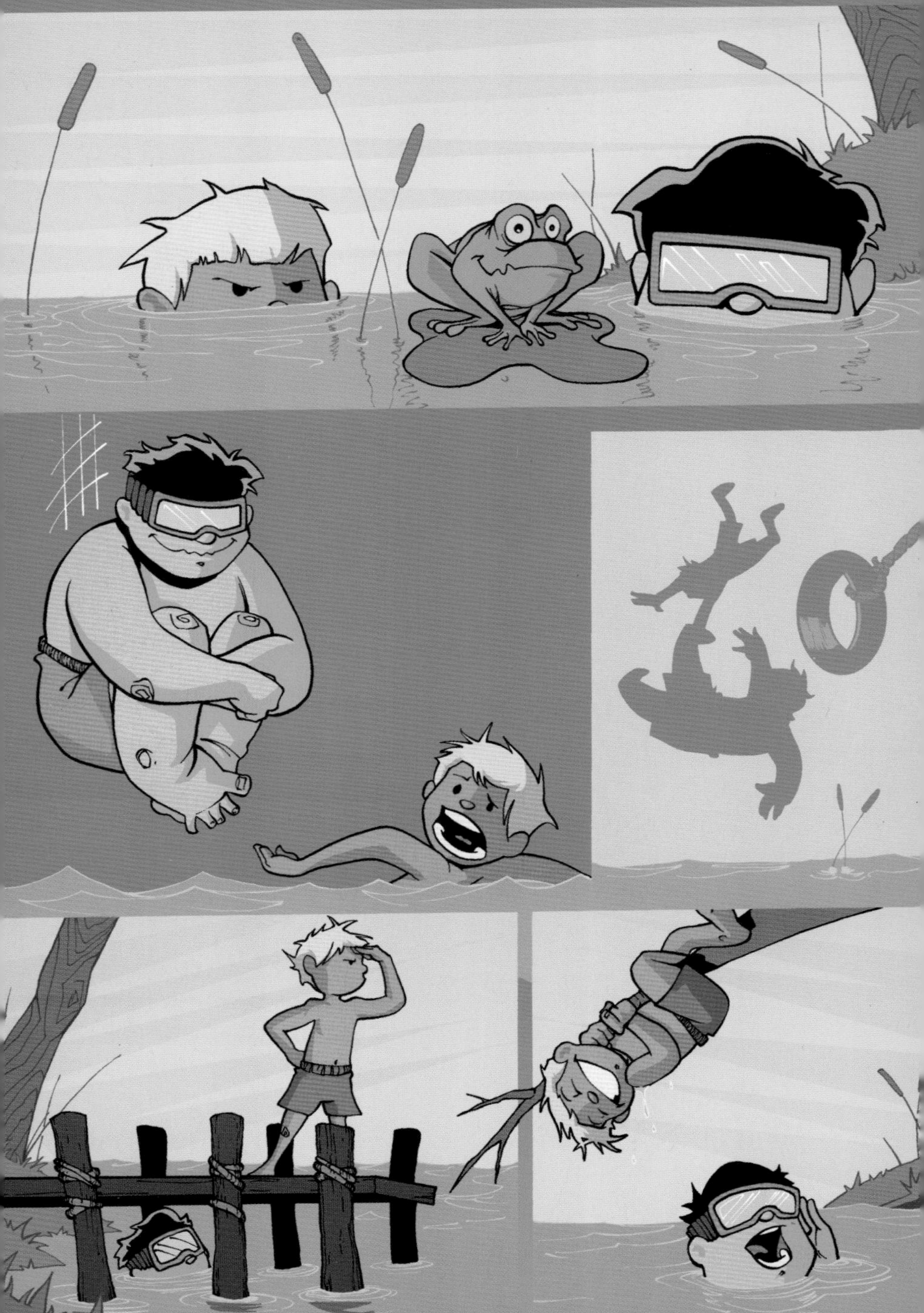

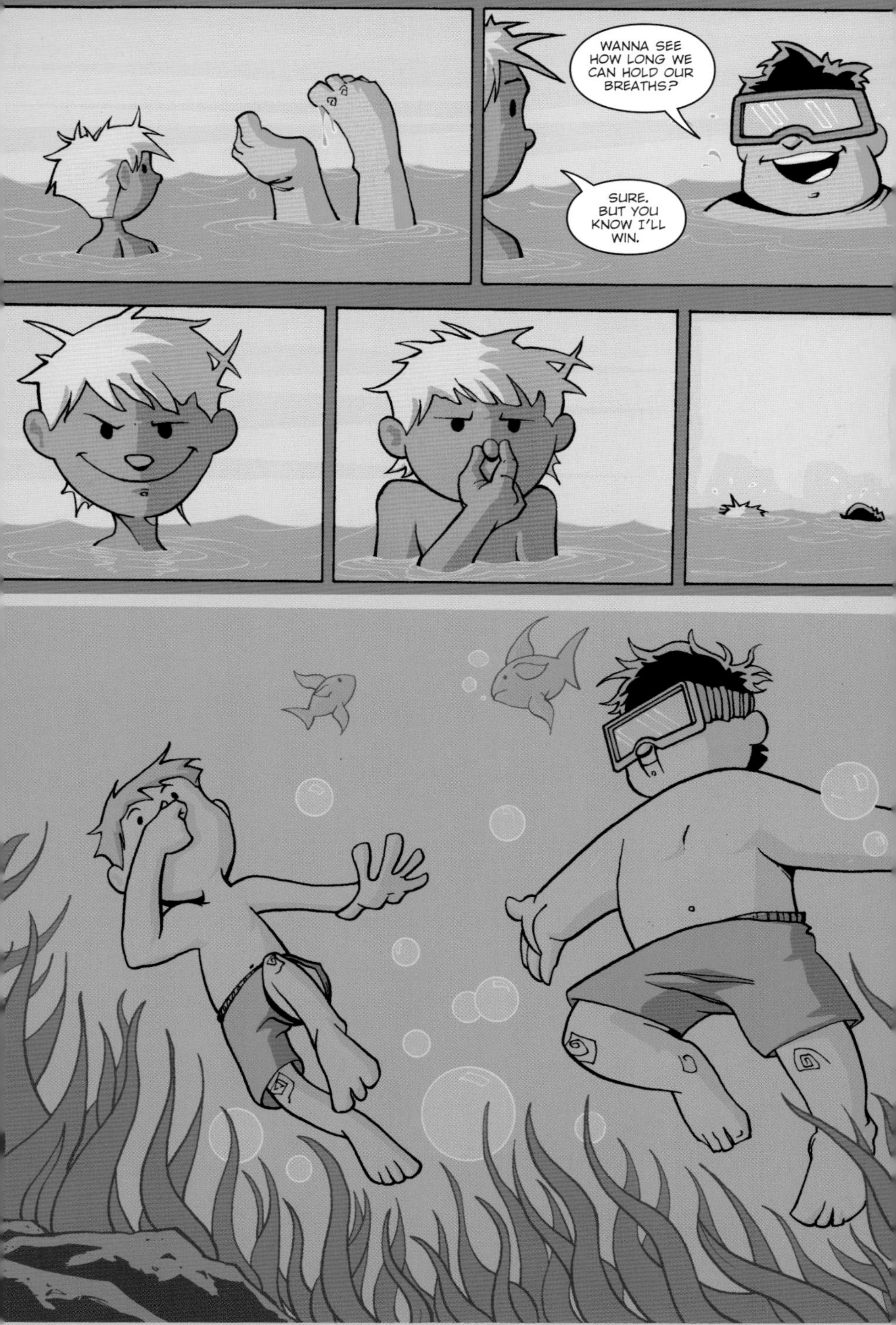
WANNA SEE HOW LONG WE CAN HOLD OUR BREATHS?
SURE. BUT YOU KNOW I'LL WIN.

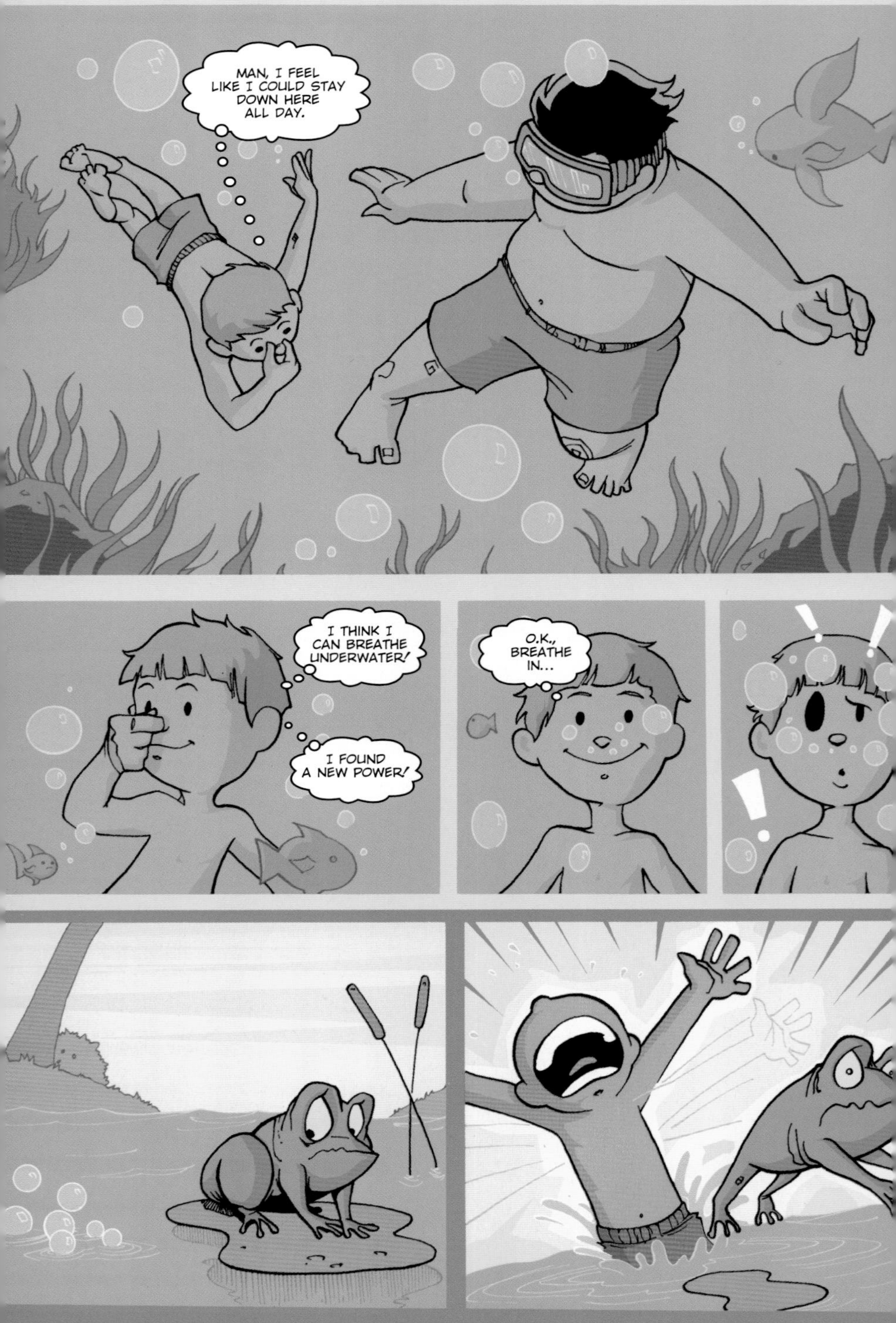
MAN, I FEEL LIKE I COULD STAY DOWN HERE ALL DAY.
I THINK I CAN BREATHE UNDERWATER!
I FOUND A NEW POWER!
O.K., BREATHE IN...

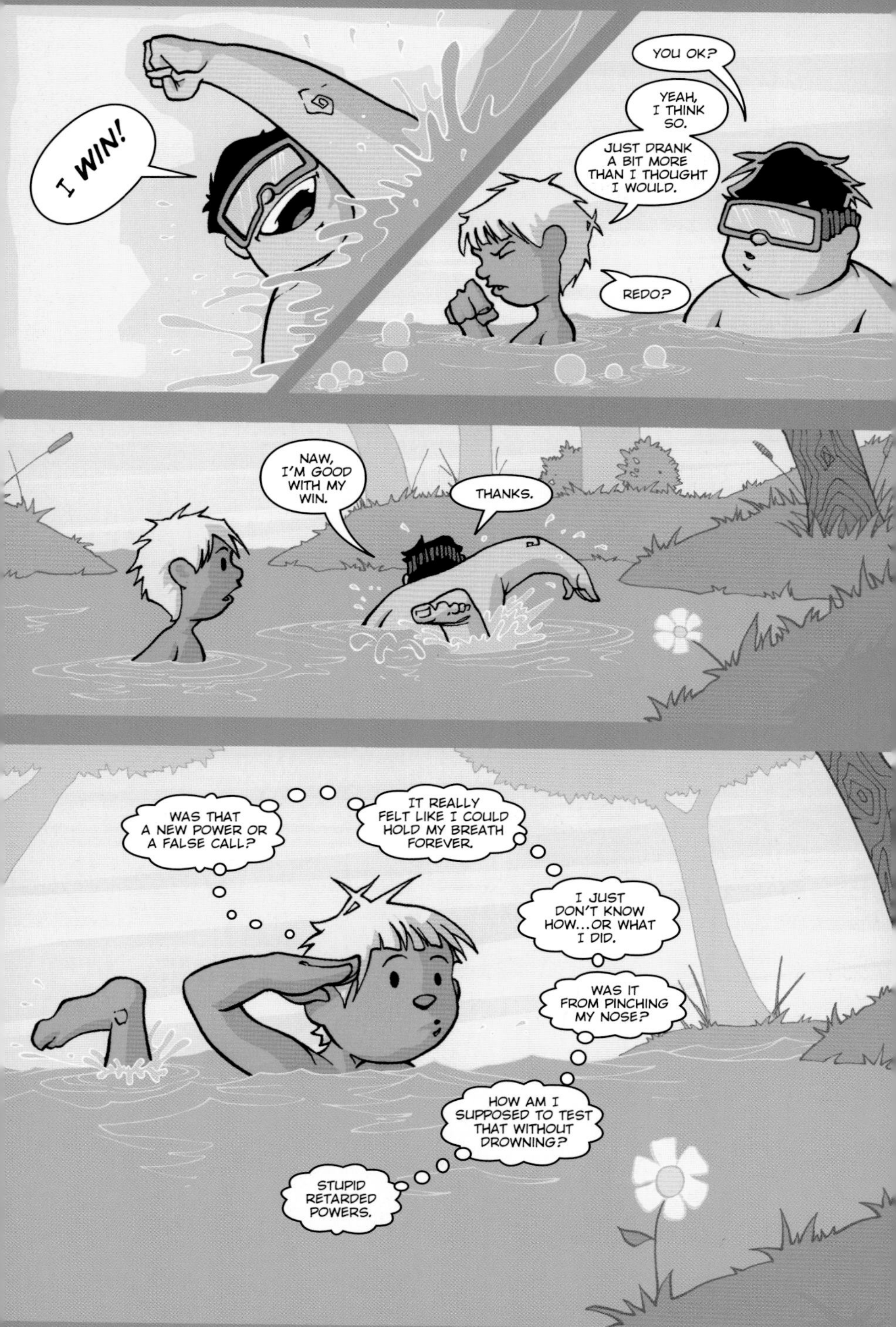
I WIN!
YOU OK?
YEAH, I THINK SO.
JUST DRANK A BIT MORE THAN I THOUGHT I WOULD.
REDO?
NAW, I'M GOOD WITH MY WIN.
THANKS.
WAS THAT A NEW POWER OR A FALSE CALL?
IT REALLY FELT LIKE I COULD HOLD MY BREATH FOREVER.
I JUST DON'T KNOW HOW...OR WHAT I DID.
WAS IT FROM PINCHING MY NOSE?
HOW AM I SUPPOSED TO TEST THAT WITHOUT DROWNING?
STUPID RETARDED POWERS.

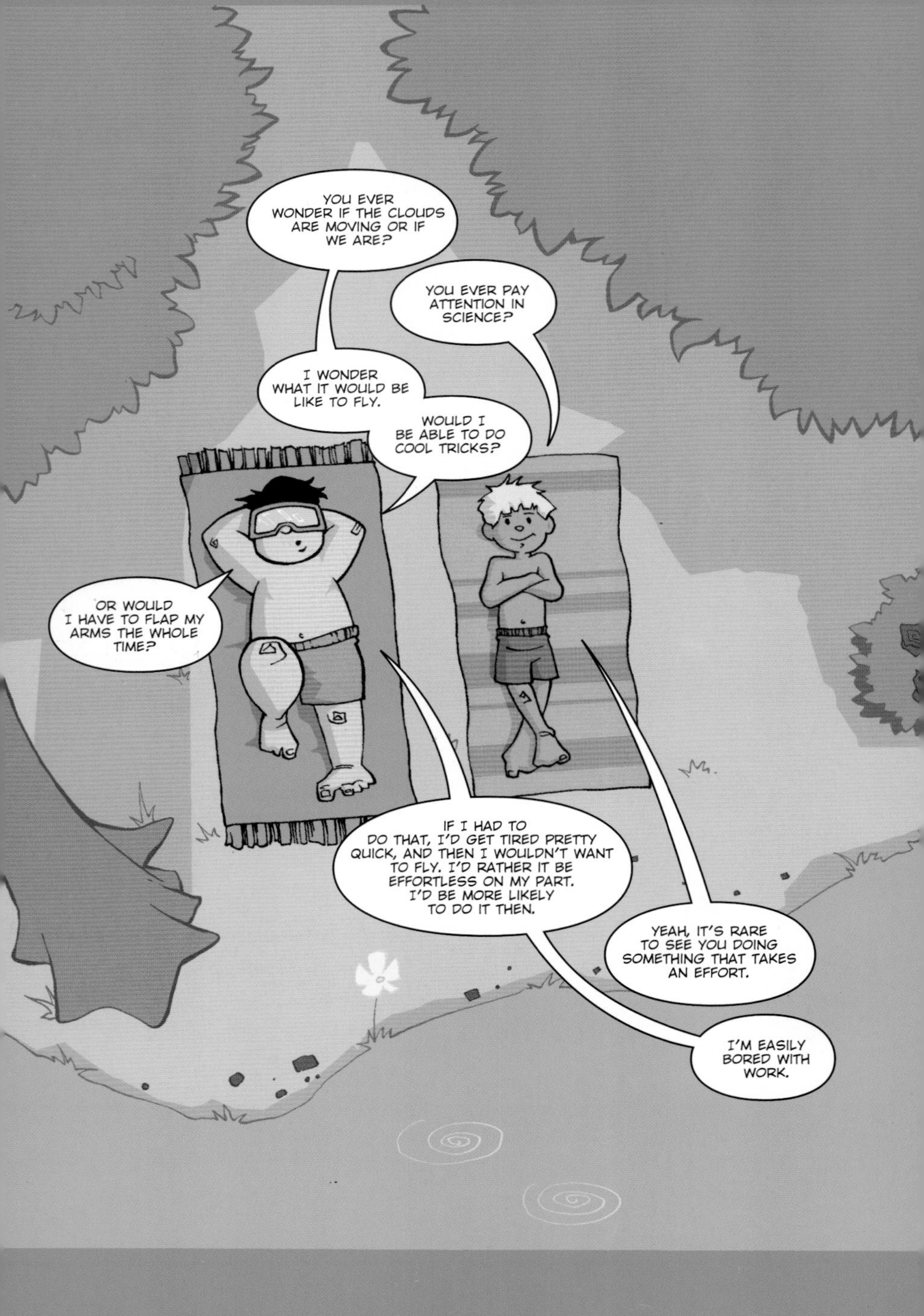
YOU EVER WONDER IF THE CLOUDS ARE MOVING OR IF WE ARE?
YOU EVER PAY ATTENTION IN SCIENCE?
I WONDER WHAT IT WOULD BE LIKE TO FLY.
WOULD I BE ABLE TO DO COOL TRICKS?
OR WOULD I HAVE TO FLAP MY ARMS THE WHOLE TIME?
IF I HAD TO DO THAT, I'D GET TIRED PRETTY QUICK, AND THEN I WOULDN'T WANT TO FLY. I'D RATHER IT BE EFFORTLESS ON MY PART. I'D BE MORE LIKELY TO DO IT THEN.
YEAH, IT'S RARE TO SEE YOU DOING SOMETHING THAT TAKES AN EFFORT.
I'M EASILY BORED WITH WORK.

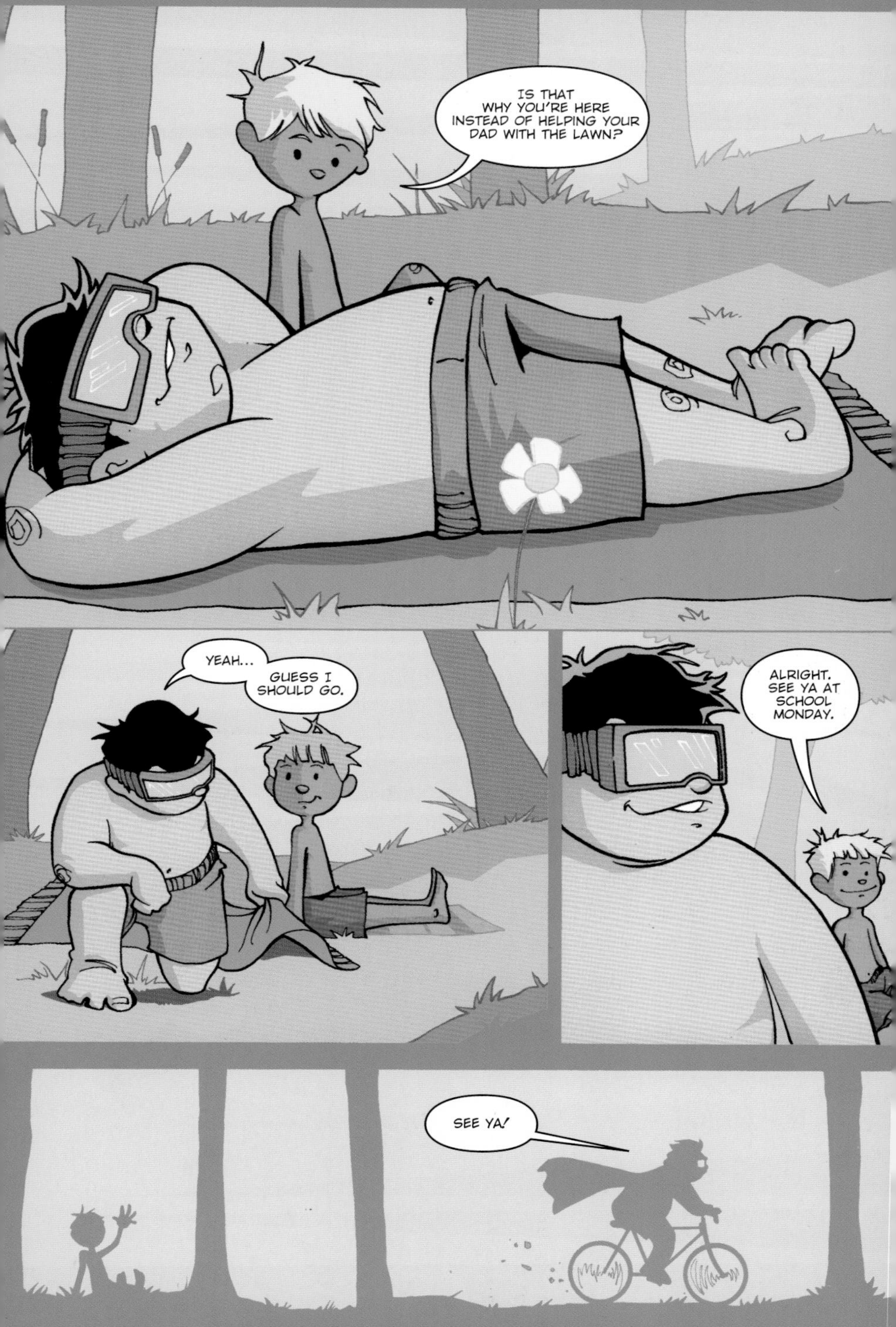
IS THAT WHY YOU'RE HERE INSTEAD OF HELPING YOUR DAD WITH THE LAWN?
YEAH...
GUESS I SHOULD GO.
ALRIGHT. SEE YA AT SCHOOL MONDAY.
SEE YA!

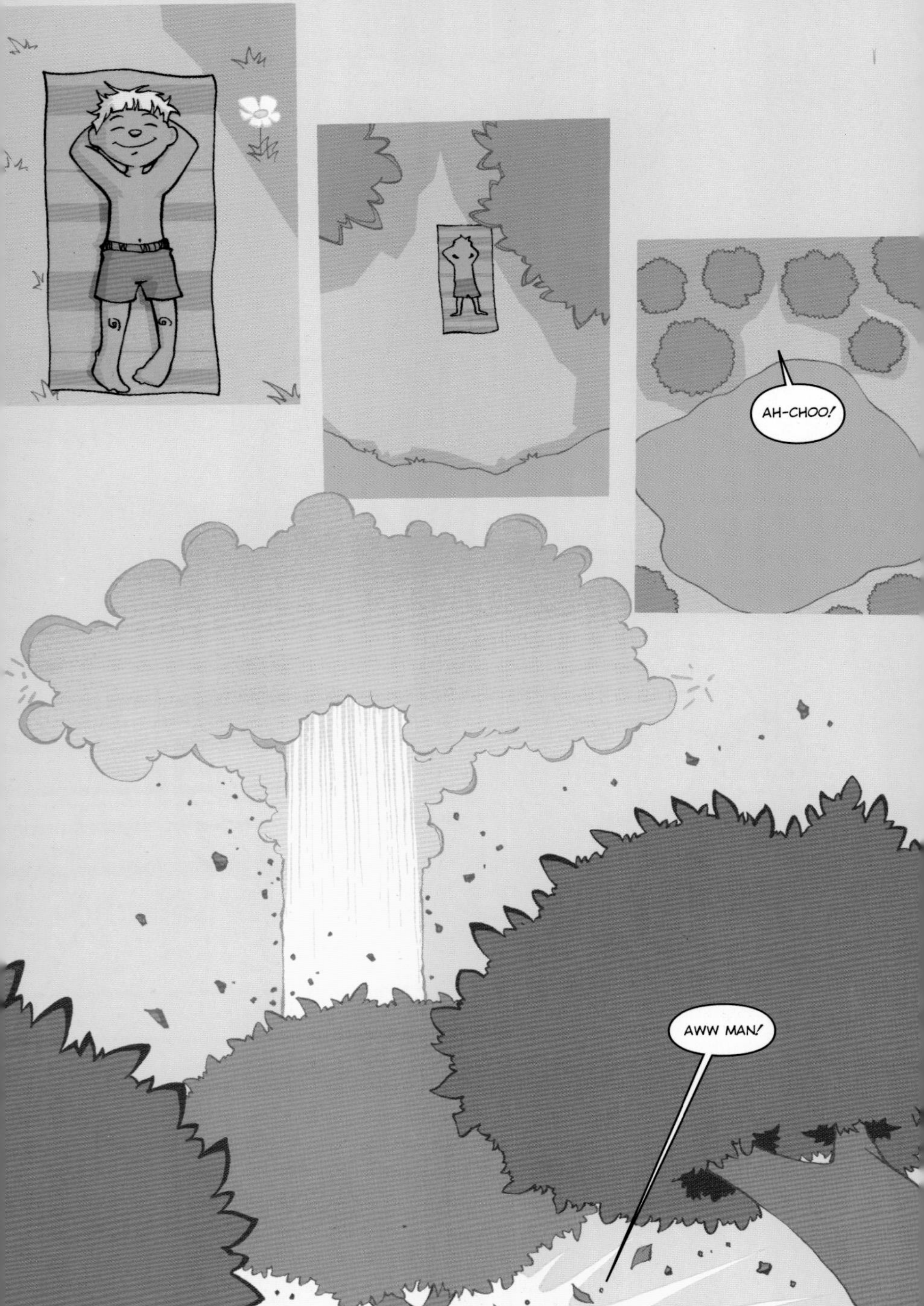
AH-CHOO!
AWW MAN!

chapter 4
DAD SAID NO POWERS

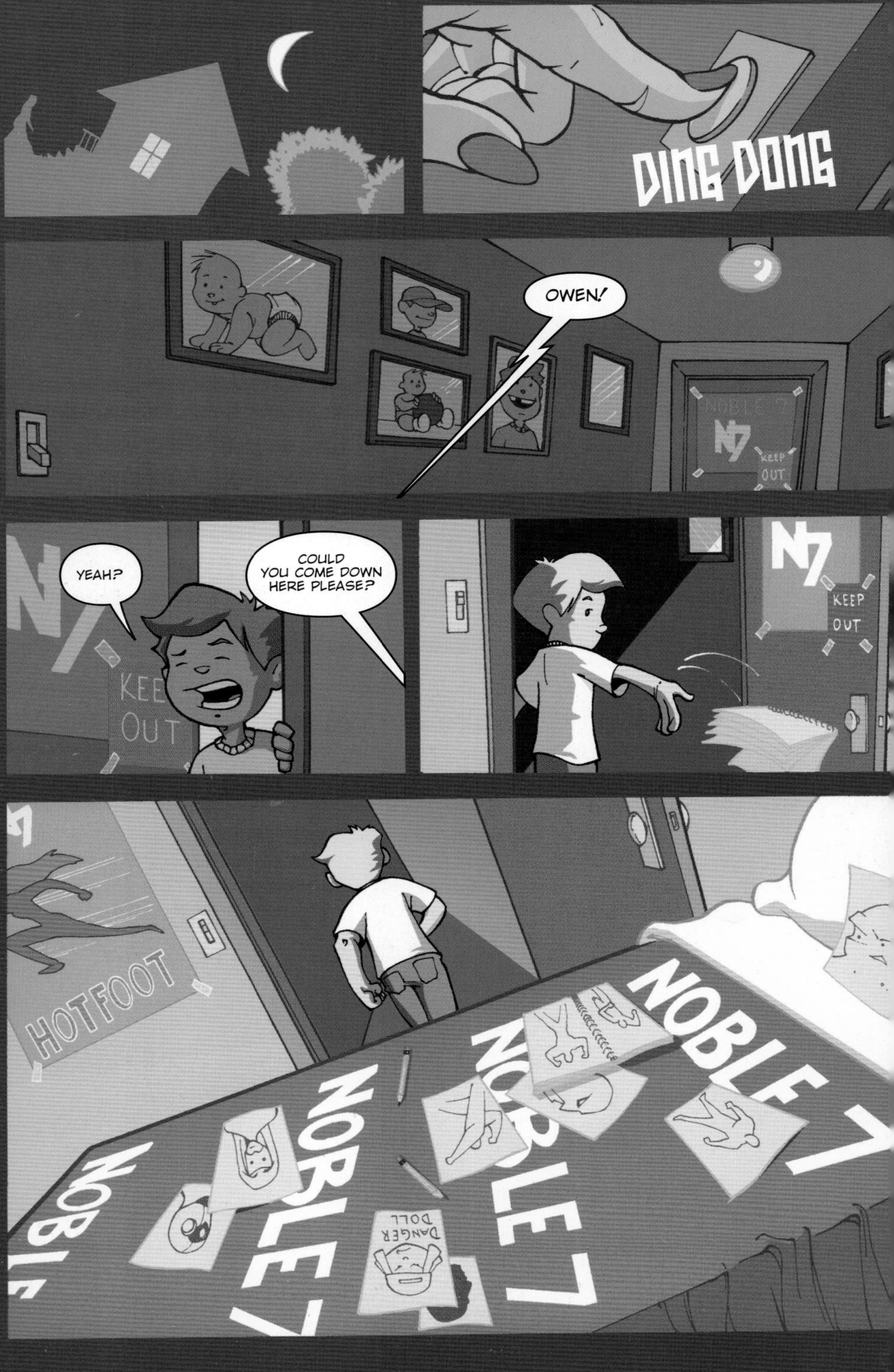
DING DONG
OWEN!
N7
KEEP OUT
YEAH?
COULD YOU COME DOWN HERE PLEASE?
KEEP OUT
HOTFOOT
NOBLE 7
DANGER DOLL

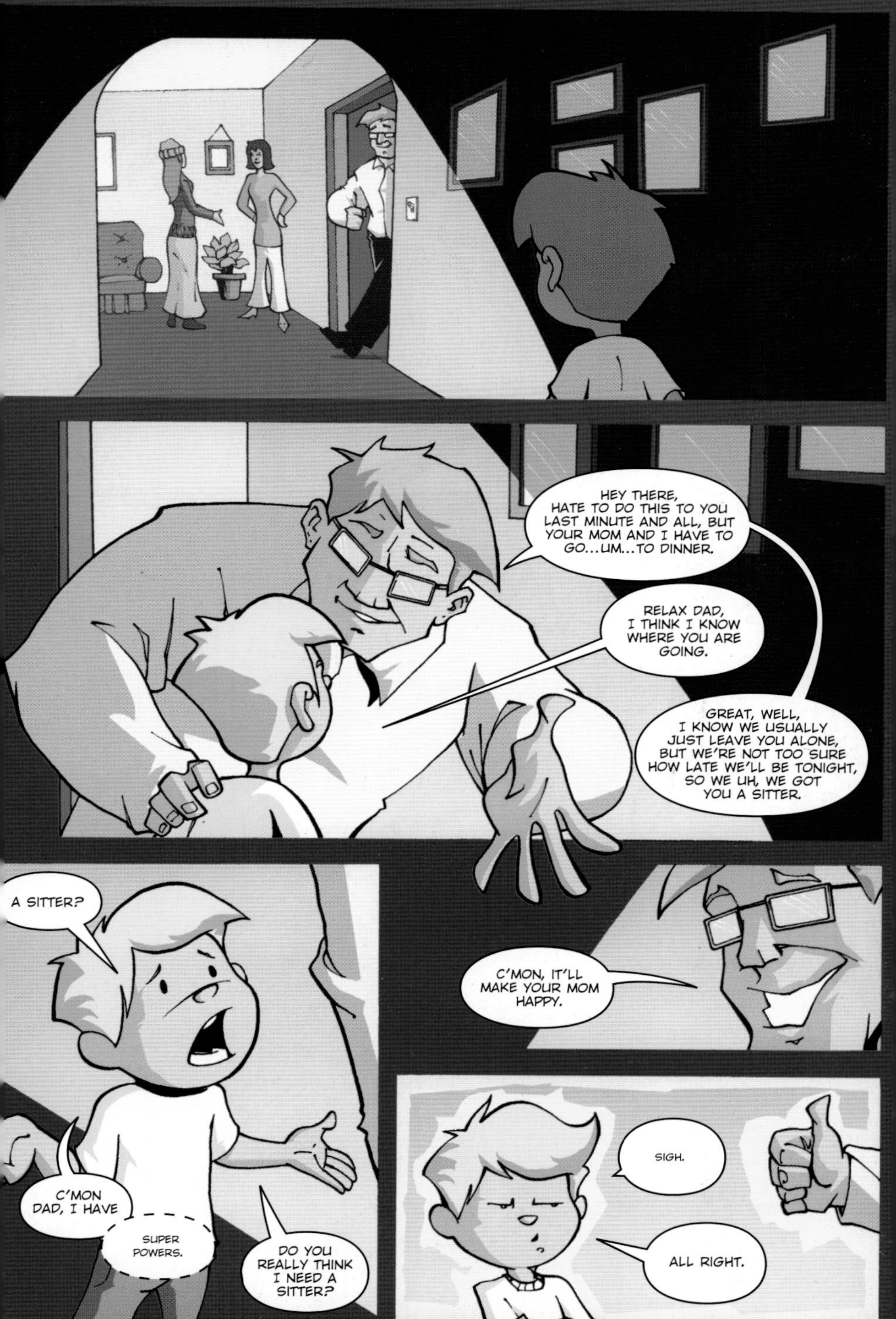
HEY THERE, HATE TO DO THIS TO YOU LAST MINUTE AND ALL, BUT YOUR MOM AND I HAVE TO GO...UM...TO DINNER.
RELAX DAD, I THINK I KNOW WHERE YOU ARE GOING.
GREAT, WELL, I KNOW WE USUALLY JUST LEAVE YOU ALONE, BUT WE'RE NOT TOO SURE HOW LATE WE'LL BE TONIGHT, SO WE UH, WE GOT YOU A SITTER.
A SITTER?
C'MON DAD, I HAVE
SUPER POWERS.
DO YOU REALLY THINK I NEED A SITTER?
C'MON, IT'LL MAKE YOUR MOM HAPPY.
SIGH.
ALL RIGHT.

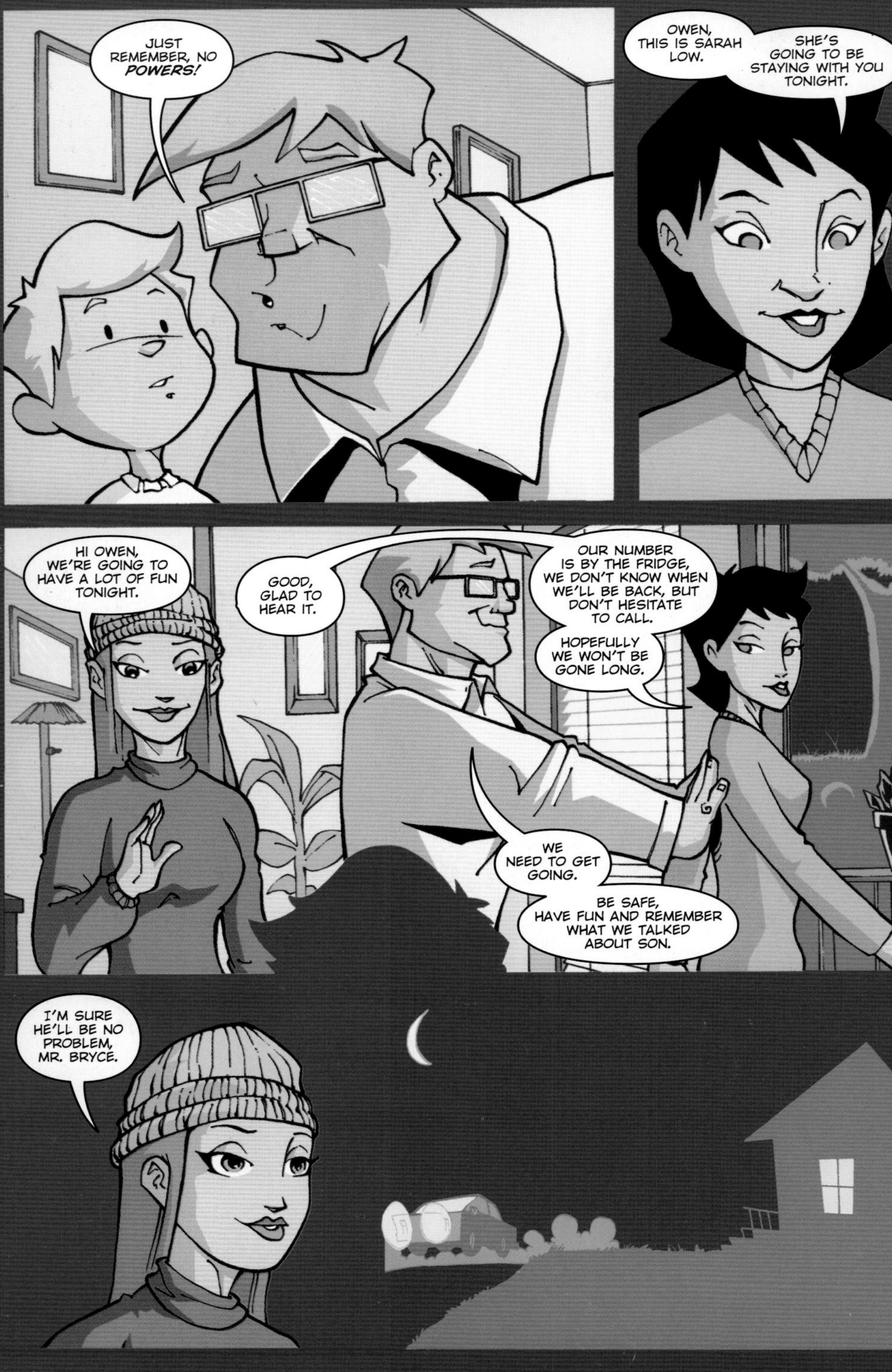
JUST REMEMBER, NO *POWERS!*
OWEN, THIS IS SARAH LOW.
SHE'S GOING TO BE STAYING WITH YOU TONIGHT.
HI OWEN, WE'RE GOING TO HAVE A LOT OF FUN TONIGHT.
GOOD, GLAD TO HEAR IT.
OUR NUMBER IS BY THE FRIDGE, WE DON'T KNOW WHEN WE'LL BE BACK, BUT DON'T HESITATE TO CALL.
HOPEFULLY WE WON'T BE GONE LONG.
WE NEED TO GET GOING.
BE SAFE, HAVE FUN AND REMEMBER WHAT WE TALKED ABOUT SON.
I'M SURE HE'LL BE NO PROBLEM, MR. BRYCE.

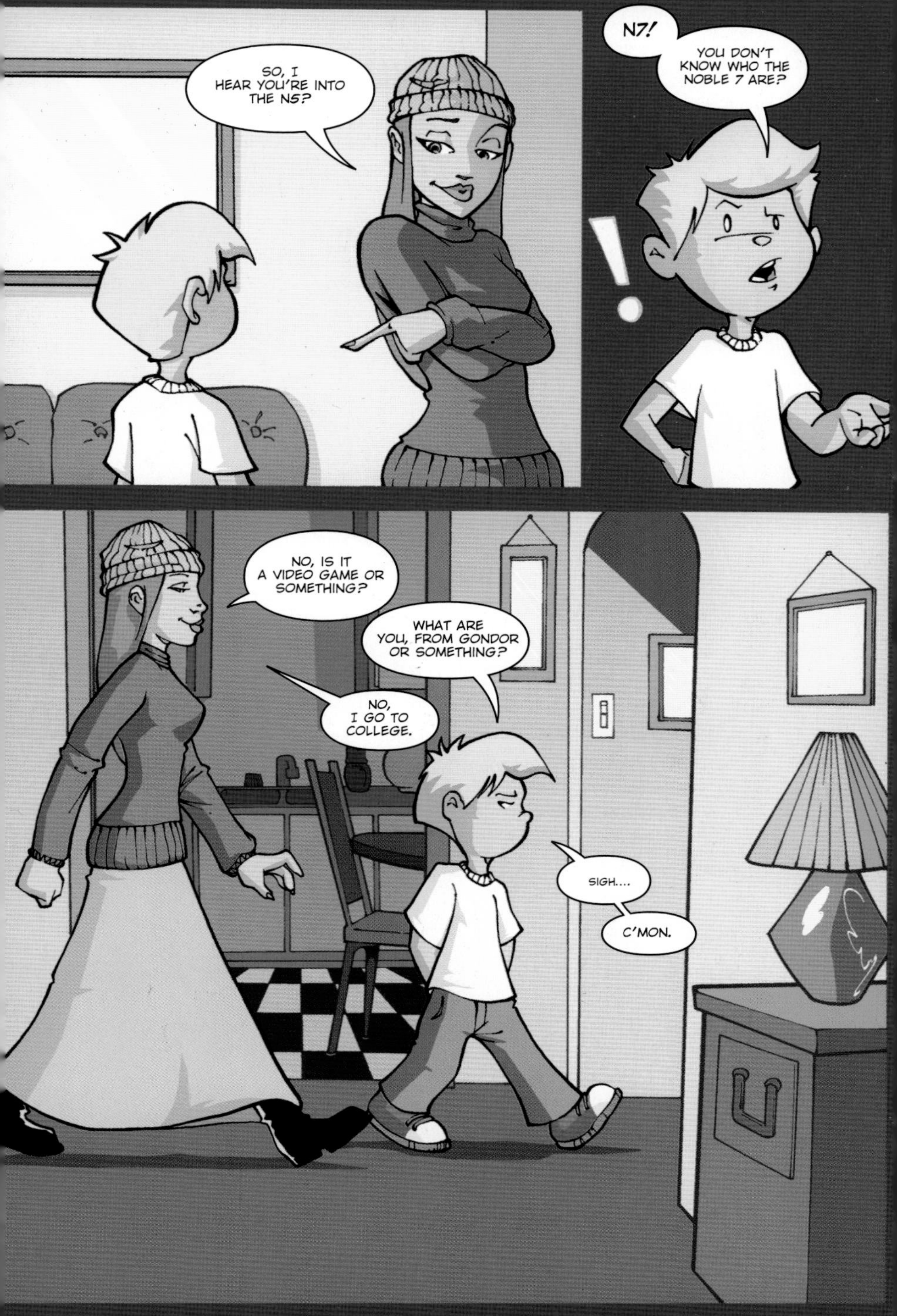
SO, I HEAR YOU'RE INTO THE N5?
N7!
YOU DON'T KNOW WHO THE NOBLE 7 ARE?
NO, IS IT A VIDEO GAME OR SOMETHING?
WHAT ARE YOU, FROM GONDOR OR SOMETHING?
NO, I GO TO COLLEGE.
SIGH....
C'MON.

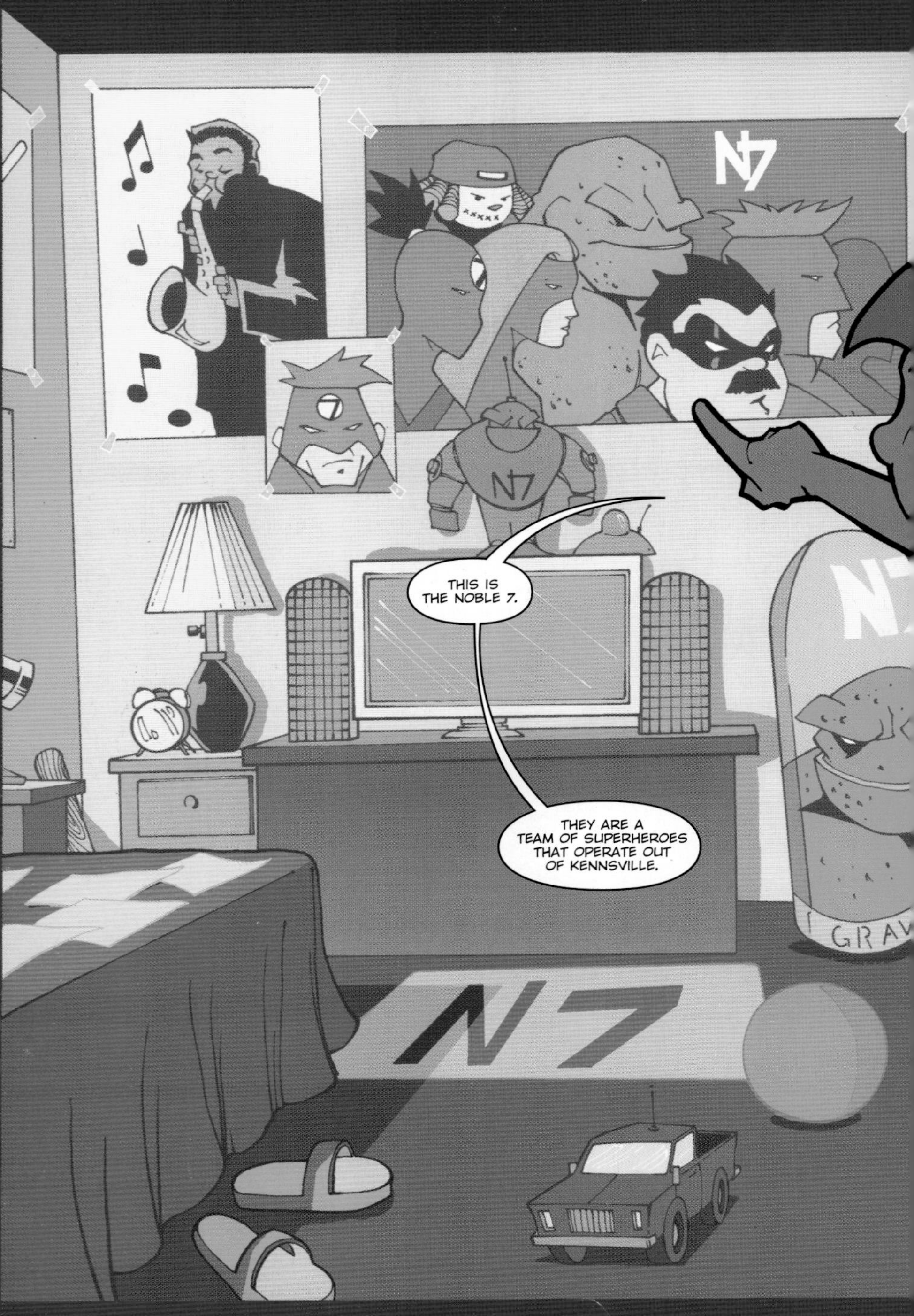
THIS IS THE NOBLE 7.
THEY ARE A TEAM OF SUPERHEROES THAT OPERATE OUT OF KENNSVILLE.

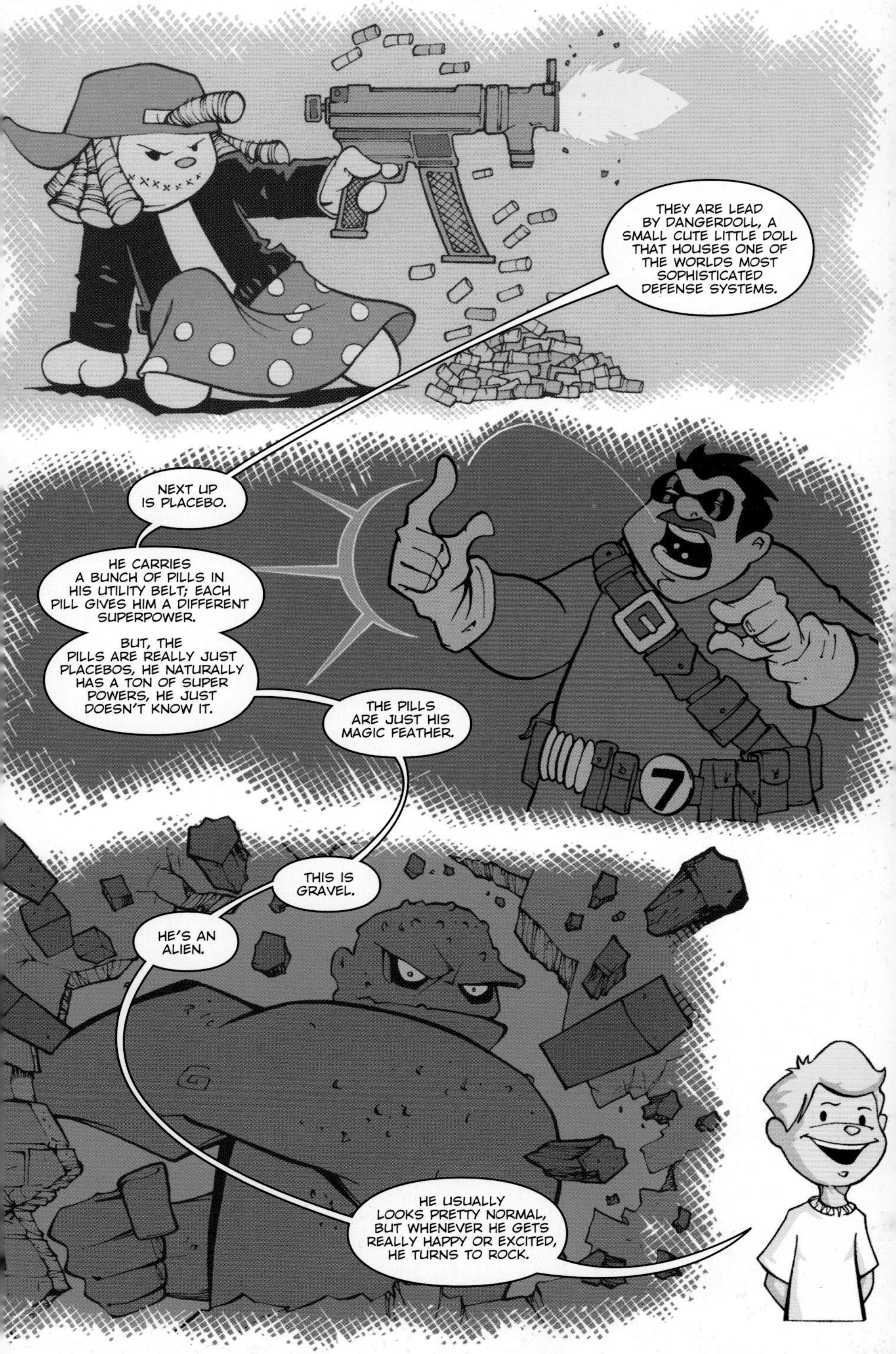
THEY ARE LEAD BY DANGERDOLL, A SMALL CUTE LITTLE DOLL THAT HOUSES ONE OF THE WORLDS MOST SOPHISTICATED DEFENSE SYSTEMS.
NEXT UP IS PLACEBO.
HE CARRIES A BUNCH OF PILLS IN HIS UTILITY BELT; EACH PILL GIVES HIM A DIFFERENT SUPERPOWER.
BUT, THE PILLS ARE REALLY JUST PLACEBOS, HE NATURALLY HAS A TON OF SUPER POWERS, HE JUST DOESN'T KNOW IT.
THE PILLS ARE JUST HIS MAGIC FEATHER.
7
THIS IS GRAVEL.
HE'S AN ALIEN.
HE USUALLY LOOKS PRETTY NORMAL, BUT WHENEVER HE GETS REALLY HAPPY OR EXCITED, HE TURNS TO ROCK.

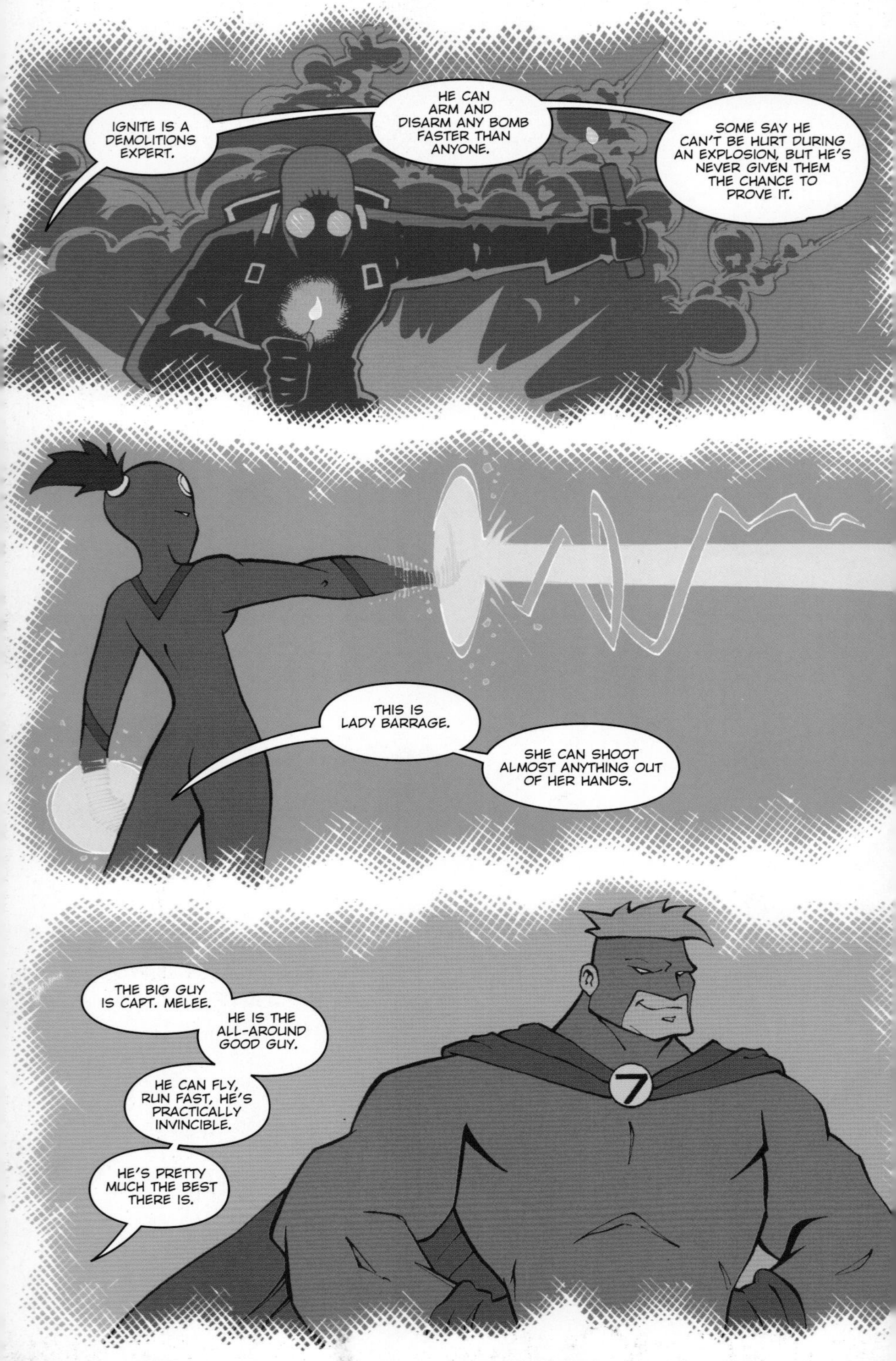
IGNITE IS A DEMOLITIONS EXPERT.
HE CAN ARM AND DISARM ANY BOMB FASTER THAN ANYONE.
SOME SAY HE CAN'T BE HURT DURING AN EXPLOSION, BUT HE'S NEVER GIVEN THEM THE CHANCE TO PROVE IT.
THIS IS LADY BARRAGE.
SHE CAN SHOOT ALMOST ANYTHING OUT OF HER HANDS.
THE BIG GUY IS CAPT. MELEE.
HE IS THE ALL-AROUND GOOD GUY.
HE CAN FLY, RUN FAST, HE'S PRACTICALLY INVINCIBLE.
HE'S PRETTY MUCH THE BEST THERE IS.
7

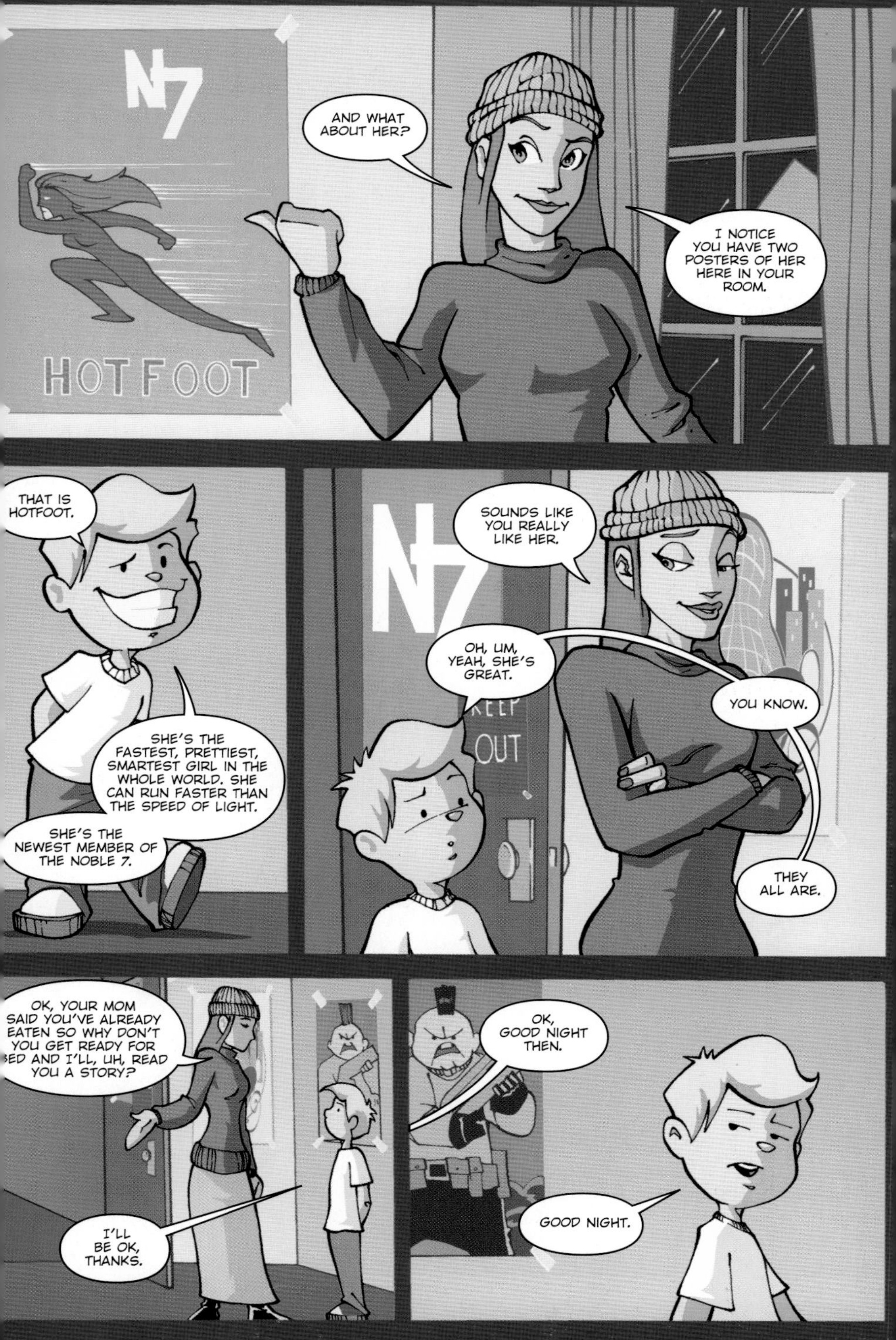
N7
HOTFOOT
AND WHAT ABOUT HER?
I NOTICE YOU HAVE TWO POSTERS OF HER HERE IN YOUR ROOM.
THAT IS HOTFOOT.
SHE'S THE FASTEST, PRETTIEST, SMARTEST GIRL IN THE WHOLE WORLD. SHE CAN RUN FASTER THAN THE SPEED OF LIGHT.
SHE'S THE NEWEST MEMBER OF THE NOBLE 7.
N7
SOUNDS LIKE YOU REALLY LIKE HER.
OH, UM, YEAH, SHE'S GREAT.
YOU KNOW.
THEY ALL ARE.
OUT
OK, YOUR MOM SAID YOU'VE ALREADY EATEN SO WHY DON'T YOU GET READY FOR BED AND I'LL, UH, READ YOU A STORY?
I'LL BE OK, THANKS.
OK, GOOD NIGHT THEN.
GOOD NIGHT.

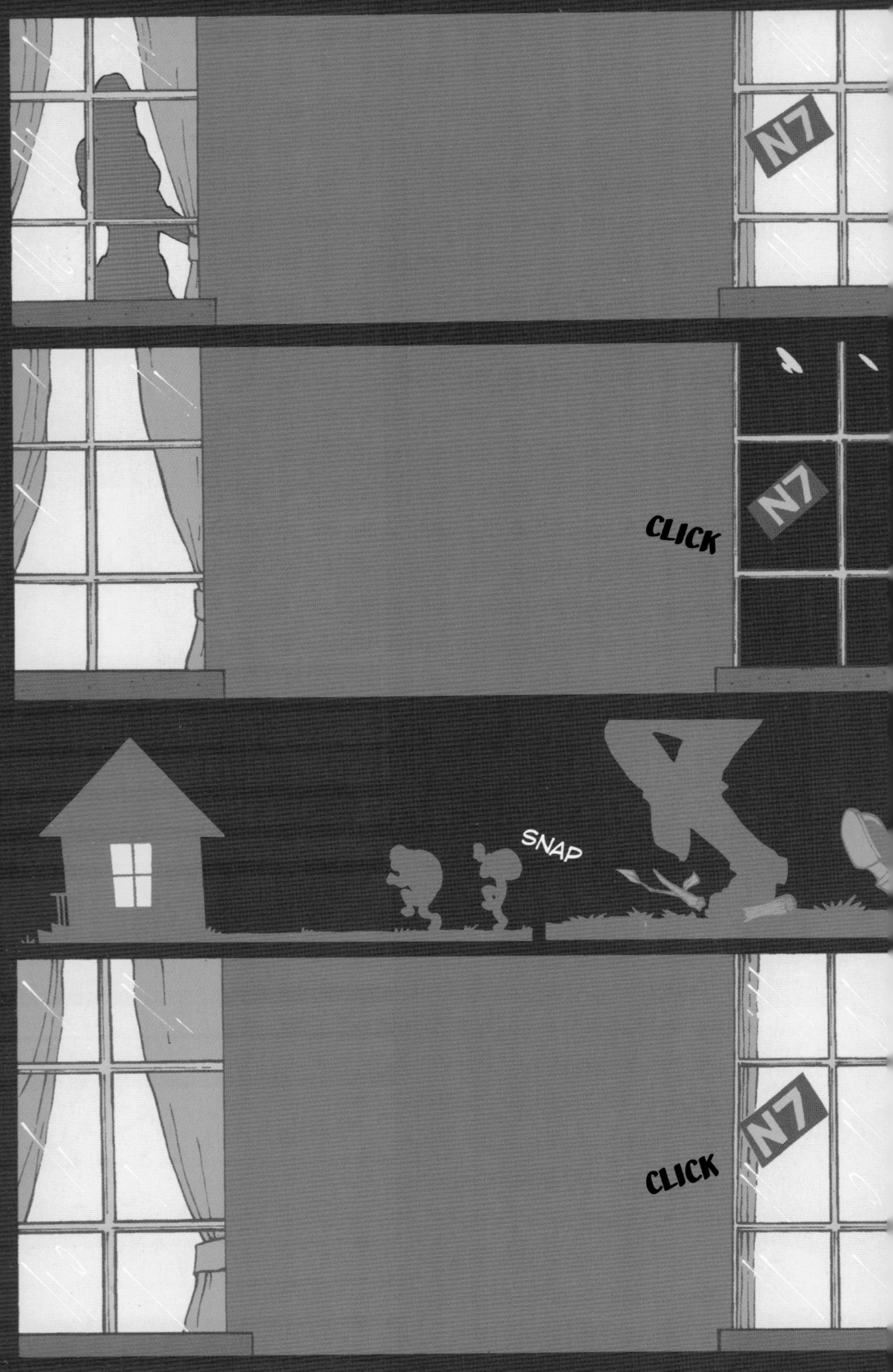
N7
N7
CLICK
SNAP
N7
CLICK

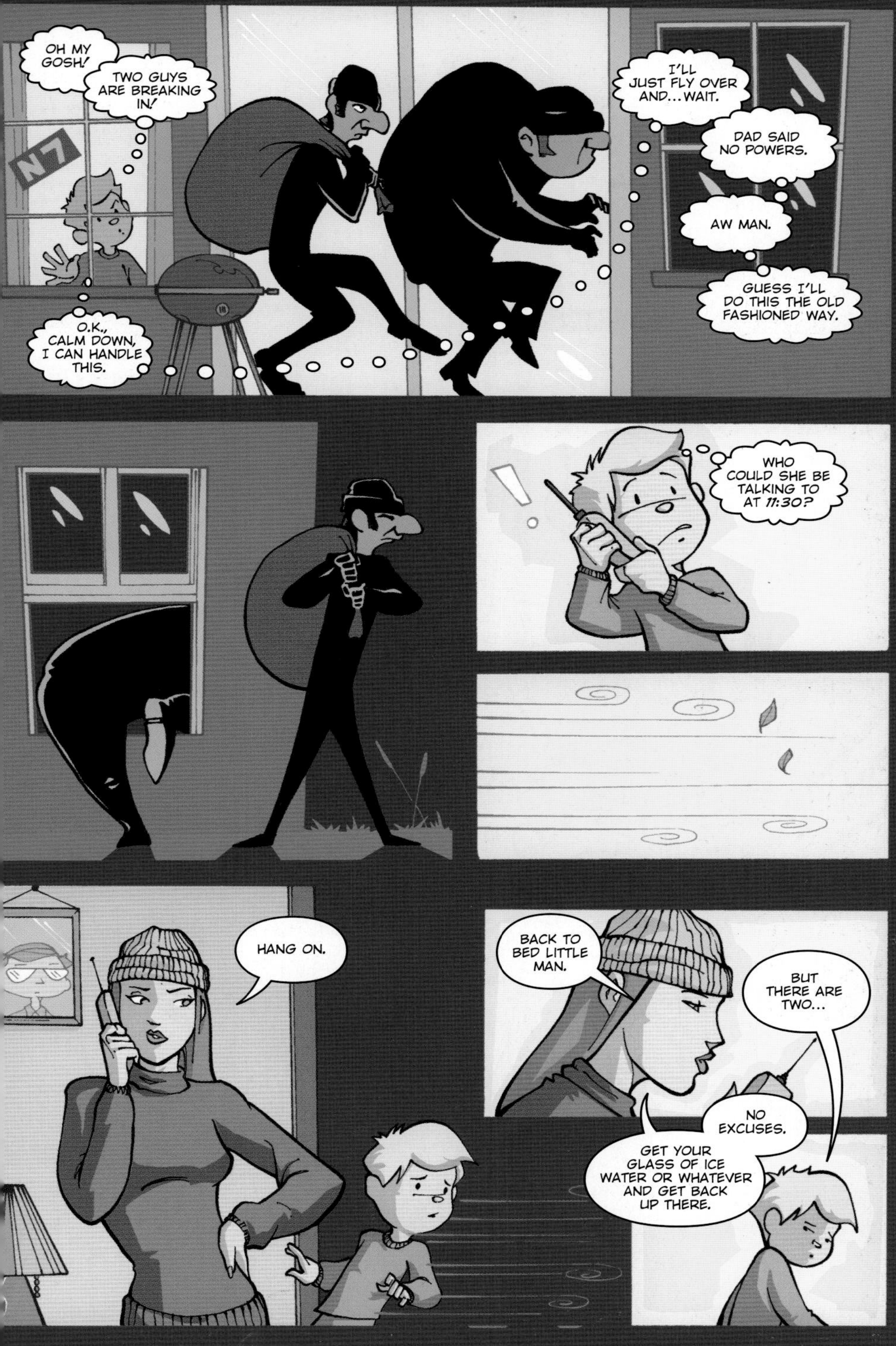
OH MY GOSH!
TWO GUYS ARE BREAKING IN!
O.K., CALM DOWN, I CAN HANDLE THIS.
I'LL JUST FLY OVER AND...WAIT.
DAD SAID NO POWERS.
AW MAN.
GUESS I'LL DO THIS THE OLD FASHIONED WAY.
WHO COULD SHE BE TALKING TO AT 11:30?
HANG ON.
BACK TO BED LITTLE MAN.
BUT THERE ARE TWO...
NO EXCUSES.
GET YOUR GLASS OF ICE WATER OR WHATEVER AND GET BACK UP THERE.

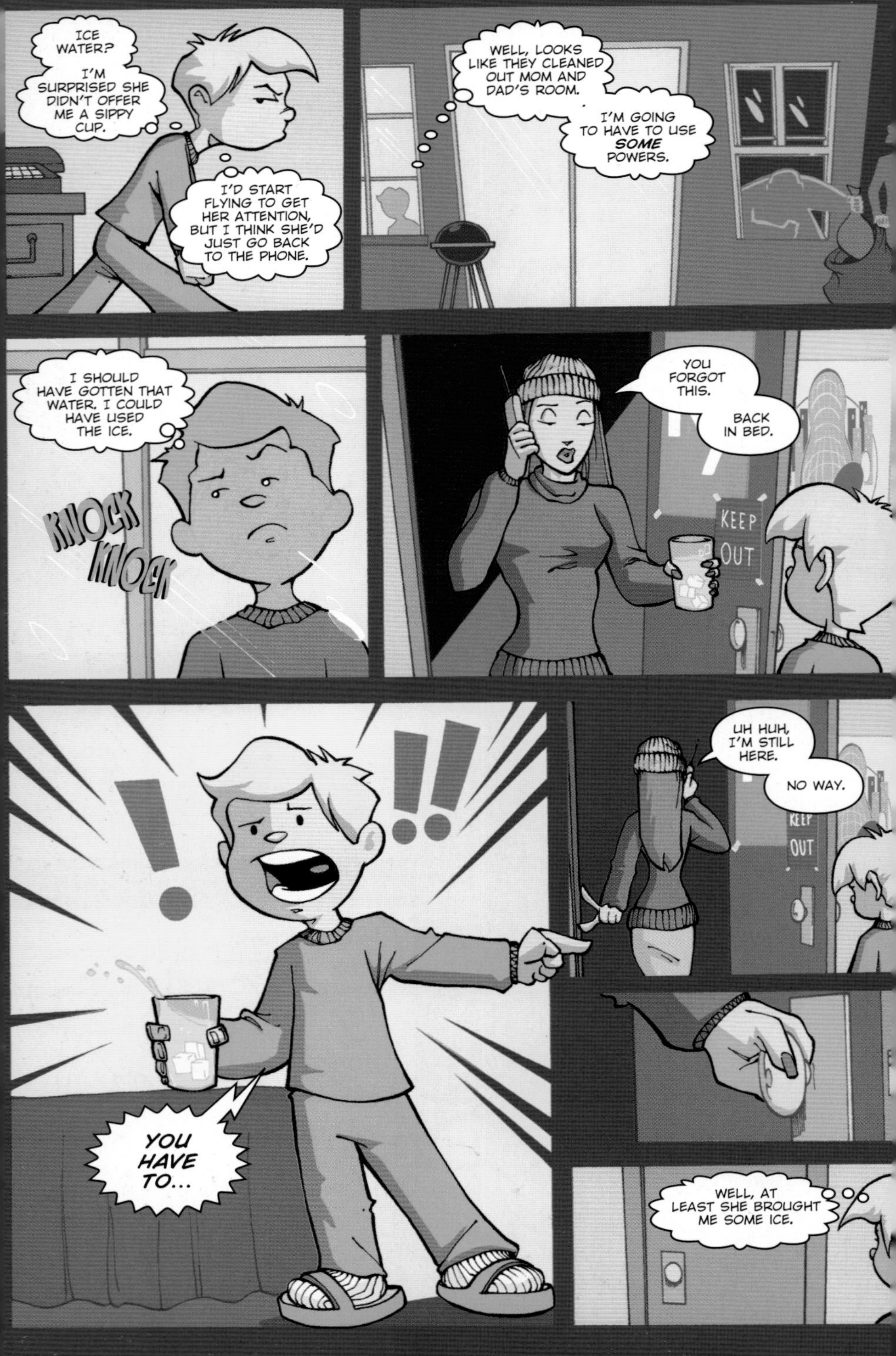
ICE WATER?
I'M SURPRISED SHE DIDN'T OFFER ME A SIPPY CUP.
I'D START FLYING TO GET HER ATTENTION, BUT I THINK SHE'D JUST GO BACK TO THE PHONE.
WELL, LOOKS LIKE THEY CLEANED OUT MOM AND DAD'S ROOM.
I'M GOING TO HAVE TO USE SOME POWERS.
I SHOULD HAVE GOTTEN THAT WATER. I COULD HAVE USED THE ICE.
KNOCK KNOCK
YOU FORGOT THIS.
BACK IN BED.
KEEP OUT
YOU HAVE TO...
UH HUH, I'M STILL HERE.
NO WAY.
WELL, AT LEAST SHE BROUGHT ME SOME ICE.

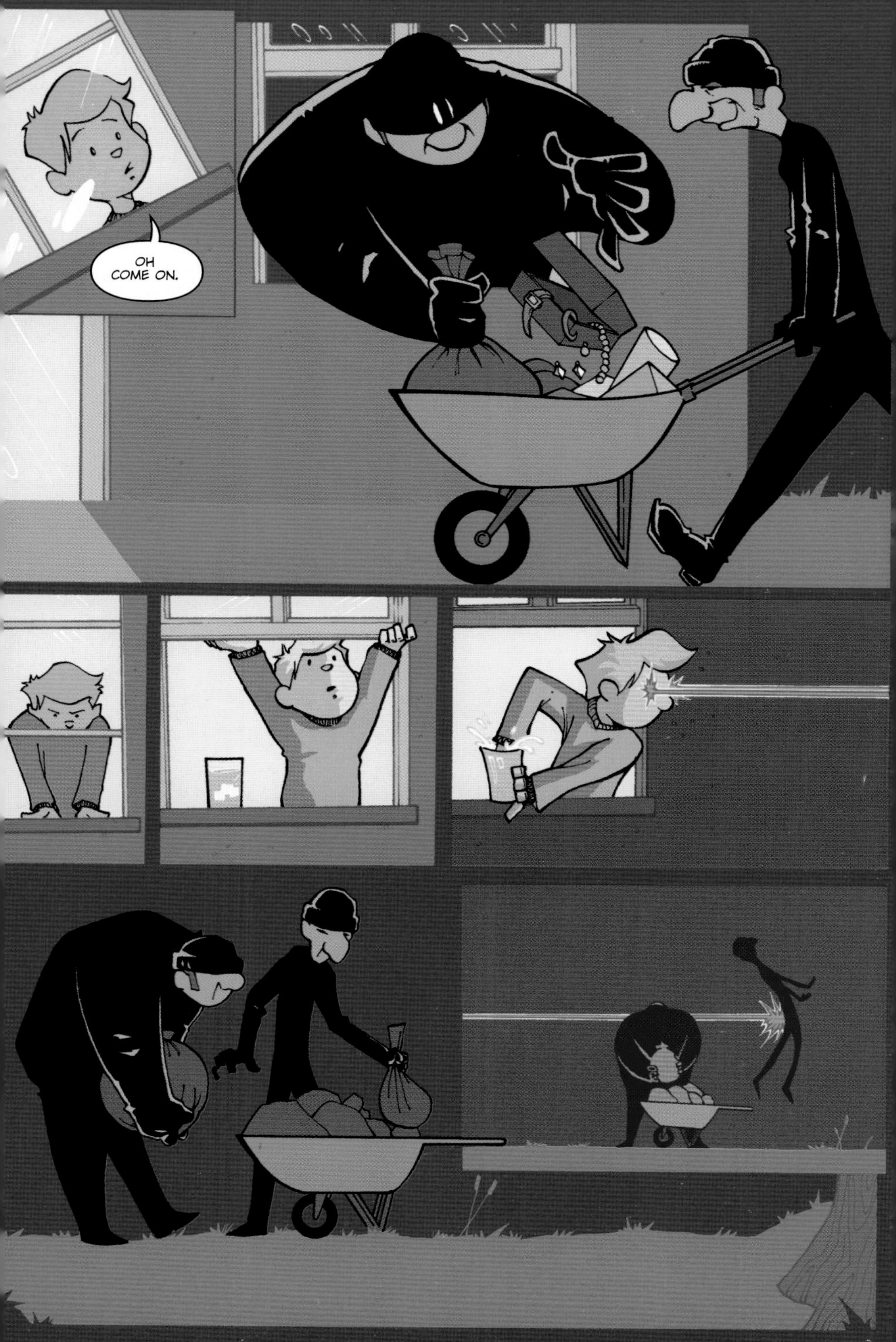
OH
COME ON.

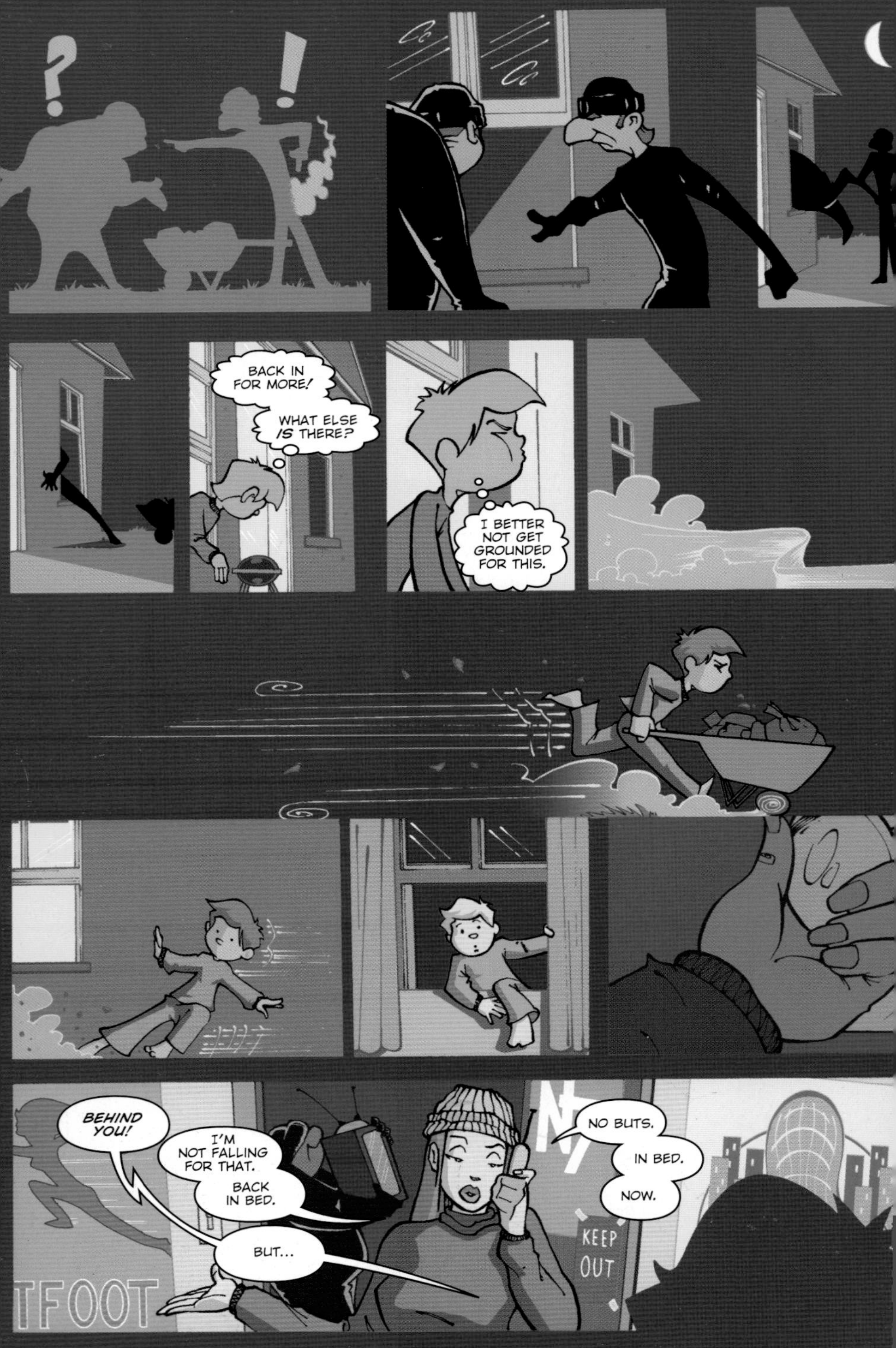
BACK IN FOR MORE!
WHAT ELSE *IS* THERE?
I BETTER NOT GET GROUNDED FOR THIS.
BEHIND YOU!
I'M NOT FALLING FOR THAT.
BACK IN BED.
BUT...
NO BUTS.
IN BED.
NOW.
KEEP OUT
TFOOT

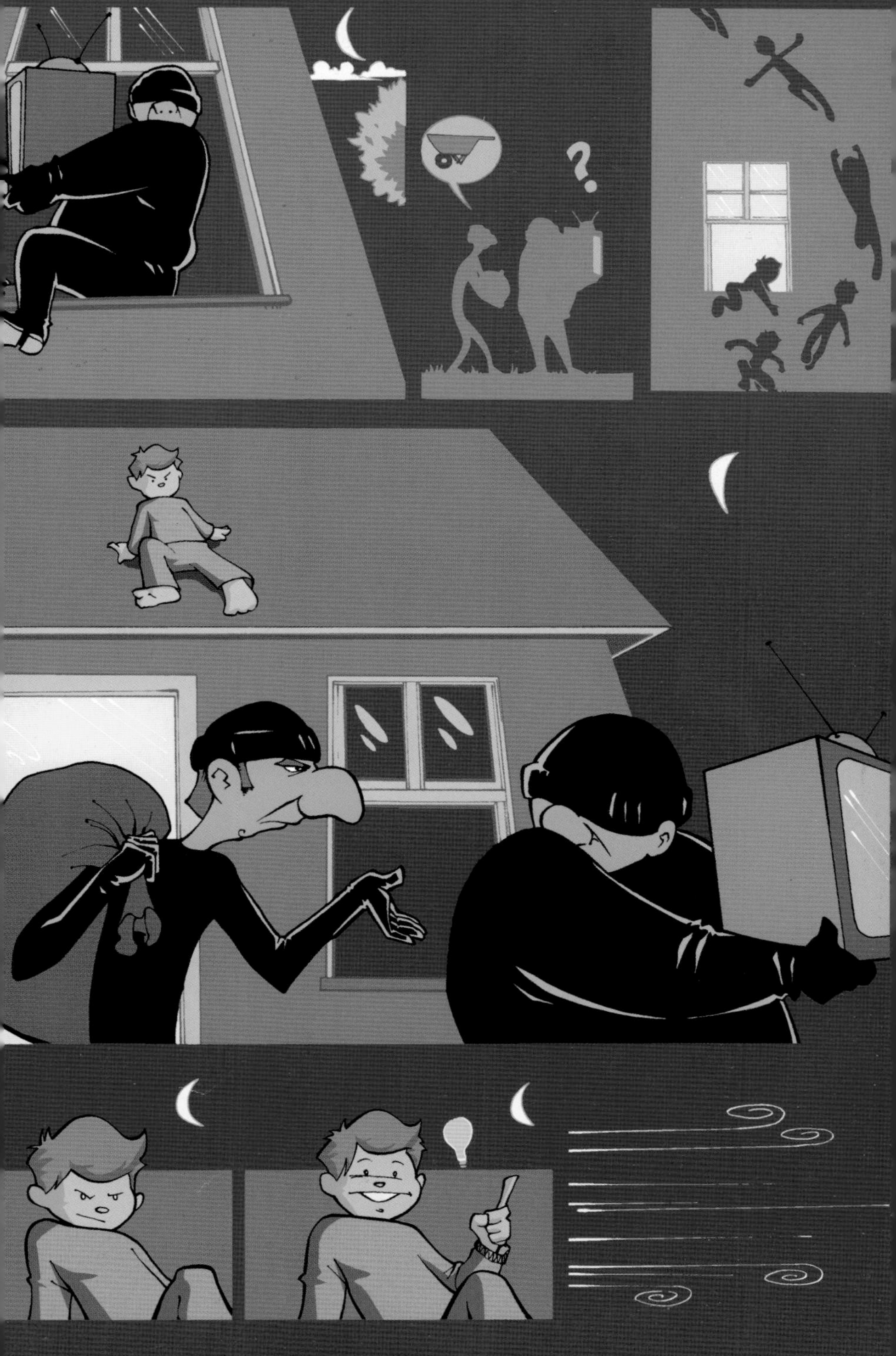

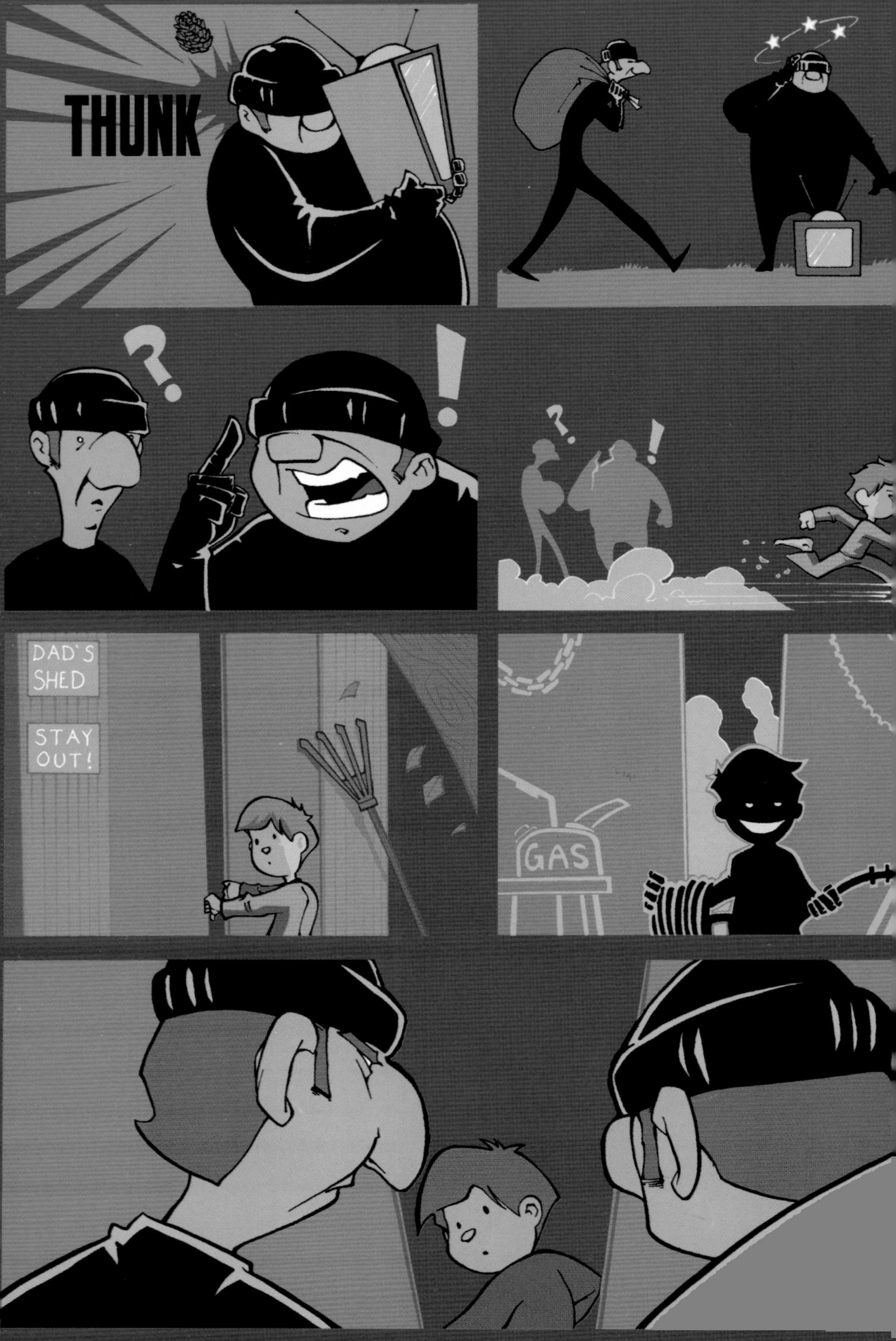
THUNK
?
!
?
!
DAD'S SHED
STAY OUT!
GAS

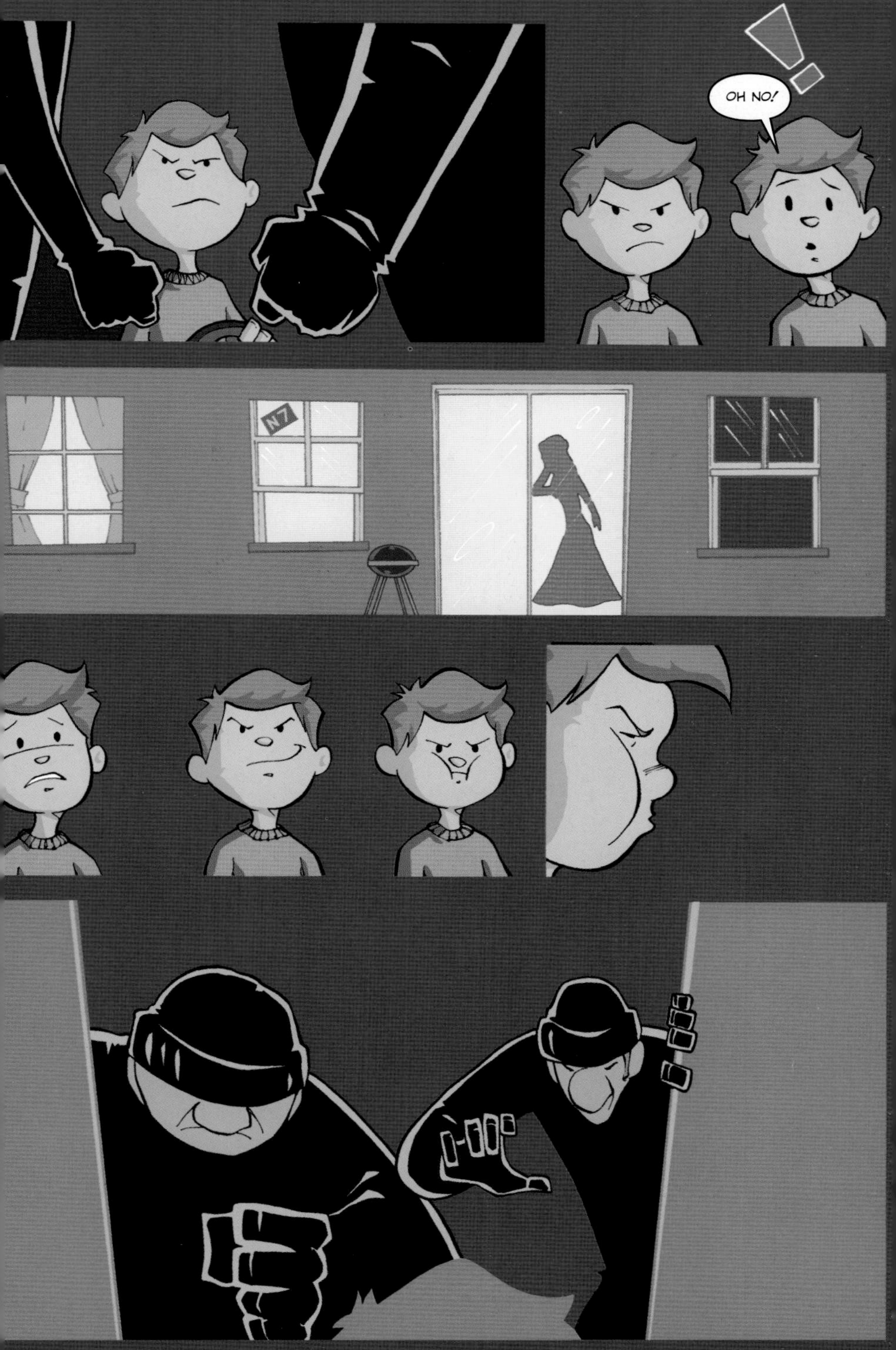
OH NO!

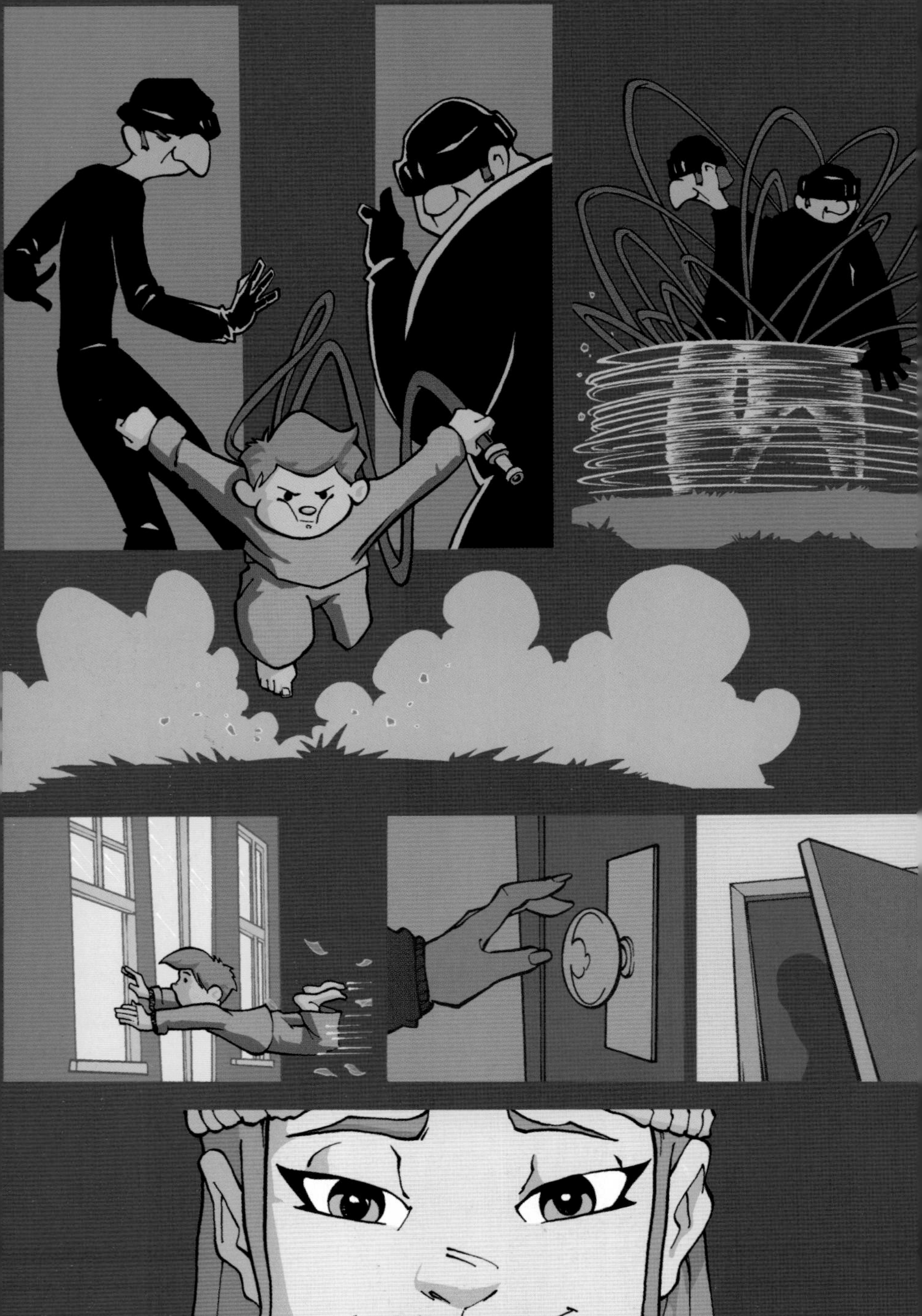

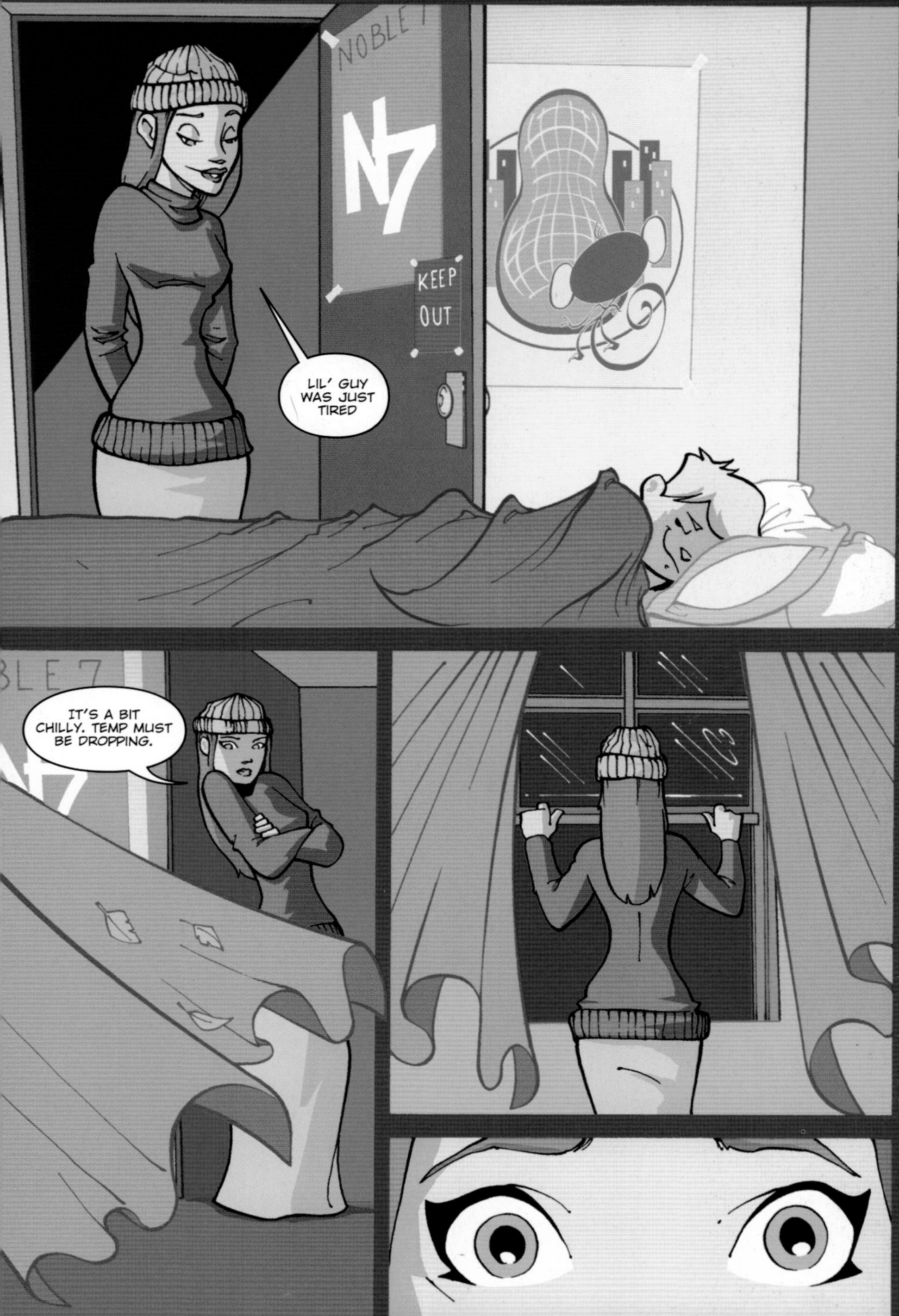

NOBLE 7
N7
KEEP OUT
LIL' GUY WAS JUST TIRED
IT'S A BIT CHILLY. TEMP MUST BE DROPPING.

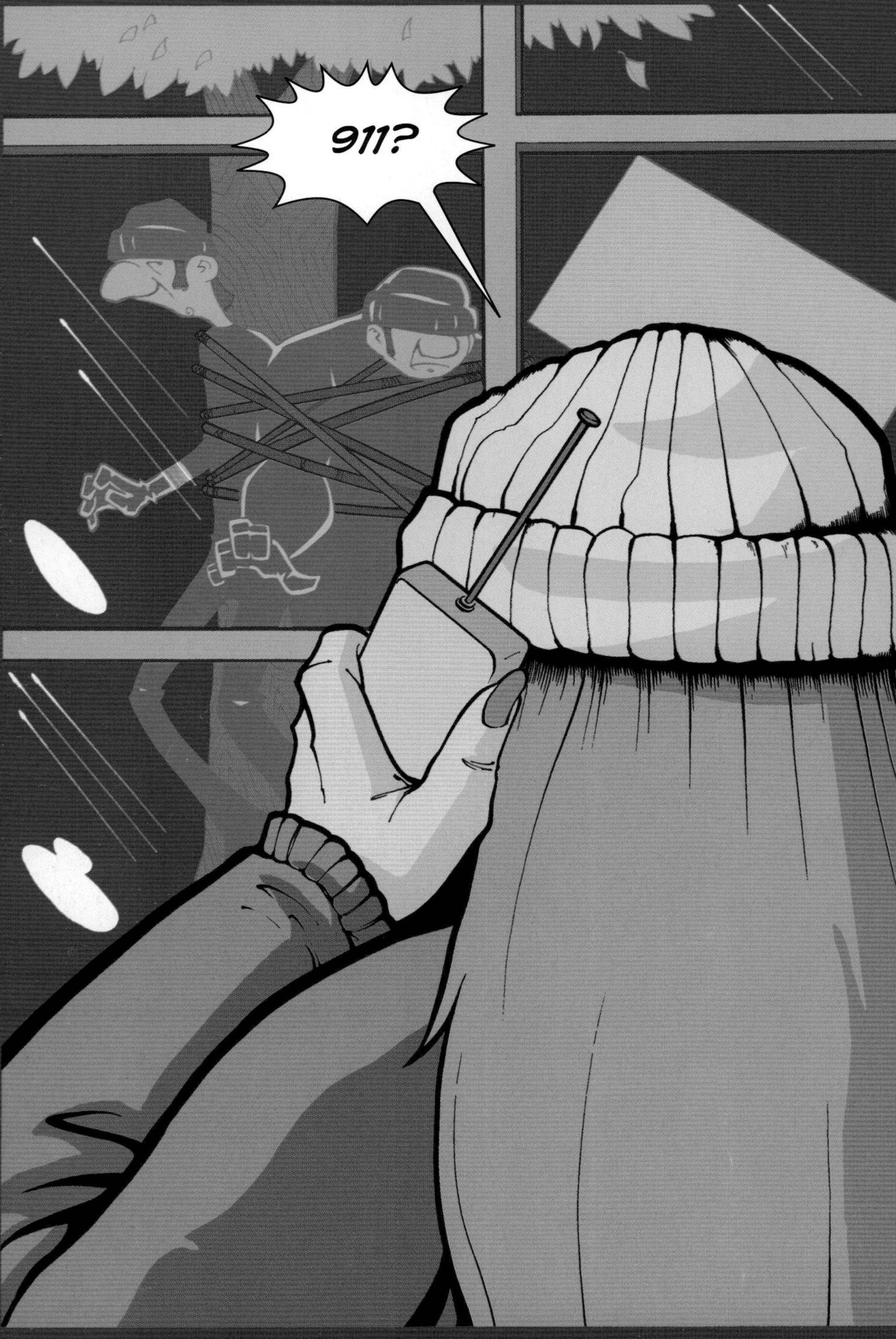
911?

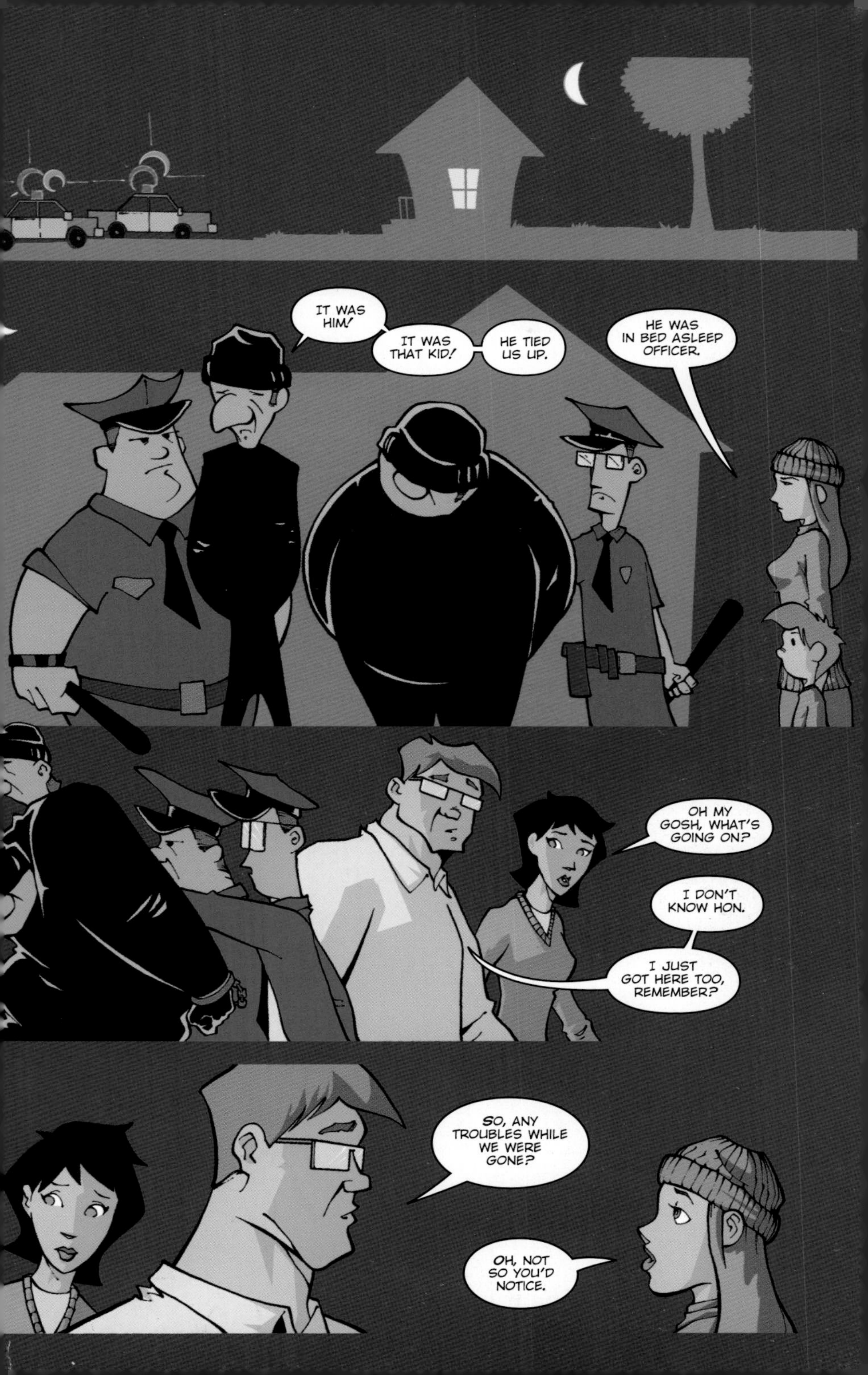
IT WAS HIM!
IT WAS THAT KID!
HE TIED US UP.
HE WAS IN BED ASLEEP OFFICER.
OH MY GOSH, WHAT'S GOING ON?
I DON'T KNOW HON.
I JUST GOT HERE TOO, REMEMBER?
SO, ANY TROUBLES WHILE WE WERE GONE?
OH, NOT SO YOU'D NOTICE.

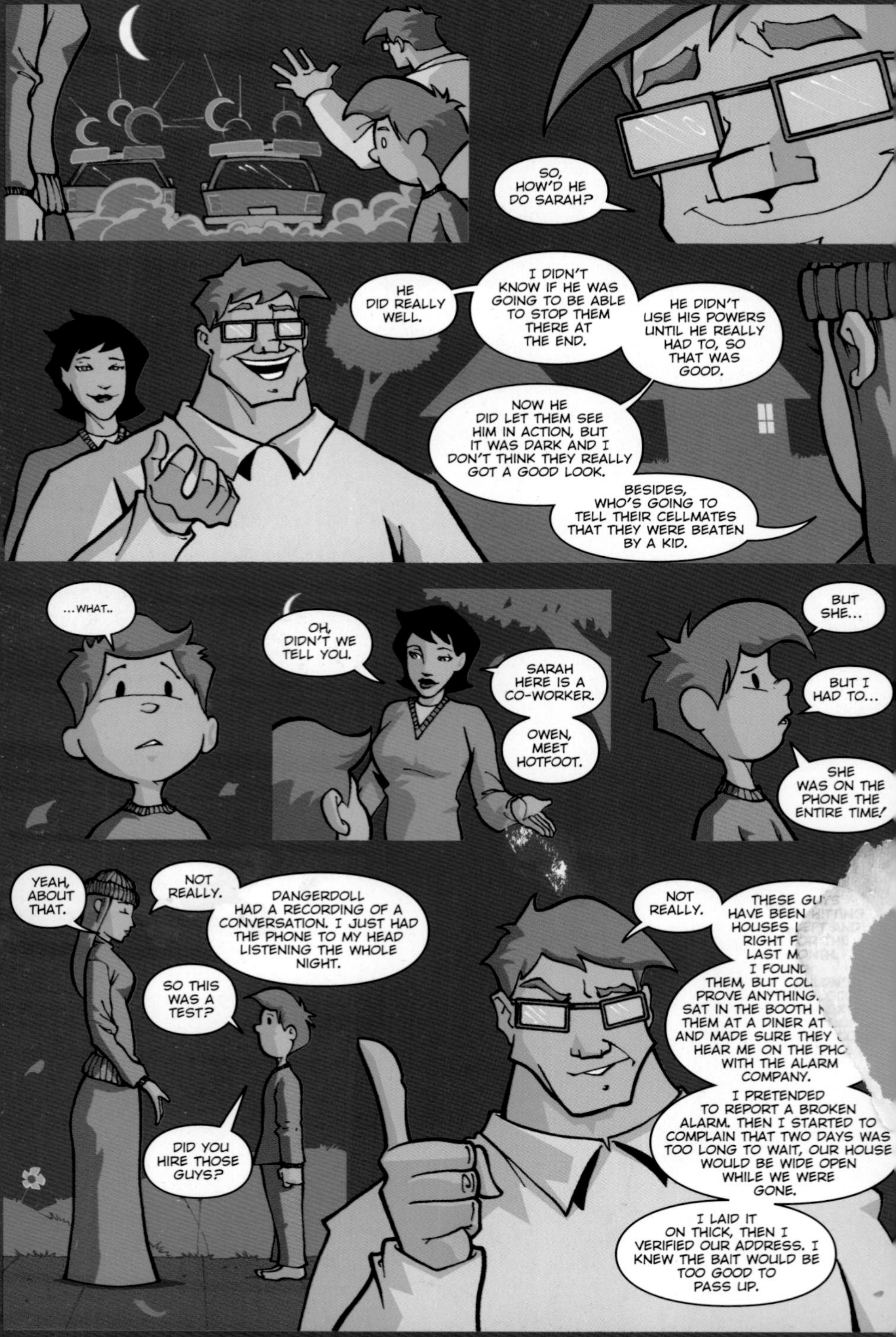

SO, HOW'D HE DO SARAH?
HE DID REALLY WELL.
I DIDN'T KNOW IF HE WAS GOING TO BE ABLE TO STOP THEM THERE AT THE END.
HE DIDN'T USE HIS POWERS UNTIL HE REALLY HAD TO, SO THAT WAS GOOD.
NOW HE DID LET THEM SEE HIM IN ACTION, BUT IT WAS DARK AND I DON'T THINK THEY REALLY GOT A GOOD LOOK.
BESIDES, WHO'S GOING TO TELL THEIR CELLMATES THAT THEY WERE BEATEN BY A KID.
...WHAT..
OH, DIDN'T WE TELL YOU.
SARAH HERE IS A CO-WORKER.
OWEN, MEET HOTFOOT.
BUT SHE...
BUT I HAD TO...
SHE WAS ON THE PHONE THE ENTIRE TIME!
YEAH, ABOUT THAT.
NOT REALLY.
DANGERDOLL HAD A RECORDING OF A CONVERSATION. I JUST HAD THE PHONE TO MY HEAD LISTENING THE WHOLE NIGHT.
SO THIS WAS A TEST?
DID YOU HIRE THOSE GUYS?
NOT REALLY.
THESE GU HAVE BEEN HOUSES RIGHT F LAST M I FOUND THEM, BUT COL PROVE ANYTHING. SAT IN THE BOOTH THEM AT A DINER AT AND MADE SURE THEY HEAR ME ON THE PHO WITH THE ALARM COMPANY.
I PRETENDED TO REPORT A BROKEN ALARM. THEN I STARTED TO COMPLAIN THAT TWO DAYS WAS TOO LONG TO WAIT, OUR HOUSE WOULD BE WIDE OPEN WHILE WE WERE GONE.
I LAID IT ON THICK, THEN I VERIFIED OUR ADDRESS. I KNEW THE BAIT WOULD BE TOO GOOD TO PASS UP.

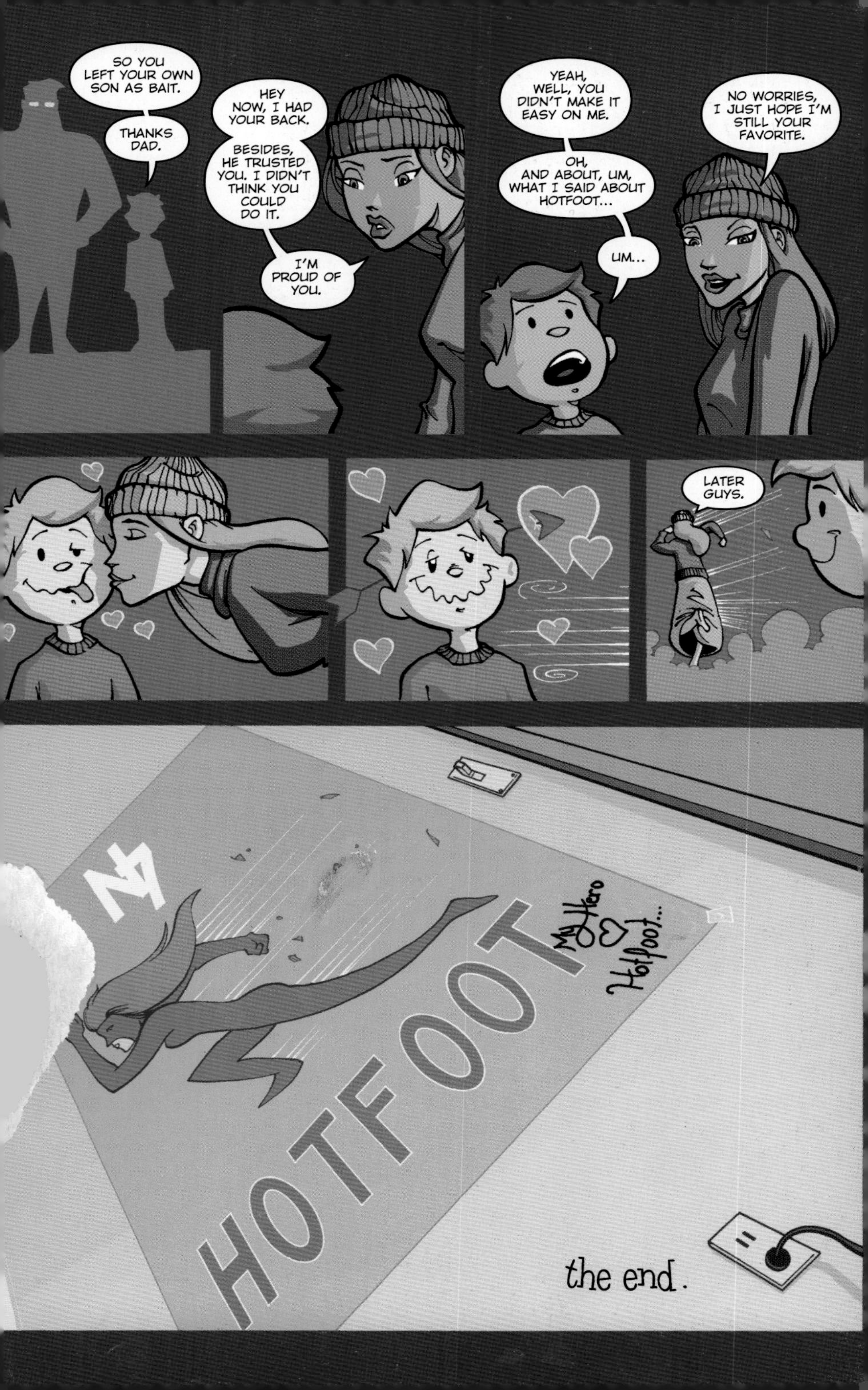
SO YOU LEFT YOUR OWN SON AS BAIT.
THANKS DAD.
HEY NOW, I HAD YOUR BACK.
BESIDES, HE TRUSTED YOU. I DIDN'T THINK YOU COULD DO IT.
I'M PROUD OF YOU.
YEAH, WELL, YOU DIDN'T MAKE IT EASY ON ME.
OH, AND ABOUT, UM, WHAT I SAID ABOUT HOTFOOT...
UM...
NO WORRIES, I JUST HOPE I'M STILL YOUR FAVORITE.
LATER GUYS.
HOTFOOT
My Hero
Hotfoot...
the end.

ACKNOWLEDGEMENTS

courtney huddleston

Hello. Thanks for giving "A Bit Haywire" a try. This comic book is one of the many ideas I've wanted to do for some time. The biggest problem was the fact that I can't write. Anyone can come up with an idea, but putting it on paper and making it interesting is an entirely different story. I wasn't sure who would be a good writer for it, so I left it on one of the shelves in my head until I knew. The opportunity fell into my lap while working on an anthology with a bunch of buddies and rising talents. Scott Zirkel, whom I met on Mike Kunkel's Astonish Factory years ago, did a short story for the book that was hilarious. At first I thought that maybe I was a little biased since we had known each other for a while. But, to my surprise, everyone else responded the same as I did to his writing. I read his story a few more times and had the same chuckling reaction every time. That's when the light went off in my head. I approached Scott with the idea, and he was immediately on board. The rest is pretty much history.

Special thanks to Jessie and Jim over at Viper Comics for taking a chance with this title. Also a special thanks to Mike Garcia for taking the time in his busy schedule to color the book. It's no easy task making my art look good.

A Warm thanks to my parents, Brandee Adams, Court and Phoenix, Michelle Nichols, and of course Scott Zirkel. You guys helped me out with your kindness, support, and suggestions on making this story a lot better.

And a final thanks to Trainor Houghton, Ken White, and Marlaine Maddux.
There is no me without you guys. Well, you guys and my parents of course. But, that's a no-brainer that I just don't wanna think about.

scott zirkel

Court exaggerates a bit; it took a lot of begging and pleading on his part. I mean, the rough idea he came up with looks nothing like the book you see before you. His idea was to have a guy with no powers just wander around town, talking to himself, riding the bus, and crying in his soup. I thought it sounded a bit too much like Court's biography, so I did some tweaking.

But I digress.

Actually I knew this book was going to be great when I heard the pitch. A kid with powers that don't quite work right. The possibilities are endless. I owe a lot to Court, from that first pin-up I did for him to this book, he sees talent in me that I largely overlook. And for that I thank him.

I also have to thank Jessie Garza and the Viper crew for giving our little story a chance. Viper is an awesome group of folks and I'm glad we were able to find a home with them.

I hope you enjoy this book, and whatever else we dream up.

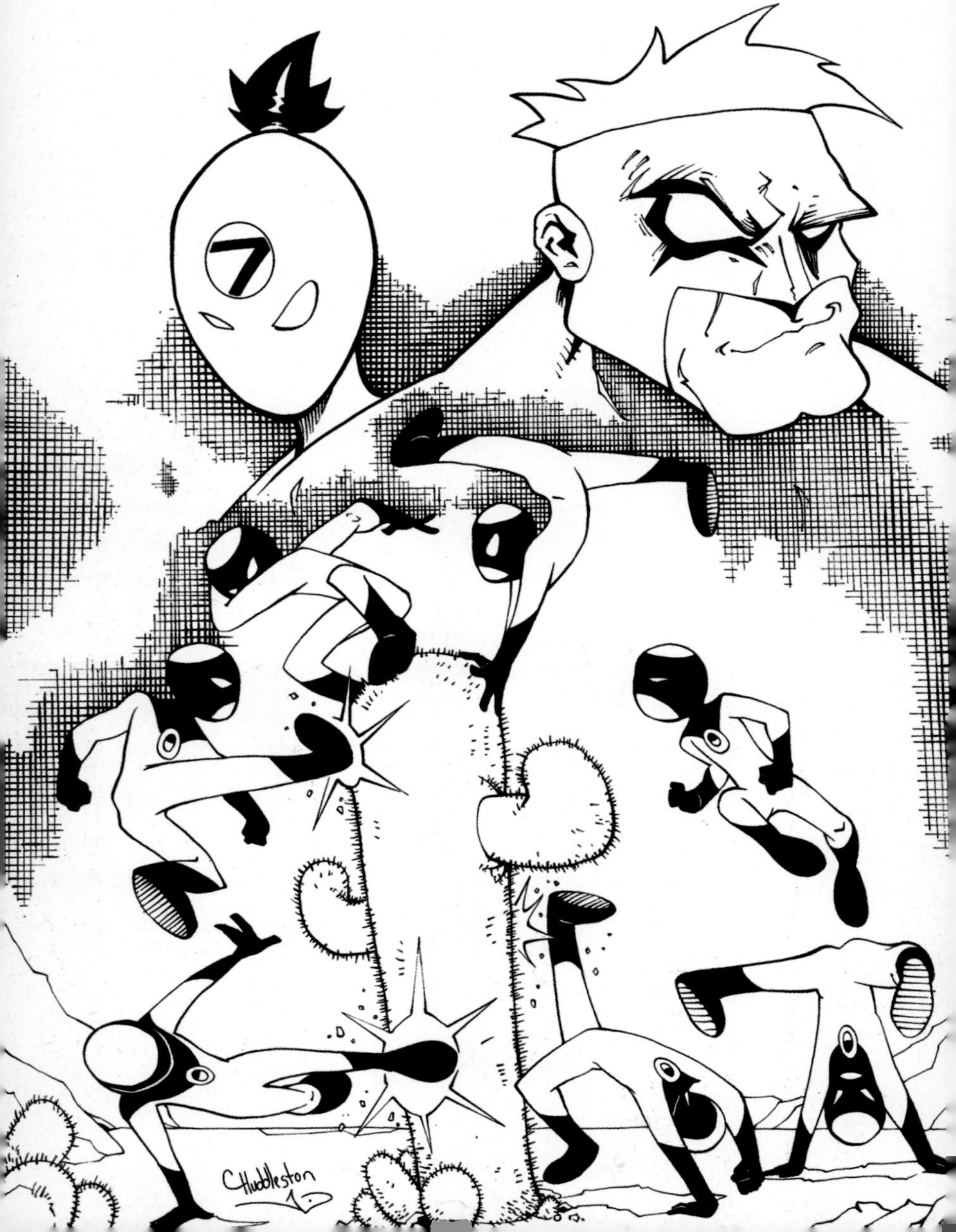
CHuddleston

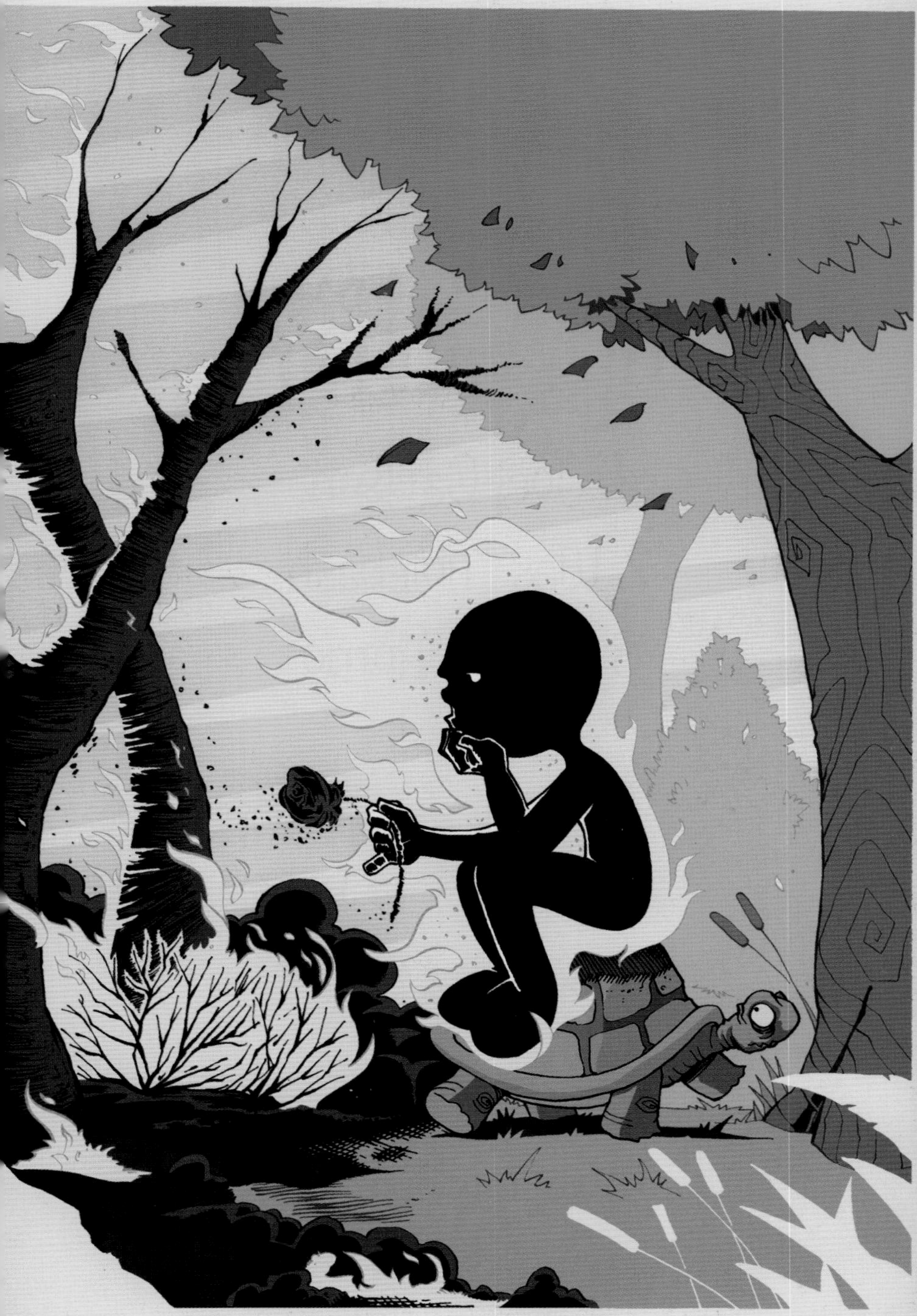

PIN-UPS

1. Joel Carlson
2. Wes Molebash
3. Aaron Romo

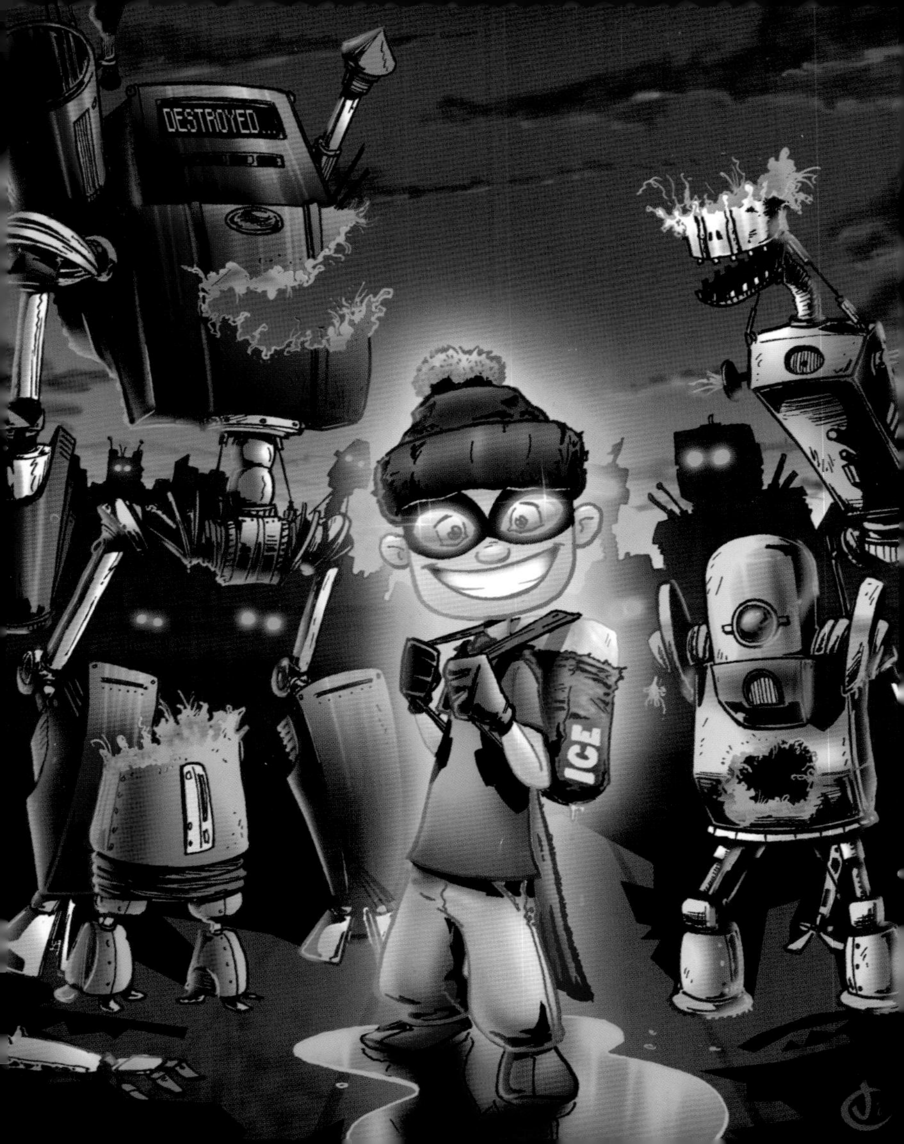
DESTROYED...
ICE

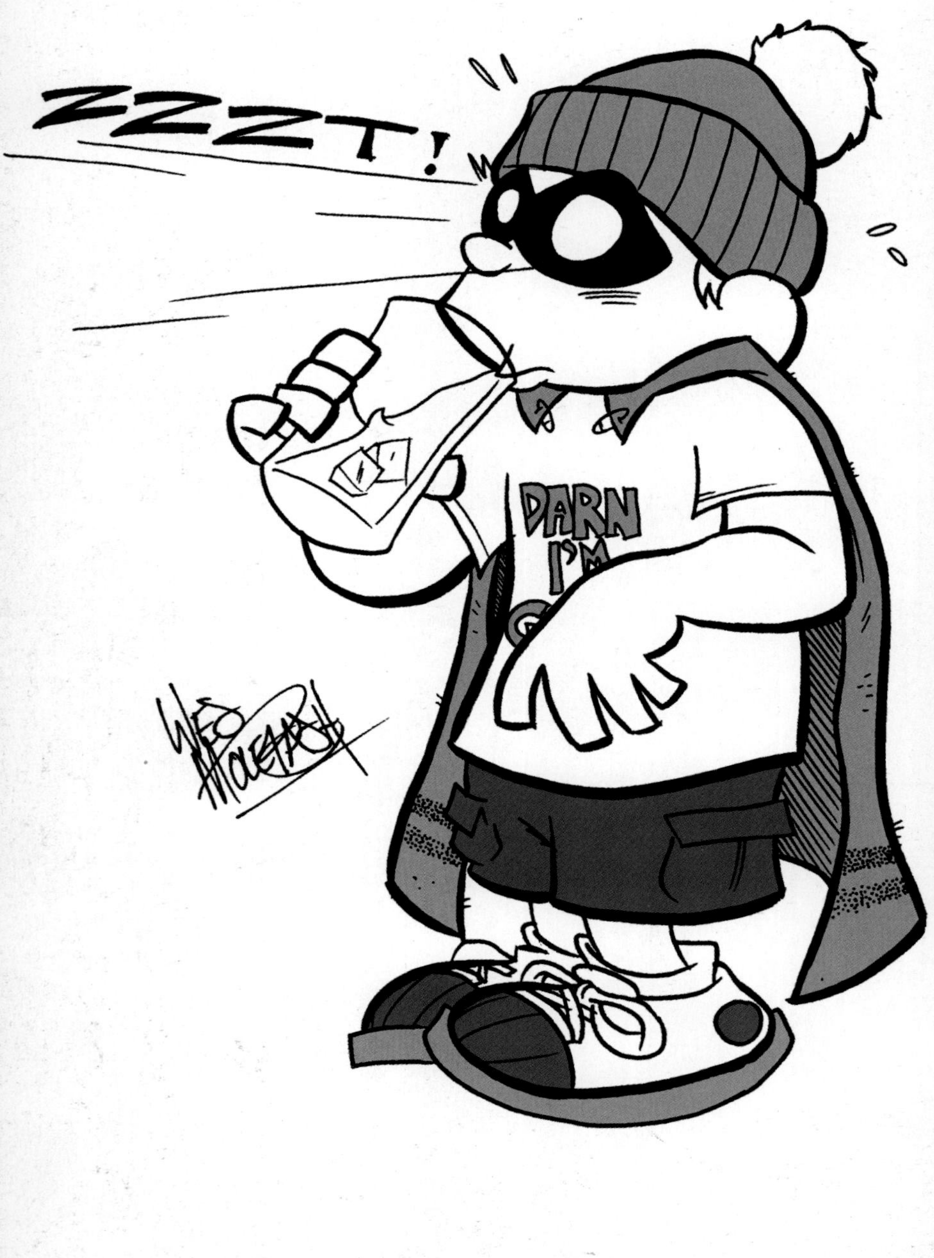
ZZZZT!
DARN
I'M

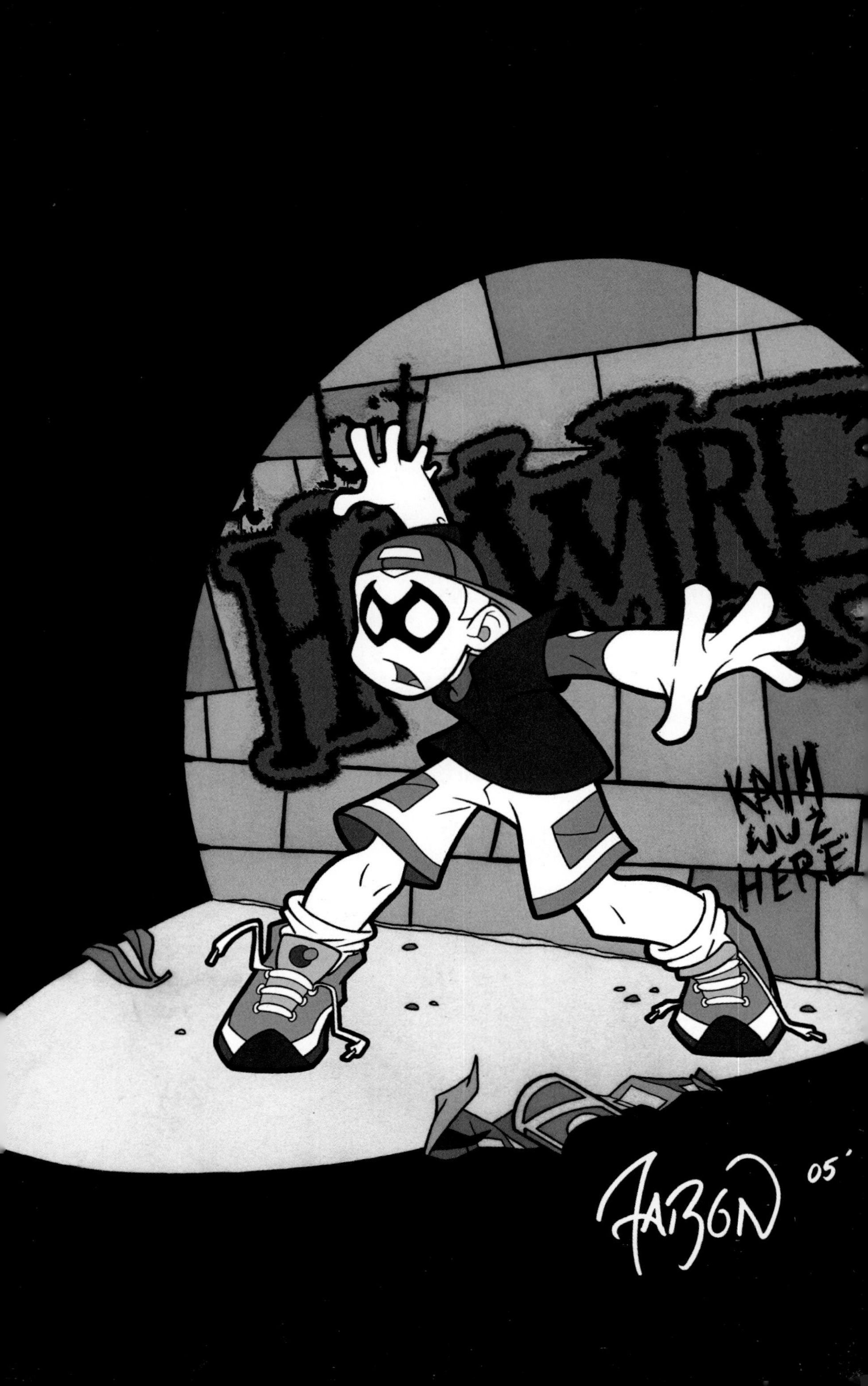
KAIN WUZ HERE

ALSO AVAILABLE FROM VIPER COMICS

DEAD AT 17: THE COMPLETE FIRST SERIES (REPRINT)
ISBN: 0-9754193-0-7

DEAD AT 17: BLOOD OF SAINTS
ISBN: 0-9754193-1-5

DEAD AT 17: REVOLUTION
ISBN: 0-9754193-3-1

DAISY KUTTER: THE LAST TRAIN
ISBN: 0-9754193-2-3

RANDOM ENCOUNTER: VOLUME 1
ISBN: 0-9754193-8-2

ODDLY NORMAL: VOLUME 1
ISBN: 0-9777883-0-X

EMILY EDISON
ISBN: 0-9777883-2-6

THE MIDDLEMAN: THE TRADE PAPERBACK IMPERATIVE
ISBN: 0-9754193-7-4

THE MIDDLEMAN: THE SECOND VOLUME INEVITABILITY
ISBN: 0-9777883-4-2

THE EXPENDABLE ONE
ISBN: 0-9754193-9-0

MOSH GIRLS + MONSTERS: THE ART OF JOSH HOWARD, VOL. 1
ISBN:0-9777883-3-4

YOU'LL HAVE THAT: VOLUME 1
ISBN: 0-9777883-1-8

YOU'LL HAVE THAT: VOLUME 2 (DECEMBER 2006)
ISBN:0-9777883-6-9

VILLAINS: VOLUME 1: (DECEMBER 2006)
ISBN:0-9777883-7-7

AVAILABLE ONLINE AT WWW.VIPERCOMICS.COM